To my friends Simba, Pierrot, Bella, Venus
and Sophie, in the hope that a goodly crew
of their fellow lions, rhinos, elephants, chimps
and all the rest will soon be heading for
the New World on board my "Noah's Ark" . . .

ANIMAL
KITABU

Another Fawcett Crest Book
by Jean-Pierre Hallet:

CONGO KITABU (*with Alex Pelle*)

ANIMAL KITABU

By Jean-Pierre Hallet

With Alex Pelle

A FAWCETT PREMIER BOOK

Fawcett Publications, Inc., Greenwich, Conn.

ANIMAL KITABU

THIS BOOK CONTAINS THE COMPLETE TEXT OF
THE ORIGINAL HARDCOVER EDITION.

A Fawcett Premier Book reprinted by arrangement with
Random House, Inc.

Library of Congress Catalog Card Number: 67-22666.

Printed in the United States of America.

CONTENTS

INTRODUCTION

There is really no debate about the need for conservation. Laws have been enacted, even in the new nations of tropical Africa, to protect and preserve the natural heritage of the land. But those laws have proved, at least so far, to be sadly ineffectual, due in large part to the people's simple lack of understanding of the problem and their consequent indifference or even hostility to it. The efforts of international conservationist groups, which must go begging for funds as a "charity," have alike been hindered by this same popular indifference. Education, or rather the dissemination of factual information, is at present our most sorely needed and important road of attack.

Jean-Pierre Hallet learned, firsthand, the true facts upon which any worthwhile and effective promotion of real conservation must be founded. He learned them from a near life-time spent in Africa, and in travels through other parts of the tropics. In his first book—*Congo Kitabu*—Hallet gave us a good jolt with respect to the human problems of equatorial Africa, showing by actual accounts just how *mis*informed we really are about that troubled subcontinent. Now in *Animal Kitabu* he has hit us again, and hit us harder than ever.

On almost every page readers will come upon some fact that flies in the face of what they had previously believed and been taught—not only taught in school and college, and from textbooks, but from movies, television, popular works, travelogues, magazines and newspapers. When it comes to animals and their behavior, the volume of tosh that has been bombarding us from all sides for the past century has superseded even the rubbish that was bruited about in earlier ages when myth, legend and folklore were accepted as fact. Just where all this misinformation came from is hard to say. Much of it harks back to the old medieval legends, but a monstrous sort

9

of fungoid growth of untruth, non-truth, and just plain outright lies has grown up around that core, fostered to a large extent by the tall tales of travelers and hunters. Any real analysis of causes must necessarily be specific, and Hallet is very, very specific when he goes to work on the subject.

The science of ethology—not ethnology, be it clearly noted —describes and studies animal behavior in a *natural* environment or in a foreign but simulated natural environment (as with the specimens of Arabian oryx which have been established under free-living conditions in the American Southwest). The behavior of animals kept in an *unnatural* environment, such as that provided by zoos, circuses and other exhibits, or in laboratories, does not form a part of ethology but is rather described and studied as "behaviorism." There are, of course, borderline cases such as large animal farms, ranging from enclaves for indigenous animals in their own environment, to reserves or parks for foreign animals in other areas. Nevertheless, the distinction is fairly clear-cut as between animals in their native milieu and uprooted or "displaced" animals, however they are subsequently housed or kept.

I was trained, and have spent nearly forty years off and on, as a working ethologist in the field. During the past twenty years I have also collected and read as much of the literature as time has permitted on the studies and findings of the behaviorists. And I have to say, reluctantly and without attributing conscious intent to the behaviorist school, that they have contributed not a little to the general store of misinformation. The behavior, for example, of a troop of baboons on an artificial, naked, concrete hill in a northern climate bears, in the final analysis, very little correspondence to their behavior on the African savannahs. On the concrete hill they simply cannot perform the major part of their normal activities —such as "sifting sand"—or carry on their normal social life. But since they are highly ingenious creatures, they appear to devise new laws or "patterns of behavior" (according to the behaviorists' favorite expression) that were never needed in their free-living past and are in fact quite alien to animals living in an undisturbed natural environment.

But there are few environments that remain "undisturbed" by the hunters and the so-called "sportsmen." Now baseball, cricket or soccer are fine, healthy sports by which man can let off some of his aggressive and a lot of his competitive steam. What is more, he can do so by either watching the action or engaging in it personally. But why is it considered "sporting" to shoot at animals who cannot shoot back? I have always deplored hunting or killing any creature except for food, or to reduce wild stock that would otherwise eat itself into starvation, or to obtain scientifically needed specimens —and then only the very minimum. Only when it is necessary for maintaining nature's balance (or rather, what is left of it) is hunting permissible or praiseworthy. But just to go blasting away at living creatures for the "fun" of it, or to obtain trophies, strikes me as the worst form of immature and uncivilized behavior. Will man *never* grow up?

Hallet is one of the "sportsman's" most inveterate opponents. I only met him a few years ago, but that meeting was to me a classic one. I can count on my fingers (alas!) the men and/or women I have met in my life with his knowledge and his opinions. As you read on in this book—and read on you will, even if you have little interest in animal life—you will come to see and appreciate how he differentiates between fact and fancy with regard to animal life, not only in theory but in down-to-earth practice. When confronted by a crouching leopard (a notorious pretext for the "sportsman" to start blasting away with his gun), Hallet sends the animal packing with a stentorian cry of "Grandpa, get lost!"; when threatened by a stampeding herd of Cape buffalo, he stands in his tracks "trying to look like a new species of baobab tree" while the herd thunders by, quite harmlessly, on either side. Both of these incidents, and many others he describes, will shock or at least surprise those who have read too many hunters' tales of Africa's alleged "vicious killers." They are based, however, on a thorough knowledge of animal behavior —and the whole point is that animals simply do not behave in accordance with our own cherished fancies.

It is my opinion that we cannot proceed with any really effective schemes for conserving animals until we know just how they *do* behave. Here we come to some special aspects of the problem, aspects that are particularly applicable to Africa, and first and foremost is the matter of the human beings who also inhabit the land. It is seldom realized that indigenous peoples are often the best conservationists; it is the immigrants, and particularly those of other races, who often upset the established balance (as in North America, where the Indians once lived in almost perfect balance with the continent's animal life). But "colonialism," which can be debated endlessly from a political point of view, was not actually as harmful to the wild life, especially in the tropics, as has been made out. It tolerated the "sportsmen" and the "white hunt-

11

ers"—who are still tolerated, even encouraged in today's independent African nations—but it must be remembered that the colonial governments launched Africa's first promising conservation projects. There was nothing quite comparable to the American Buffalo Society, but the Belgians in the Congo and the British in the upland eastern area had made a very good start. (My father instituted one of, if not the first private game reserve in Africa and died in Kenya in 1924 due to a pure accident with a rhinoceros while aiding Martin Johnson in the making of his famous film *Simba*. Thus, unlike many critics who disparage and deplore *every* action of the "white colonialists," I know something of what I'm talking about.)

One of the deadliest activities that has plagued colonial and independent Africa alike, has been the scourge of poaching. In early times it could hardly have been given such a name, since there were no laws against the mass slaughter of animal life for commercial purposes, such as occurred with the white rhinos, brought to near extinction by the insatiable Asiatic market for their "aphrodisiac" horns, or the beautiful colobus monkeys who were massacred for their pelts. Today there *are* laws, but this blight remains and has spread throughout Africa, seemingly beyond control, despite praiseworthy governmental efforts in at least some of the new nations.

Between poaching, increasing population, overcultivation, and the invasion of the grasslands by vast herds of native cattle (which actually constitute local currency rather than a source of food), it seems almost a miracle that any game still remains on the savannahs. The potential value of that game, in the most practical and realistic terms, was spelled out in a proposal made by Julian Huxley. He suggested that the nations protect and conserve their vanishing game, and encourage breeding, to ensure their people a desperately needed source of meat to supplement or augment their protein-deficient diet. Hopefully, the African governments will latch on to this suggestion, aided perhaps by a grant of United Nations funds.

But there is one disheartening thing about conservation as a whole. It seems, to some extent, to be a matter of semantics —the word "conservation" simply has not caught the fancy of the young, it infuriates the rifle-toting boys, and it has somehow acquired a namby-pamby aura of maiden-auntish do-goodism. If someone would only come up with a new, punchy term and a few slogans that would really alarm the public, we would move much faster. There is nothing like shock treatment in propaganda, and the cause of conservation needs all the propaganda it can get. But how can we expect a tired and confused humanity to get excited about the extermination of animal life when we are in the midst of what seems to be a worldwide period of sociopolitical upheaval? Hallet and I discussed this once and he was as concerned about the outlook as I. Now, having read this book, I have come to the conclusion that its author, with his Congoland project, is just the man to generate that badly needed conservationist *excitement*. But we still need a new word, a slogan, and a concentrated campaign that will shock the public, the bureaucratic stuffed shirts, and maybe—just maybe—the unthinking "sportsmen."

So far, we have mostly been talking about "open country" like the savannahs. Almost for the first time that I know of, from the zoological point of view, Jean-Pierre Hallet gives us here some firsthand knowledge on collateral problems in the closed-canopy forest areas, popularly called the "jungles." These problems are very different ones since, in any closed forest, there are no great herds of herbivores, either wild or domesticated, fewer predators, and far fewer human beings. It is impossible to take any census of the forest's animal population, and compared to the ethology of the savannahs, virtually nothing is known of the forest animals' behavior. Meanwhile the forests are steadily shrinking year by year. Their animal populations shrink with them and may perish before we even begin to understand them.

As I read this magnificent work I found myself wanting to stand up and cheer for almost every page. Jean-Pierre Hallet knows his animals, and his approach to them and his observations constitute one of the most vivid and realistic contributions to natural history, ethology and zoology that I have ever read.

IVAN T. SANDERSON

Blairtown, New Jersey, October 1967

ANIMAL
KITABU

People vs. Animals

People living together on our planet fondly call the resulting community a "society" or even a "civilization." Animal communities, however, are treated on a somewhat different level. The scientists call it ecology, or interrelations between animals and their environment, and ethology, the new science of "normal" animal behavior. The rest of us, for the most part, see only a chaotic horde of creatures that spawn, live, kill, and die without apparent reason. We generally interpret this vision according to three basic styles of thought and action: the well-meaning but usually uninformed nature enthusiasts who "love" but sometimes try to housebreak both ends of an animal; the lords of a clockwork creation who feel free to exterminate animals when they are in man's way; and the would-be White Hunters—ignorant or even compulsive killers who have turned the African savannahs into a hunter's version of Las Vegas.

The first tribe of men, probably a majority, has some interest and enthusiasm for the earth's nonhuman species. They express it by the care and sympathy they extend to domesticated dogs, cats, birds, or horses, by their liking for those free-living animals who seem gentle and endearing, like the soft-eyed deer, the antelopes, and the squirrels, and by their admiration for "dangerous" but exotic creatures such as lions, elephants, and tigers. But their humane attitude has certain built-in limitations: they usually regard the lesser predators and scavengers as "sneaky," "cowardly," or even "evil"; and they will kill wolves, hyenas, vultures, or coyotes without the least consideration for their vital roles in nature's balance.

Toward animals who diverge more widely from the human form, this group of men extends even less humane treatment. Reptiles are feared and killed on sight although most are entirely harmless; those who present some actual degree of menace, such as cobras or crocodiles, are of course "evil." Spiders, insects, and other invertebrates are rarely even recognized as animals; they are frightening or loathsome "bugs" which must be squashed or sprayed.

Yet this first tribe of men is almost always well meaning, despite their unreasoning prejudice and animosity toward animal outcasts and pariahs. They want to like "Mother Nature," even to love her, but they think that she should be reformed—strictly for her own good. In many so-called nature books and films, they sentimentalize the animals beyond recognition, transforming them into fluffy greeting-card characters that prance eternally through a technicolor Garden of Eden. Even in some alleged documentaries, the "hero" animal has all our human virtues while the "villain" is afflicted with our human flaws. Neither has any real or valid personality of his own.

The fact that in extreme cases, fanatical nature lovers try to reform the animals themselves is no exaggeration. Even during the 1960's within the borders of the world's most advanced industrial civilization, a substantial number of American citizens were eager to join an organization whose purported goal was to trouser "naked horses" and install petticoats on "nude cows." This fantastic project was sponsored by a group known as SINA, The Society for Indecency to Naked Animals—a name which should have been a dead give-away to its founder's playful intentions. Nonetheless there were many eager volunteers, ready to march under SINA's streaming banners on the great crusade to clothe America's naked animals.

18

Now I am not criticizing American manners and mores, only the ways of nature fanatics wherever they may be found. Back in Belgium, where I was born, the impassioned cat-lovers of my father's home town, Liège, once formed a society for "the improvement, mental and moral, of the domestic cat." After announcing that goal—a far less feasible project than trousering cats—you might expect that the Belgian cultists organized feline poetry classes. Not at all. They had a more practical scheme: since *Felis catus* has an excellent sense of direction, they planned to train cats to carry messages and thus eventually replace carrier pigeons. The steady employment, they felt, was bound to improve the cats' moral tone in that it left them much less time to frolic on the back fence. Fired by this magnificent vision, the cat-lovers of Liège made some preliminary tests, depositing their cats up to twenty miles from home. Shortly afterwards, as the supply of feline mailmen waned, the plan was dropped and the great cat society was quietly dissolved.

The second tribe of men, as I see them, are quite indifferent to the animal world. Consciously or not, they believe with Christian dogmatists that animals have no souls, or with the French philosopher Descartes that animals are mere instinct machines, little higher than the plants, "brutes who act by force of nature and by springs like a clock." Since the rest of animate creation is just a pile of clockwork toys, they feel that man may do with it exactly as he pleases. That includes exterminating entire nonhuman populations, especially if they impinge in any way on his rapidly accelerating program for turning our planet into one vast concrete-surfaced, steel-structured, plastic-furnished, and grimly tedious housing tract.

The third and smallest tribe of men seizes upon the opportunity to satisfy their passions in a world where, apparently, anything goes. They join eagerly in the animals' alleged killing spree; they become "hunters." Now this was once a decent word, and still is if men are hunting for meat. But when they are looking for trophies or sport, it often becomes obscene—especially in Africa, where civilized standards quickly wither under the tropical sun. Here the self-styled sportsmen often display themselves as the classic on-safari types so well described by the late Robert Ruark: ". . . boors and bores and bitches and cowards and braggarts and creeps and occasional homosexuals who have the eye more on the hunter than on the game."

But in addition to these three attitudes there is also a sound, unsentimental and truly humane approach toward the problems of animal-human coexistence. I feel very strongly that the animal life of any area can be viewed as a true society running parallel to our own. It may be a *foreign* society, but no more foreign, really, than Germany to an Italian or the United States to an incredulous (and probably disapproving) Congo Pygmy. As such, and even though immensely less advanced, the world's animal societies deserve our curiosity and respect—not our condescension. We should not flinch in pious indignation at unexpected sights, sounds, and smells, nor should we attempt to impose our own allegedly superior customs—social or sexual. It is vital to their survival, however, that we give the world's animal societies a sort of "foreign aid."

Maintaining this attitude won't be easy. It isn't even easy with people. I found that out during the ten years I served as agronomist and sociologist for the Congo's former Belgian colonial government. There I taught brush tribesmen many things needed for their continuing survival: how to rotate crops, prune trees, reforest barren slopes, dig septic holes, fight a score of different insect pests, and even how to stop eating each other; but the hardest problem was to render aid, material or social, without menacing their established cultures and more valuable traditions.

To put it simply, I liked the people of the bush, even loved them *for themselves,* finding their human differences as deeply meaningful as their human similarities, and *not* as raw material for imitation Europeans. My feeling wasn't by any means a colonialist opinion, but diametrically the opposite; in fact, it much resembles the feeling now being expressed by native Africans who do not wish to model themselves after white men but prefer to preserve and further develop their own cultures—to be proud of their "négritude," as they call it.

I must have succeeded in conveying that attitude, since I was accepted as an initiated member of Kenya's Masai tribe, and as a blood brother of the Congo's Balega and Banande. In the Ituri Forest, despite my cumbersome size, I became for all practical purposes a Bambuti Pygmy, sharing in every respect the merciless realities of my adopted people's existence. In 1957, in the Ituri, I took a poison arrow in the leg and somehow managed to survive the crude Pygmy surgery that followed. Previously, blackwater fever had nearly killed me in Katanga, a native knife slashed my leg in Kasai, and in Burundi, late in 1955, a dynamite explosion blew off my right hand at the wrist, taking most of my hearing with it. My body is a patchwork quilt of old African scars, but none of them, oddly enough, resulted from contact with the animals.

Though I never carried a gun or even a knife while living among Africa's "vicious wild beasts," observing them at close quarters and even playing with so-called killers like the buffalo and rhino, I was never hurt by them. That remained the case, on leaving government service in 1958, when I took up animal taming and training as a steady hobby, keeping a full-grown lion in my backyard at Kisenyi, North Rwanda, and a full-grown rhino and two elephants in a nearby compound. I took what seemed to be amazing liberties with all, but because I knew and respected their individual natures, I was neither clawed, gored, nor trampled.

Then I left Africa in 1960, immigrating to the United States, and nearly everyone I met assumed, automatically and with the friendliest enthusiasm, that I was a Hollywood-style White Hunter. Some of them even asked, nodding sympathetically at my missing hand, "Did a lion do it—or a crocodile?" I suppose they assumed this because I came from Africa, I was experienced with animals, and I was rather large and durable-looking. In fact, my physical appearance tallied exactly with a description Robert Ruark once gave of the public's stereotyped White Hunter image: "He stands about six foot five and sports a full beard."

This American welcome was intended as a sort of compliment, but it came as an ironic one, since "White Hunter Hallet" was a life-long conservationist known on the other side of the ocean as *Le Père Noé Belge*—the Belgian Father Noah. I now hoped to moor my ark on American soil by attempting to found a huge game sanctuary, Congoland U.S.A., to save a part of Africa's fauna from native poachers and invading foreign hunters.

Writing my first book, *Congo Kitabu,* I told the story of my African adventures. Toward the end of *Animal Kitabu,* I recount some of my subsequent misadventures, which occurred mostly in Southern California where Congoland was nearly established. It would have become a reality, I think, if various public officials and the public itself had enjoyed a little knowledge of the African fauna. It may still be realized, and I am working toward that goal. As it was, however, the first Congoland attempt became a center of public controversy, beset by rumors that were wilder than the wildest wild beast. At one time I was even accused of planning to bury the state of California under a seething mass of African boa constrictors.

That charge was launched by the Monterey County Board of Supervisors, headlined in local newspapers, sent out over the wire services, and printed without question or comment by the national press, including *The Philadelphia Inquirer* of February 22, 1961, and the *New York Journal-American* of the same date. No one rose to challenge the validity of my oncoming African boa invasion, or even to laugh at it, despite the fact that boa constrictors or boas of any kind do not and have never lived anywhere on the African continent. Curiously, two members of the boa family—the rosy boa and the rubber boa—happen to be native Californians. If the Monterey Board of Supervisors ever finds out, they may be deported to Africa.

The boa panic, such as it was, arose from a misconception of the very simplest sort, a lack of information as to what animals live where. It happens all the time and "Darkest Africa" is usually the victim, made a little darker by a legendary crew of Indian tigers and water buffaloes, plus South American boa constrictors, jaguars, and monkeys that hang by their tails. On a slightly higher level, if the real animals are known, they are usually believed to live together, one and all, in the teeming, omnipresent "jungle" of the Tarzan-style movies, although two-fifths of Africa is desert and another two-fifths rolling savannah, very similar to America's western prairies. On the highest level of misinformation, when the animals are properly sorted out into their respective habitats, their habits are generally misinterpreted or they are credited with unfounded behavior.

There are many excellent existing works on natural history which, if read, would clear away the picturesque confusion. But few people want to read them, having neither the desire nor the patience to pore over technical minutiae—and frankly, I don't blame them. In the last analysis, it is almost impossible to get a vivid, meaningful picture from disconnected facts or stories of one animal or another, even if they are told on a more or less popular level.

Thus, my intention in writing *Animal Kitabu* was to draw a series of overlapping animal portraits that would blend together, taken as a whole, to recreate the complex animal society of Equatorial Africa. Each portrait should be complete in itself, having a many-angled view of the subject, with family, friends, acquaintances, and enemies sketched into their proper background places. As one passes from one level of society to the next, the camera angle shifts, the first animal blends into the background, and a new figure comes into close focus.

My animal society is stratified along familiar human lines, with king, warriors, gentlemen, bourgeois citizens, and proletariat, and even delinquents, hobos, and eccentrics. I doubt that anyone will find it sentimental, but some may possibly contend that this kind of structure tends to over-humanize the animals. I don't believe that is true. Although animal societies may be foreign, they can be translated.

Animal-human differences are a matter of degree, not of kind; few can doubt that fact after sitting down and watching, just for a couple of hours, a pack of very intelligent, highly gregarious and ever-loquacious baboons. But it's a little harder to grasp the basic similarities between human and elephant, between human and vulture, between human and giraffe, until you see a herd of elephants, drunk on fermented fruit, playing practical jokes, or watch an Egyptian vulture pick up a stone, heave it at a tough-shelled ostrich egg, and break it for breakfast, or glimpse giraffes babysitting for other giraffes and getting involved in homosexual love affairs.

Some may find my frank descriptions rather repellent. They think of Africa and see in their mind's-eye the cloudlike vision of Mount Kilimanjaro or the green-haired beauty of the Congo's Grand Forest. Africa can indeed be a place of vast, almost overwhelming beauty, but it is also a place of mud, blood, and excrement. Remove them from the scene and it is Africa no longer, just a pretty picture postcard.

Despite their lack of polished manners, in my opinion animal societies are less aberrent than our own. They are more solidly rooted in the ancient laws of selection and survival, and more frankly oriented toward the basic problems of territory, food, and procreation.

Death comes very quickly to the weaker animal, but life is rich, vivid, pungent, and, above all, honest.

JEAN-PIERRE HALLET

Los Angeles, 1967

CHUI

The Real King of Beasts

Who is the real "King of Beasts"?

Aesop and La Fontaine, spinning the same fables in Greek and in French, pictured the lion as ruling over all other animals, "a monarch provident and wise." This sentimental misconception has persisted through the ages and still dominates popular opinion. Naturalists and nature-lovers, smitten by the elephant's size, power, and very appealing ways, have sometimes given him the crown, while hunting fans usually try to seat the Cape buffalo on Africa's animal throne, and Hollywood portrays the black rhino, or "horned fury," as he is usually billed, as the reigning or most dangerous beast.

All of them, from Aesop to MGM, are judging by appearances and not by action.

A king cannot be a lazy, good-natured idler like the lion, letting his ladies kill for him and living on the profits like a pimp. He cannot, like the elephant, spend sixteen hours a day in the simple act of eating and lead a family life that is blatantly bourgeois. He cannot travel with the common herd, grazing and chewing the cud like a cow—even a very shrewd and tough cow like the Cape buffalo. And least of all, he cannot be a snorting, dim-witted windbag like the rhino, who rarely knows exactly what he is charging.

The real king never travels, hunts, or feeds in a pride, pack, or herd. He stands or dies alone, as a king has to. He has no real friends, even among his own kind, and will not settle for a banal family life, but mates briefly, soon divorces, and never sees his offspring. He either kills his own meat—and kills it superbly!—or commandeers a lesser predator's kill. Pound for pound, he is the strongest animal on earth, seemingly assembled out of steel muscles and tendons. He is also one of the most intelligent; coolly calculating, patient, and immensely wary.

His Swahili name is Chui, and its sound somehow conjures up slinking, silken-coated, Oriental-flavored visions. They are quite appropriate, since the stealthy monarch ranges all the way from Africa, through Persia, Syria, and India, to China, Malaya, and even Java. He is, by reason of his intelligence and great adaptability, the most successful and widely distributed of all big cats, ruling regions that lions have never been able to invade and surviving where lions have long been extinct.

The real King of Beasts is the leopard.

This unsung sovereign is also, in my opinion, Africa's toughest, most elusive, and most hazardous animal to hunt, deserving top rank in the so-called Big Five, the hunters' cherished and contantly discussed listing of Africa's most dangerous game. I know that many hunters and hunting buffs will object, especially on the basis of his size; a full-grown male leopard often weighs little more than a hundred pounds and usually measures less than eight feet from tip of nose to tip of tail. How can such a little cat, they ask, be ranked above a four-hundred-pound lion, a one-ton buffalo, a ton and a half of charging rhino, or a six-ton elephant? In their opinions, his size seems to exclude him from being recognized as Number One; in fact they often rank him last.

But when one considers very briefly the problems faced by hunters in their attempts to find and kill the various members of the Big Five—often ranked in descending order as Cape buffalo, elephant, rhino, lion, and leopard—the picture changes.

Seeking out a black rhino, Cape buffalo, or elephant presents no major difficulties, except in regions where they have been hunted to near-extinction. These are all animals of the wooded savannah rather than equatorial forest—the only true "jungle"—and they are all large, even cumbersome creatures who cannot hide themselves except in the very thickest bush, handicapped by the very bulk which seems to be an asset. The buffalo stays closer to cover than either rhino or elephant, but the hunters often spot his presence by the circling flight of snowy-winged egrets, or "cattle herons," overhead.

The hunter, or more often the hunting party, can spot any of these enormous targets from a distance and take a more or less studied shot. If the first bullet fails to hit a vital spot and the wounded quarry charges, there is nearly always time for another shot if not a whole salvo. If the wounded animal retreats, attempting to take cover, the hunter who follows him into the bush (and this rough job is usually left to professionals) again has the advantage of stalking a heavily built animal who cannot easily conceal himself and who cannot move as silently as the soft-padded lion or leopard.

Considering this shared handicap, I have to relegate the three giant herbivores to the bottom rungs of my reluctant Big Five. The black rhino, addlepated and terribly nearsighted, is a poor fifth; the Cape Buffalo, wary and equipped with superior physical senses, is a much more dangerous fourth. The elephant, despite his poor vision and the huge target he presents, displays such shrewd intelligence when hunted, combined with such a versatile array of lethal weapons—massive head, trunk, tusks, and great trampling feet—that he makes a very strong third. But any hunter so inept that he cannot stop the charge with his .450- to .600-caliber elephant gun fully deserves his fate; he might just as well have started an argument with a locomotive while standing on the railroad tracks.

The lion, also restricted to the savannahs, I rank second. Intelligent like the elephant and equipped with superior senses like the buffalo, he has the added virtue of being designed for a hunting, not a browsing or a grazing life. Speedier and far more agile, he presents a smaller target when goaded into charging, and if the first bullet doesn't stop him, the clumsy hunter often has no time to fire again; he may be knocked unconscious as the lion lands and badly mauled or killed before his hunting companions can get off another shot. But the lion has a fatal flaw: lazy and overconfident, he lolls about on the open savannah, watching distant hunters complacently and allowing them to make an easy approach.

This not only keeps him from assuming top rank in the hunters' trivial Big Five, but has led to his extermination over vast stretches of his former range.

The Number One animal commits no tactical errors, has no physical handicaps of any kind, and never permits a man or beast to approach him—he does the approaching himself. Ranging from tree-clad savannah to deep equatorial forest, Chui follows the same elusive pattern of life in both: prowling in his fanatically cautious way during the night, he kills his prey, dines, hangs the ravaged carcass high in a tree, and holes up for the daylight hours in heavy cover—rockpile, cave, or the most impenetrable thornbush thicket he can find. If the cover is less dense than he prefers, his lithe body with its camouflaging spotted coat can be tucked away almost invisibly in places where a housecat seemingly couldn't hide. He climbs trees with more agility than Tarzan and takes to the water readily, sometimes hiding out on wooded islands in the larger rivers or lakes.

If the hunter spots the leopard's tree-hung kill or stumbles across his freshly made spoor and tries to track it, he usually finds nothing. The hunter then departs, deciding that Chui has abandoned the neighborhood. Meanwhile, Chui himself has probably been observing the hunter with casual contempt. He rarely bothers to attack—why should he? If he has seen and heard a gun before, he knows its ominous possibilities. If not, he still distrusts the situation; rifle-bearing white men are neither his customary prey nor a part of his customary landscape. Their appearance, scent, clothing, equipment, and even the way they move are all novel, suspect, and, in the mind of this supremely clever cat, potentially dangerous. He doesn't believe in taking unnecessary chances, so he will either watch from hiding or make a quick, unobtrusive departure.

Sometimes, very rarely, he will hunt the hunter. Such a highly unusual course of action can be expected only from a leopard partially crippled by an old bullet wound or nearly senile with advancing age, and in either case unable to prey on swifter, more alert quarry. Yet, almost invariably, even a desperate leopard will not launch an actual attack unless the man is alone and unless he can attack from the rear. If he does, the hunter is soon finished: no one can fight effectively or survive for more than a few minutes with a leopard gnawing and wrenching at the nape of his neck, tearing his shoulders with razor-sharp talons, and demolishing his buttocks and thighs with even more powerful hindfeet.

Only if the lucky (or unlucky!) hunter surprises him at

close quarters and has him cornered, or manages to wound him first, will Chui make a frontal attack. Then he will go for the jugular while ripping the shoulders with his front feet and using the hind ones to tear out the hunter's entrails. Either way, front or rear, few men survive unless someone rushes to their aid. Unlike a lion, who will sometimes cuff his victim and depart, especially when he isn't very hungry, Chui never lets go until his opponent is dead and, preferably, disemboweled.

Considering the leopard's stealthy and largely nocturnal habits, deliberate or organized leopard hunts are just about impossible, either in Africa or India. But strictly to satisfy their clients' insatiable desire to get a leopard, professional hunters often stage a sorry little farce that has neither dignity nor danger. They take an antelope or zebra quarter, hang it in a tree for bait, and build a *boma,* or hunting blind, at a safe distance. Sometimes, as a variant, they stake out a goat or dog on the ground. If the leopard rises to the bait toward sunset, as he often will, he can be picked off by the hunters' telescopic-sight rifles with no risk at all to their concealed persons. Somehow or other they manage to call it sport.

Such a baited "leopard hunt" from a concealed blind was featured in January, 1967, on the documentary television series *American Sportsman.* Movie actor John Saxon played the role of intrepid amateur hunter, crouching in the *boma* with his guide, squinting through his scope, and getting off a killing shot; but like most novices in Africa, he let the hunting talk convince him that the leopard hunt was for real.

Critic Cleveland Amory commented in *TV Guide* on the spectacle of what he called "white hunters in living color":

> . . . one thing is easy, and that is picking the *worst* show on the air. To me, beyond question, beyond argument, beyond even the faintest shadow of a doubt, it is an appalling apparition entitled *The American Sportsman* . . . a show which every week assassinates grizzly bears, leopards, elephants, rhinos, and other animals in danger of extinction. If the men who run ABC themselves find enjoyment in such "sport," it is sad news. But it is their private business. When they inflict it on the public, however, under the guise of "sportsmanship," it is the public's business and an outrage. . . .

That old saw about the thrill of the chase falls rather flat when the so-called chasers sit in hiding. But the underlying motive of these staged leopard hunts is not merely a false

29

sense of danger or excitement; it is, as with most amateur hunting in Africa, the avid quest for trophies. The gullible tourist, bent on preserving and publicizing the memory of his African triumphs, needs tangible proof to bolster his hunting and social status. So, to immortalize his victories over the other members of the Big Five, taxidermists will transform elephant feet into trash baskets or bar stools, rhino feet into ashtrays, and Cape buffaloes or lions into mounted heads. Chui's head is also mounted, complete with glass eyes and plastic tongue, gums, and palate, but unlike the other Big Fivesters he bears as well a beautiful spotted pelt.

What happens to that pelt has been described by Vernon Bartlett in his poem "The Leopard Coats," which originally appeared in the *New Statesman:*

> Once in a moment of great generosity
> God has shown to me
> A leopard running free.
> How, from that moment, could he expect of me
> Born without his tolerance, calmly to see
> All those women, those bloody awful women,
> Dressed up in leopard skins and sitting down to tea?

Most of the skins that go into leopard coats, hats, and other accessories are not obtained, however, by the staged antics of White Hunters and their clients. Only a limited number of licenses to shoot leopards are issued, so the deficit must be remedied by middlemen who purchase pelts for a pittance from Africa's own native poachers. The poachers, long ago corrupted by the far-spreading influence of the safari racket, lay wire slip-noose snares that may sentence trapped leopards or other animals to days of agony before the poacher comes to finish them off. Smuggled out of Africa, often via Somalia, the pelts are sold to Western markets at an enormous markup.

Those who provide the skins, and those who hunt Chui for a nonexistent thrill, are the only animals who ever prey on full-grown leopards, although allegedly cowardly hyenas will sometimes run far more risk to snatch a straying cub. Yet compared to other animals, Chui seldom falls prey to man; he hangs on where lions and every other kind of large game have been blasted off the map. If present-day game slaughters continue, the leopard will soon give the final proof of his supremacy: he will be the last surviving member of the Big Five.

With African natives, who are more familiar and predictable from his point of view, Chui grows more daring. Prowling round the fringes of their villages, he will pick off stray goats, pigs, and dogs, snatch up a wandering baby or, much more rarely, kill and haul away a careless woman. Yet he will almost always hesitate and turn aside before attacking a full-grown man, even a poorly armed or unarmed native.

The fact that Chui takes so very few human victims is partially explained, once again, by his caution. But I have always felt that leopards and the other predatory cats actually have little liking for our human flesh and prefer almost any other kind of meat. For obvious reasons I have never been able to make actual experiments, but theoretical confirmation recently came from the very highest authority. Dr. Louis S. B. Leakey, the world-famed anthropologist who first unearthed many of our fossilized ancestors in East Africa's Olduvai Gorge, has suggested that both human body odor and taste are highly offensive to the great cats, unlike the more pleasingly scented flesh of baboons. He mentioned also that chimpanzees are preyed upon only rarely, since they are far more manlike than baboonlike in their anatomy, physiology, and aroma. Conceivably, man's evolution and survival in the prehistoric world may have depended, to some extent, on his unsavory reputation.

So far as I know, the leopard's character and style are consciously recognized and countered by only one of the varied peoples who live in the Congo's leopard-teeming Ituri Forest —the Bambuti Pygmies, who are not a Negro tribe but a separate and distinct human race. Nomadic in their ways, they have no fixed villages, but when they spot a leopard prowling near a temporary encampment, they stand fast and frighten him off, shouting and twanging their bowstrings. If a single Pygmy is moving through fairly dense brush and suddenly comes upon a leopard, he brandishes his little three-foot hunting bow, shouting loudly, *"Odu, ogu muradi!"*—"Get out of my way, Grandfather!" Startled and perturbed, the leopard flees. The cocky Pygmy goes his own way, sometimes later claiming that he made the leopard "put his tail between his legs like a dog."

While living with a Pygmy band in the Ebuya sector of the forest, I gave the old Bambuti slogan a try. I had been gathering mushrooms with the women when I strayed into a small clearing, eyes searching the ground. Suddenly sensing an alien gaze, I looked up and saw a full-grown leopard crouching on the mossy ground some twenty-five feet away, and staring at

31

me with an expression of avid curiosity. Living in the deep forest as he did, he had probably never seen a white man; but I wasn't carrying anything that might be interpreted as a weapon, only a basket of mushrooms, and I wore familiar Pygmy garb, a beaten-bark loincloth. Perhaps the poor animal was trying to decide exactly what I was.

Playing my Pygmy role to the hilt, I stepped forward saying, *"Odu, ogu muradi!"* "Grandfather" coughed a harsh, grunting cough, but he didn't look very worried or bother to put his three-foot tail between his legs. He simply stared a little harder. I didn't feel like switching tactics so I switched to another language, learned during a recent year-long visit to the United States. "GRANDPA!" I thundered. "GET LOST!"

The leopard turned and vanished into the bush. They almost always do. So does every so-called dangerous predator when confronted and outfaced, but given a chance to retreat. Yet people—perhaps from watching too many televised "jungle" films on Sunday afternoon—still believe that animals leap out of the bush, one after another, to attack passing humans. They will probably continue to believe it, even though the myth has been debunked many times, and perhaps most notably by the outstanding naturalist and writer, Ivan Sanderson. As Sanderson wittily summed it up in his *Book of Great Jungles:*

> To all of these creatures I simply said something like "Boo!" in a very loud and peremptory manner and they shoved off at the double. . . . As a matter of fact, after nearly forty years of meandering about jungles under the most vulnerable conditions . . . I have yet to be actually jumped by anything larger than an ant.

The Pygmies not only agree with Ivan Sanderson, but go him one better. Mutuke, an old gentleman of Ebuya, once explained to me that the leopard-hailing cry wasn't really intended to frighten Chui but to display filial respect. Long, long ago, Mutuke told me, a leopard lay down to kitten and had a litter of talkative Pygmies instead. The father leopard accepted the situation stoically, but after a long series of Bambuti litters, he lost all patience. "Either stop your chattering," he told his Pygmy cubs, "or go away from me and make your own living." The Pygmies, who are probably the most loquacious, noisy, high-spirited people on this earth, at once trooped away. Now, whenever they meet their distant ancestor, they're merely reminding him of the old family ties.

Other human tenants of the Grand Forest, Sudanese and Bantu tribes alike, take a very different view of Chui. Their folk tales cast the leopard as a shrewd, grasping, brutal tyrant-king, an animal reflection seen by the African "man in the bush" of his own tribal despots. They act accordingly, encouraging leopard depredations by that same attitude of pessimistic fatalism which enabled native rulers of the past to exploit their people, sell them into slavery, or even devour their children. (King Munza of the Ituri's otherwise advanced Mangbetu tribe was encountered in 1871 by the German explorer Georg Schweinfurth. Schweinfurth visited Munza's royal court and was stunned to find that the Mangbetu ruler subsisted on a diet of "one plump infant per day.")

When one of these Bantu tribesmen has an unexpected meeting with a leopard, he usually screams and then turns and runs, sometimes heading for the nearest tree. This procedure, a dangerous course of action to take with any animal, is absolutely senseless when dealing with a highly intelligent cat who watches carefully for any sign of weakness, has an innate feline tendency to snatch at anything that runs, and climbs trees more rapidly and efficiently than any man born.

Considering that pattern of behavior, diametrically opposed to spunky Pygmy tactics, it isn't too surprising that full-grown men are occasionally attacked; what *is* amazing is the fact that Chui attacks so seldom.

A leopard panic of this sort, racing through an entire file of Banande porters, led to the closest call I ever had with any free-living African animal. It happened shortly before I went to live with the Pygmies, in January, 1957, in the Watalinga bush country between the Semliki River and the northwestern edge of the Ruwenzori Massif—the famed "Mountains of the Moon." My sixteen-man caravan was winding its way along a narrow trail leading through heavy brush toward the village of Muregeta. Our *kapita,* or head man, was in the lead, chopping away with his machete at the overgrown foliage, while I brought up the rear. It was a quiet, even banal on-safari scene; then it suddenly dissolved into hysterical chaos.

The second porter, near the column's head, had spotted a large leopard crouching on a tree branch. The cat was well concealed, but as leopards sometimes do he had let his tail dangle beneath him. Predictably, the porter shrieked, dropped his load, turned and tried to run away. The other porters and the *kapita* either bolted into the bush or shinnied up into the trees. Meanwhile, the leopard had sprung on the second porter from the rear, hurling him forward onto his face and belly. By the time I raced up the trail and reached them, the great cat had torn the shrieking man's shoulders, calves, and thighs, but hadn't as yet gone for the neck.

Weaponless and one-handed as I was, I couldn't force myself to stand by and do nothing while a man died. So foolishly or not, I did the only thing that seemed feasible: I attacked the leopard, leopard-style, from the rear. As I jumped onto his back, he tried to turn and we rolled sideways, freeing the porter who staggered bloodily into the bush.

Taking advantage of the leopard's initial surprise, I passed my arms under his forequarters from behind, partially dislocating his shoulders and forcing the upper end of each humerus into the side of his neck. The stump of my right forearm was long enough to hook around his right front leg, and I locked the hold by gripping my right elbow with my hand. Simultaneously, I scissored his hind legs with my own, forcing them stifly and widely apart.

The leopard writhed and heaved, coughing and choking but he was now completely spread-eagled. So was I. Mounted on his back like the proverbial man who rides the tiger, all I could do was hang on as he rolled me over and over on the trail and in the brush. For although I outweighed him by a factor of two to one, he tossed my 250 pounds about as though I were a mere toy.

"Kisu! Kisu!" I shouted to my scattered porters. "A knife! A knife!"

But the leopard panic had done its work well: none of the terrified porters would leave their stations in the treetops of the bush, either to aid directly or even to throw me a knife. In fact, not one of them tried to help for twenty agonizing, nightmarish minutes while I fought what was literally a holding battle. Then, as I approached the end of my endurance, the *kapita* got up enough courage to come within a hundred feet and throw me a huge, very clumsy knife with a foot-long blade.

It landed twenty feet away.

While the pair of us kept rolling over and over, I managed to wrestle the leopard toward the knife. As we got within reach, I released his left foreleg and pinned it under his body with a sudden shift of my weight. That enabled me, momentarily, to snatch at the knife with my hand while I kept his forequarters pinned with my truncated right arm. I barely caught the tip of the blade, shifted my grip to the hilt, and clutching the unwieldy knife, managed to regain my original

34

hold. Now, still rolling with the leopard, I tried to stab him through the heart.

The knife slipped, and I nearly lost it. The great cat leaped in my arms, and it was only by a terrible effort that I prevented him from breaking loose. I tried again, but the leopard suddenly writhed to the side and I just missed stabbing myself in the chest—I could feel the cold metal of the huge blade slide across my ribs. On my next attempt, I turned sideways, forcing the knife into his chest. The one-foot blade sank almost to the hilt, but he fought for another three or four minutes before he died.

At battle's end, I lay exhausted on the ground. The leopard hadn't once managed to bite or claw me, but my arms and legs were covered with a network of jagged red lines. They were scratches from the thornbush we had rolled through.

Other leopard-human battles, more well known, have usually involved grave or fatal wounds to the man. Such was the bloody struggle between Carl Akeley, the famed American naturalist and conservationist, and an eighty-pound leopardess. Akeley had rashly fired two rifle bullets, breaking one of her feet and creasing her neck, when she charged and sprang upon him. She went for the jugular with her jaws, but hampered by her broken foot (as Akeley himself was quick to remark), she missed her target, catching him by the upper arm instead. He tried to choke her as she chewed his arm from shoulder to wrist; he shoved his right hand down her throat so hard that she couldn't close her mouth, and he managed to crack a rib or two with his knees before he finally finished her off with a knife.

The leopard that I fought hand-to-paw, giving him a one-paw advantage, was an unwounded 120-pound male, in the prime of life and apparently healthy. I found no old scars on his body, so it must have been extreme hunger that drove him, despite all gourmet prejudice, to take advantage of the porters' panic.

Had he broken free at any time, the story might have had a more picturesque ending. He would have mauled and killed me within minutes; then he would have dragged the 250-pound cadaver into a dense thicket and torn out the entrails and buried them. Starting at the face and working his way down, he would have eaten rather daintily—unlike the lion who ploughs into the hindquarters and works his way up. Once he had polished off the nose, tongue, ears, heart, liver, and lungs, plus a quantity of skin and flesh, he would have hauled the remainder aloft and stuffed it into a tree crotch.

Considering my size it wouldn't have been an easy job, but leopards have been known to carry fully three times their own weight into the trees, even baby giraffes weighing over 300 pounds. Night after night, he would visit and revisit his aerial larder, relishing the stock of meat more keenly as it putrefied and grew tender, for leopards and lions alike adore carrion and will eat it just as readily as will any ill-reputed hyena, vulture, or crocodile. They will, in fact, take carrion away from hyenas whenever they get a chance. Of all the great African cats only the cheetah dislikes putrefying meat and seldom returns to a kill.

Carrion-eating, as well as their alleged "cowardice," accounts for much of the prejudice against hyenas and other scavengers—an illogical position to take unless we first condemn "man's best friend," the carrion-loving dog, punish the barnyard chicken who pecks at carrion and worse, and excommunicate America's national bird, the bald eagle, who feeds on carrion as well as fresh meat. We should also have to damn beyond redemption some ethnic groups such as the Eskimos, who like their meat green with putrefaction, or the Congo's cannibal Balega, who macerate their human meat, crocodile-style, under running water. And to be thoroughly honest, we might as well condemn ourselves for eating well-aged steaks and high-smelling cheeses rather than sinking our teeth into quivering, freshly killed prey.

There is one minor mystery connected with the leopard's upstairs pantry: vultures, who usually descend within minutes on any unprotected corpse, seldom touch Chui's kill even though Chui himself may be sound asleep in a cave or thicket half a mile away.

Vultures soar at fairly high altitudes, relying almost exclusively on their magnificent vision to spot any dying or dead animals on the savannah. They may well find it difficult to detect carrion that is stashed away under a shielding mass of branches and leaves, but that isn't a fully satisfying explanation, although it seems far more likely than some of the wild theories I have heard from professional hunters. A few of them even claim that Chui makes a "transaction" with the bateleur eagle: the eagle allegedly guards the leopard's larder all day long, driving away the vultures, and for his services receives a couple of pounds of meat per day.

The crested, brightly-colored bateleur eagle will certainly take meat from a leopard's kill, but hardly under contract. He usually cruises no more than a few hundred feet from the ground and is likelier than the vulture to detect tree-hung carrion. Since he is also much less common, and less gregarious in his ways, it usually happens that a single bateleur eagle finds the leopard's kill and visits it for some hours, snacking from time to time. He is a smaller bird than the vulture—some twenty inches long, compared to the vulture's more than forty—and his needs are relatively modest.

As for Chui, I cannot imagine a leopard making any kind of transaction with a bird, except a rather final one. A leopard doesn't do business with anyone, even another leopard. Besides, a story such as this one implies a certain amount of abstract reasoning on both sides, plus other human qualities which neither party possesses.

Congolese natives concoct similar fanciful tales about transactions between animals of widely differing species. Some are amazingly valid, based on symbiotic or social relationships; others, like the hunters' folk tale, show human rather than animal behavior. Reflecting native life itself, the characters in this type of legend live in comfortably furnished huts, cultivate fields or groves, and engage in some highly commercial activities: lizards borrow money from leopards, antelopes take crocodiles to court, and turtles write letters of protest to Belgian District Commissioners. It is all one big native-style *palabre,* an endless round of haggling argument, agreement, disagreement, feud, and even actual litigation.

In many of the legendary lawsuits, Chui himself plays the role of defendant. The court cases often involve stolen dogs, and in real life, leopards usually get into trouble for that very reason—they have an insatiable passion for dog meat. To get it, even in so small a portion as a Pekingese, this normally wary animal will take risks that he wouldn't otherwise consider. Some leopards will not only prowl around native villages but will invade the huts; a few may even enter white planters' gardens, sometimes their very houses—the sort of unknown territory they detest and fear.

Native storytellers usually explain that Chui has an ancient grudge against the dog. According to a version I heard in the eastern Ituri, the leopard once planted a field of peanuts which was then raided by a lizard. To escape punishment, the lizard told the leopard that he had seen a dog digging in the field. Enraged, Chui went to search through all the forest for the thief who stole his peanuts. "To this very day," I was told, "he is still trying to find the right dog."

His attempts to find it have led to more human deaths than any other phase of leopard activities. The daring dog hunts, and goat raids to a lesser extent, bring him into close contact with people, most of them unarmed, unprepared, and prone to panic. Seeing their weakness, an aging leopard who is having trouble catching wiser prey and growing desperate for meat of any kind, may grow bold enough to become a confirmed man-eater. If and when he does, employing all of his fantastic stealth, ingenuity, agility, and strength, he exacts a greater toll of human life and is much more difficult to find and deal with than any man-eating lion or tiger.

In Central Africa, where accurate records are extremely difficult to keep, individual leopards have made twenty or thirty kills in one village, preying for the most part upon children. In India, where more detailed reports are available, the man-eating leopards of Bhagalpur took an estimated 350 human lives over a period of three years, from 1959 to 1962, while desperate government officials used tear-gas bombs and dynamite on any suspected lairs.

While frightful, the danger in Bhagalpur hardly compared to the reign of terror conducted by a *single* leopard, probably the most notorious and widely-feared animal in all of human history: the great man-eating leopard of Rudraprayag, shot and killed on May 2, 1926, after a ten-week stalk by the late Colonel Jim Corbett, who had pursued it off and on for two years.

Clearly identifiable by his distinctive pug marks, the Rudraprayag leopard roamed over five hundred square miles in the Kashmir region of northern India, killing at least 125 human beings and sometimes hauling their bodies distances of up to four miles. Four thousand persons in the area held officially licensed guns; three hundred more took out special licenses, hoping to collect the huge government-offered reward; soldiers of the Garhwal regiments tried to track him down; government officials poisoned his kills whenever they could find the bodies; villagers tried to capture him, erecting baited drop-door traps; and European sportsmen hunted him with skill, experience, and the finest modern weapons. But the Rudraprayag leopard defied them all, ruling for *eight* years.

When Colonel Corbett finally caught up with him, shooting him in the shoulder from a goat-baited *machan,* or hunting blind, this arch killer and tyrant-king of all past or present cats was revealed to be a large and very aged male, his teeth brown and broken, his tongue and mouth black in color—perhaps from ingested poison he had survived—and his left hindfoot mutilated by an old bullet wound.

38

Commented Colonel Corbett himself, writing in his classic book, *The Man-Eating Leopard of Rudraprayag:*

> Here was only an old leopard, who differed from others of his kind in that his muzzle was gray and his lips lacked whiskers; the best-hated and the most-feared animal in all India, whose only crime—not against the laws of nature, but against the laws of man—was that he had shed human blood, with no object of terrorizing man, but only in order that he might live. . . .

Ironically, in light of those words, humans have themselves invoked the leopard's name and aura so that they might terrorize and take human life. I refer to Africa's notorious Leopard Man secret societies, especially the Congo's still-active *Anyoto* which was nearly extirpated by the former colonial government and then revived by Ituri Forest tribes after the Congo received its independence.

One of the worst *Anyoto* outbursts occurred in 1934, west of Lake Edward on the Ituri's eastern fringe, centering around Beni, a small town where I spent the first six years of my childhood and later worked among the Banande tribe and the Bambuti Pygmies. Here the Leopard Men murdered forty-two natives in three months, far outdoing the Rudraprayag leopard who had averaged only fifteen victims per year. Since their methods and weapons were patterned after those of their namesake, it was often difficult to determine whether deaths had actually been caused by a leopard or a man.

Describing those methods, I wrote in *Congo Kitabu:*

> The *Anyoto* masqueraded grotesquely in bark-cloth tunics and hoods marked with black spots and rings to resemble a leopard's skin. The tail of a real leopard dangled from the human leopard's rear, attached to a belt which held other important accessories: a small earthenware pot, a stick carved in the shape of a leopard's paw, and a very sharp knife. He blew into the pot to mimic the leopard's muffled snarl, he pressed the stick into the soft earth surrounding his victim's body to copy the animal's spoor and he used the knife to sever his prey's carotid arteries. The final and the most characteristic tool was an iron bracelet equipped with four dangling knives: when his hand was extended, the blades were concealed under his palm, but when he made a fist they jutted out between his clenched fingers—like a leopard's claws.

The *Anyoto* hunted at dusk, prowling the forest paths or picking off victims at the edges of plantations and villages. Like their animal prototypes, they rarely attempted to kill strong young men who could fight for their lives. Instead, they hunted old men, children and especially women, and often, as an initiation requirement, they murdered their own close relatives. Like the leopard, the *Anyoto* attacked from the rear, slashing their prey with incredible fury. But then they usually gave themselves away . . . they cut off their female victim's breasts.

Sometimes the severed breasts were taken to the local *Anyoto* leader as proof of successful murder; sometimes they were eaten. As a final touch, the Leopard Men often tore the eyes out of their kill for use in making *dawa* or ritual medicine: they were simmered in a pot containing the claw-knives, and the *Anyoto* drank the resulting mess, convinced that the grisly procedure gave them the power to see in the dark. Then daylight came, and like the werewolves of European legend, the Leopard Men went calmly about their business—smiling, polite, even friendly.

Nearly twenty years after the mass killings at Beni, I talked with several Babali tribesmen jailed for complicity in another wave of Leopard Men murders. Aside from their pique at having been caught, none of them manifested the slighest itch of conscience. One, a man accused of killing his own sister, mutilating and partially eating her body, explained, "If everyone thinks a leopard did it, the cat is the guilty one and not the man."

As a man-eater, it seems that Chui has a lot to learn.

At home in raw bush, beyond temptation and corruption, Chui preys more normally. Leopard dwellers of the deep forest specialize in monkeys, rats, birds, and dwarf antelopes. Those who dwell upon the wooded savannahs hunt ground-fowl, small mammals, impalas, and the young of larger antelopes, warthogs, zebras, and giraffes. They also pick off any rash baboon who strays beyond his community limits, but never attack baboons en masse, knowing that the tough, public-spirited primates will literally tear them apart.

To capture prey Chui usually sets an ambush, pouncing down from a tree bough over a game trail, but he may stalk and spring at his quarry like a little spotted lion. He kills his victim quickly and efficiently—unlike the mild-mannered cheetah, equipped with weaker jaws and claws, who often kills by slow strangulation and sometimes starts to eat while his victim is still alive. Chui disposes of monkeys, birds, and cane rats on the spot, while the larger corpses decorate the trees.

Aside from these hunting and dining habits, we know very little. The leopard leads a cryptozoic existence—his normal pattern cannot be watched, since he will not act naturally while being observed.

Apparently there isn't any fixed time of year for breeding. When Chui runs across a leopardess in season, he probably takes her briefly, brutally but effectively, snarling and holding her by the nape of the neck as do other cats great and small. Then, unlike the patiently paternal lion, he deserts, leaving the partner-victim of his brief encounter to become a hard-working bachelor mother.

She does so, judging from zoo leopards, after a gestation period of 93 to 103 days, producing a litter of one to three cubs which are weaned at six months. Since the leopardess must hunt and care for them unaided, only one cub will generally be well-nourished and well-protected enough to reach maturity, living under her tutelage for eighteen months to two years. In India the cubs may commonly be melanistic spots or mutants—black leopards, or "black panthers," as they are sometimes called, but perfectly black leopards are extremely rare in Africa if not entirely unknown. In fact, for the filming of *Mogambo,* an "African" epic film starring Clark Gable and Grace Kelly, an Asian black leopard was imported all the way from Milan, Italy. It really would have been simpler to employ a native African, spots and all, but black leopards apparently have a mystique and glamor all their own.

Native legends, which are often helpful, fail to supply any valid insights into Chui's sex-life or its consequences. I have heard quite a few of these folk tales, some of them unrepeatable, and even a wild charge that leopards sometimes lay eggs.

According to the narrator, an Azande sage from the northeast Congo, Madame Chui once met a lady python while strolling through the forest. As ladies will, they stopped for a little chat. The leopardess was proud of her handsome cubs but complained that tending them was very wearisome. The loquacious python answered, rather smugly, that she showed her own wisdom by laying eggs and leaving them to make a living for themselves. Envious, the leopardess decided to give it a try: when it came time to kitten, she went to her cave, laid a large clutch of eggs, and departed. Returning some months later to check on her great experiment, she was stunned to find a caveful of starving, stunted little cubs. The cubs were just as horrified at the first glimpse of the mother they had never seen, and they exploded out of the cave in all directions to become wildcats, civets, genets, and servals.

The old native who told me this tale ended by giving me his solemn word that leopards still lay eggs every other year, just to keep up the population of smaller cats. Other native authorities, though less ingenious, are just as determined to connect in one way or another everything that wears spots. I have sometimes heard it claimed in East Africa that Chui mates with cheetahs, perhaps because he sometimes tolerates a cheetah's presence in the foreground. In Rhodesia, the cheetah himself is widely accused of mating and miscegenating with spotted hyenas. (But I have never heard a native claim, as do some of our own wildlife authorities, that free-living leopards will mate with spotless lions.)

That sort of integration simply doesn't go on in nature, although anything can and does happen in zoos, where llamas have mated with goats, elk with cattle, and desperate male dolphins with female turtles. Isolated from members of their own species, lonely animals will try anything to gratify their natural physical desires. More deliberate matings are induced when the zoo marriage brokers gradually and tactfully introduce a male-female pair, unmatched but belonging to related species. Caged together as they are, propinquity eventually takes its course.

Among the great cats, "ligers" and "tigons" are the most commonly produced (respectively a lion-tigress cross and a tiger-lioness cross). Though commonly believed to be absolutely sterile, as with mules and most animal interspecies crosses, they have been known to reproduce: a lady liger in the Munich Zoo mated with a lion, producing a cub which might have been called a "ligeron."

A wide variety of leopard crosses have been brought about, ranging well beyond the African natives' theory of "anything with spots." Some sixty years ago at Carl Hagenbeck's Hamburg Tierpark, a leopardess was mated with an enterprising puma, producing intermediate "pumapards." In America and more complexly during that same era, the union of a leopardess and jaguar produced a female "jagulep." Mated to a lion, she gave birth to hodgepodge animals which were, I guess, "lijaguleps." And at Japan's Hanshin Zoo in 1959 and 1961, a leopard and a lioness produced two litters of "leopons."

42

The leopons are, as I can testify from a recent visit to Japan, fairly handsome animals. Reokichi, the first litter's only male cub, now looks like a fat leopard with pale spots and a shaggy bib instead of a lion's mane. Perhaps some day he may provide a logical but lonely compromise candidate for the age-old title King of Beasts.

SIMBA

The Gentleman of Leisure

When a lion roars, according to warrior tribesmen of East Africa, he is really saying in Swahili: *"Nchi ya nani? Yangu, Yangu, YANGU!"* "Whose land is this? Mine, mine, MINE!"

It's an impressive, even poetic thought. I would like to believe it, just as I would like to hail Simba, one of my best friends among the animals, as King of Beasts. But those same Africans who praise the lion's roar chase the lion himself across the savannah, shouting insults as he runs for safety like a shaggy golden dog. More significantly, organized hunting has brought Simba to extinction in southeastern Europe, where he long ago lived; to near-extinction in India, where he once ranged widely and still remains the national emblem; extinction in the Near East and in North Africa, where the last Berber lions were slain during the 1890's; extinction in South Africa, where the huge Cape lions have been dead for

45

a hundred years; and threatened extinction, within twenty or thirty years, in his remaining East and Central African strongholds.

The species may survive, carried on by Sher—the Indian lion of the Gir Forest Preserve—rather than Simba, and by captive lions in the world's major zoos. But even if it does, a great warmth and wonder will have gone out of Africa. For behind his regal-sounding roar, his regal-looking mane, and his hackneyed regal reputation, Simba is something more—he is a thoroughgoing gentleman.

"Gentleman" may mean a courteous and open-dealing character who never gives unnecessary offense. Simba fits this definition as well as any large predator (excepting man). As Carl Akeley put it, "The lion is always a gentleman; if allowed to go his way unmolested he will keep to his own path without encroaching on yours." But according to a second school of thought, a gentleman is one who lives in idle splendor, maintaining a dignified or even dandified appearance while carefully avoiding any real work. Simba fits *that* definition better than any animal on earth, for he achieves his superbly lazy life by the classic method of his African human neighbors: he acquires one or more wives, takes his pleasure among them, and lets the ladies do the work.

Baby slung on her hip, the patient, hard-working African wife toils in the fields, pounds manioc root, washes clothes, or tends to the chickens while the man of the family lounges in the shade, smoking, sculpting wood, trading gossip or goods, and conducting endless *palabres* with his fellow gentlemen. This arrangement may appear to be unfair, but African wives, enjoying their babies and domestic chores, never develop the frustrations and neuroses of the Western world's emancipated women, perhaps because they lack the leisure for it. If and when a female suffrage movement conquers tribal Africa, its men will learn to suffer like our own. Until then, African husbands—and lions—are more to be envied than censured.

With her cubs at her side, as soon as they can keep up the pace, the lioness wife—Simba Jike, as the natives call her—stalks, runs down, captures, and kills the game while her courtly husband, Simba Dume, watches approvingly. If his wife or wives should tackle large and dangerous prey such as the Cape buffalo, he sometimes pitches in to help. But in either case, when the kill is made, he shoulders his entire family aside to take the "lion's share."

These basic principles of lion etiquette were underscored delightfully in Joy Adamson's book *Born Free*. To prepare

46

her pet, Elsa, for a return to the wild, she knew that the lioness had to be integrated into the family and social life of her free-living relatives; she had to find a husband and impress him with her housewifely talents. Mrs. Adamson aided, hauling dead zebra dowries to a series of handsome bachelors—and then consoling her bewildered pet when the suitors showed more interest in the meat than the mate. As she remarked dryly, "We hoped that if Elsa provided him with a meal he would have a favorable opinion of her."

Male and female of the other living feline species, some thirty-six in all, have little commerce with each other before or after the mating season, and then may live together only briefly. The male enjoys no fatherly relationship with cubs or kittens, and members of the same sex rarely form friendships. They are all more or less solitary, self-sufficient animals, from America's very intelligent and gentle puma to India's bold, sometimes arrogant tiger.

Uniquely social-minded, almost civilized by comparison, Simba is the world's only truly gregarious cat. Living in small communities, he contracts long-term marriages, managing several at a time without wifely friction, plays the role of kindly patriarch in the presence of his cubs, and usually associates on friendly terms with other male lions. Simba Jike, who is far more active and aggressive when lions hunt or when they defend themselves against human hunters, enjoys platonic friendships with the younger males, plays lion "aunt" by babysitting with infant cubs while their mother goes off hunting, and will often suckle cubs of litters other than her own.

Members of the lion community, regardless of their sex, enjoy each other's company and show it. Especially after brief separations—either female hunts or less productive male wanderings—they will touch noses, lick faces, or rub cheeks and bodies together with friendly enthusiasm. Older males are less demonstrative, attempting to maintain a gruff-seeming dignity, but soon relax among the rest for the day-long siesta. Lionesses and younger lions will sometimes climb into a tree, draping themselves over the limbs with utter disregard for the popular belief that no lions ever climb aloft. More often, the entire group will snooze together under a shady cassia or mimosa tree, bodies touching for companionship and often sleeping on their backs with feet absurdly raised in the air. This splayed-out heap of cat *gemütlichkeit*, which should be named a "clan" or "company," is called, ironically enough, a "pride" of lions.

A pride is not a fixed or simple social unit. Its members may patrol a roughly defined territory, usually from twenty-five to fifty square miles, or they may be animal nomads following the game. A lioness with cubs or a mated couple and their cubs make up the small "family pride." A mature, powerful, and very experienced male—a boss or pasha—his several wives and cubs of varying ages form what I call the "harem pride," often accompanied by well-mannered bachelors. Two or more lioness friends may join forces in a "ladies' pride," complete with attendant cubs, while young males may band together in a slipshod "bachelors' pride," sometimes taking as advisor an older male whose powers are waning and who has lost his lioness provider.

Casual encounters with another pride may provoke hostilities if one of the groups has staked out an actual territory. Then there is usually a great deal of roaring—"Yangu, Yangu, Yangu!"—but very little action. The residents may stage a chase or, very rarely, one of them may brawl with an intruder. More commonly, the alien lions roar briefly, just to save face, and attempt to make a dignified departure. If both prides are nomadic, their encounter is usually rather amiable; in fact, the two groups may mingle, stay together for a while, then depart with slightly altered membership. This kind of lion caucus probably explains the so-called troops of thirty to forty lions that are sometimes spotted in such rich country as the Serengeti Plains, where two or three intermingled harems may live together peacefully under the shared rule of their respective bosses.

Membership in any pride may shift from time to time as cubs mature and leave to form their own establishments, bachelors go wandering off together, or discontented lady lions pack up their cubs and leave the harem. The major shufflings and reshufflings usually occur when a lioness comes into season.

No one can foretell exactly what will happen, for each lion has a distinctive personality. He may be brilliant, mediocre, or seemingly feeble-minded, irritable or placid, playful or stodgy, careless or cautious, trainable and trustable to an amazing point, or stubborn and vindictive. And whatever his unique combination of mental and emotional traits, he will vary his behavior according to mood, whim, changing time of day, changing weather, or changing season.

Much like a man in his extreme individuality, each lion has his distinctive facial features which make him as easily

48

identified as any man, and his own distinctive way of dealing with matters of love and romance. So does every lioness.

Sometimes Simba Jike is apparently indifferent to her own biology or openly hostile to any and all male advances, snarling, clawing, and retreating from husband or importunate suitors. Sometimes she submits rather meekly. Sometimes she will play the temptress, sinuous and provocative, rolling on her back and teasing, even torturing any available male. And sometimes, at a rare lascivious extreme, she will abandon newborn cubs to run with male lions like the notorious Whore of Nairobi, an ill-famed lioness who did exactly that year after year in Kenya's Nairobi National Park.

Simba Dume on his part may approach the bored or hostile-looking lioness, finding himself either welcomed or repelled. Then again, he may watch with seemingly stony indifference while she teases, rising suddenly to touch her flank with an imperious forepaw. If she walks away disdainfully or smacks him in the face, he may wait awhile before trying again; more often, he will follow with a look of stupefied adoration, tongue hanging out while he paws at her repeatedly. If she decides to submit, she lies down on her belly and he mounts like any cat, seizing her by the nape of the neck for the five to ten seconds that the sexual act may take. As the two disengage, she may roll on her back in an ecstatic afterglow while he, attempting stolid dignity, stares at a low-hanging cloud, a cassia tree, or a distant baboon spectator. Twenty minutes later, the whole procedure may take place again; then several times more throughout the day and for several days thereafter.

If Simba Jike makes advances to a bachelor, as she very often does, her husband sometimes lies in the grass observing the courtship and actual mating with the benevolent air of a wife-lending Eskimo. He may even watch indifferently as she mates with two or three bachelors. At other times he may roar in rage, challenging any male who comes near her. If an ambitious bachelor thinks he stands a chance, he will roar his answering challenge—his intention to take over as the new boss or pasha of the pride.

Snarling, clawing, smashing with forepaw blows that would kill an ox or decapitate a man, the two lions may spar for some time without inflicting really serious wounds. Then, as one begins to tire or feels the battle going against him, he turns to run away. If his opponent presses, he may officially surrender, rolling on his back in the lion's "posture of humility"—the submission signal, like our own cry of "Uncle!,"

49

which is made by various gestures between male mammals of the same species. Invariably, the signal is honored and the losing lion flees, unpursued, across the savannah.

If the boss has been defeated but is still fairly young, he may find a place in another pride and even another mate. But although lions sometimes live for twenty years or more in captivity, a deposed boss who is ten or older has generally lost his speed, skill, and cunning during the palmy days of lioness-provided plenty. Unable to hunt for himself, he may try to prey on basking crocodiles and come to grief, or even be reduced to catching frogs, mice, termites, scorpions, and locusts. Weakened and emaciated, lonely and unprotected, the senile lion will be ringed by hyenas. They wait patiently, perhaps until he stumbles, then make their mass attack, eating the former lord and pasha while he is still alive.

Contrary to popular opinion, these hapless old lions almost never become habitual man-eaters, as do aging or partially crippled leopards and tigers. The very small lion minority who consistently attack and eat humans are usually strong, healthy, young, unmated, and seemingly demented animals. Such were the famed Man-Eaters of Tsavo, two maneless male lions who terrorized southern Kenya back in 1898, halting construction of the railway then being built from the port of Mombasa westward to Uganda. Before they were killed by Lieutenant-Colonel J. H. Patterson, this notorious pair had slain twenty-eight Indian coolies and at least thirty African natives, eating most of them. After their death, sporadic waves of man-eating continued in the neighborhood of the railway, climaxed by the fantastic actions of a lion who killed far fewer humans than the Rudraprayag leopard but should probably be called the world's most reckless and ferocious man-eater.

According to Colonel Patterson's epic account, *The Man-Eaters of Tsavo:*

A man-eating lion had taken up his quarters at a little roadside station called Kimaa, and had developed an extraordinary taste for the members of the railway staff. He was a most daring brute, quite indifferent as to whether he carried off the station master, the signalman, or the pointsman; and one night, in his efforts to obtain a meal, he actually climbed up on to the roof of the station buildings and tried to tear off the corrugated-iron sheets. At this the terrified *baboo* in charge of the telegraph instrument below sent the following laconic message to the Traffic Manager: "Lion fighting with station. Send urgent

50

succour." Fortunately he was not victorious in his "fight with the station"; but he tried so hard to get in that he cut his feet badly on the iron sheeting, leaving large blood-stains on the roof.

On subsequent nocturnal raids, this fanatical man-eater carried off the native driver of the pumping engine and several other victims. An engine-driver then sat up all night in an iron water tank, with a loophole cut in its side, hoping to pick off the lion if and when he showed up. It proved to be a false and almost fatal hope: the lion spotted the ambush, overturned the heavy tank, and tried to attack the would-be sniper through the narrow circular hole at the top. From his cramped position the native fired but missed, temporarily driving the lion away.

But he returned persistently, and in June, 1900, defeated another ambush attempt, this one laid by the Superintendent of Police, Mr. Ryall, along with two of his white friends. The three men sat up watching in an inspection carriage that was shunted onto a siding close to the station; then, believing that the local nemesis wasn't in their immediate neighborhood, the superintendent told his friends to sleep while he kept watch. When Ryall himself at last lay down and dozed, the lion swung into action: he had been watching them for some time, as proved by the survivors' incredibly simple-minded statement that they had seen "two very bright and steady glow-worms" in the dark—the man-eater's very eyes.

Mounting the high steps at one end of the carriage, the lion pawed aside the unlocked sliding door and sprang among the three sleeping men. He seized and mauled the hapless Ryall while the other two, panic-stricken, made their escape through the door without attempting to rescue their friend. The door was now held shut by an hysterical mob of coolies, but the man-eater launched himself through a closed window, shattering glass, wooden frame and all, with Ryall clamped in his jaws. He hauled the dead or dying man along the ground for a quarter of a mile, leaving the partially devoured remains in the bush where they were found next morning.

Retribution came soon after, when the man-eating lion of Kimaa was trapped, "kept on view for several days," and very properly executed. His career had been a short one, a matter of months, and would have been much shorter if really competent hunters had taken full advantage of his reckless follies.

The Rudraprayag leopard, who eluded thousands of pursuers for eight long years, would have been scandalized by the antics of any fellow cat who assailed a group of armed Europeans or pranced about noisily attacking iron rooftops; but he was a leopard, and a very sane one. The poor mad brute who terrorized Kimaa showed in stark contrast the deranged ferocity and daring that can be expected from the habitual man-eating lion, a creature who has little in common with wary old man-eating leopards or tigers.

Pressed by severe hunger and the lack of anything better to eat, any normal mild-mannered lion may occasionally attack and devour a man, afterwards returning to his normal diet. Starving humans, even "civilized" men have done the same, especially during World War II. But habitual man-eating, spreading in sporadic waves among the lions of any one area which may be well-supplied or even rich in game, is a pathological phenomenon which has never been fully or satisfactorily explained.

Many claim that man-eating lions, as well as other aberrent cats, may acquire "a taste for human flesh" from scavenging unburied corpses. That line of reasoning falls very flat even with cautious Indian leopards and tigers: although the cat population of that teeming subcontinent has had ample opportunity to dine on corpses during times of plague or famine, those who take up man-eating habits are almost invariably the handicapped who cannot get more palatable food. In Africa, where many tribes put out their dead unburied even in the best of times, such an explanation makes even less sense. Leopards and lions have dined on African corpses for untold ages, driving away the traditional hyena morticians. Yet leopards clearly show by all their actions that they vastly prefer dog meat to human flesh. As for lions, if the taste of human flesh drove normal lions to the desperate deeds of habitual man-eaters, Simba probably would have depopulated the continent long before the advent of modern firearms.

A sounder line of reasoning has been advanced by Ivan Sanderson, who described habitual man-eating among lions as a "strange contagious delinquency that sometimes affects whole lion-populations and notably the unmated juveniles."

As a tentative explanation for that strange delinquency, I would suggest that we compare the afflicted animals' apparent taste for human flesh, and the fanatical measures they will take to get it, to problems of human drug addiction and resulting crime. It may be that there is some chemical factor in the flesh of man which has an intoxicating, even addictive effect (some cannibal tribes of the Congo claim that human fat makes them "drunk"), driving the lions on as our own addicts are driven by their increasing physiological dependence upon heroin or morphine. The animals grow to need and crave the intoxication, becoming perversely addicted to food that displeases or even revolts normal members of their species.

Yet the vast majority of lions, many of whom have tasted human corpses, remain unaffected, and there is seemingly no true addiction among leopards and tigers. The explanation of this apparent paradox can probably be found in Simba's unleopardlike, untigerlike but very manlike individuality, warmly emotional nature, and strong gregarious needs.

In our own society drug addiction is confined to a minor segment of the population which includes both maladjusted adults and reckless juveniles from troubled or broken families. Other, more responsible elements of society may be dosed with narcotics in time of acute illness or may occasionally experiment with drugs, but retain the moral fiber and sound judgment to reject their habitual use. Those who suffer severe pain from chronic illness and receive sizable doses over a long term will, of course, become addicted; but aside from these unfortunates, our addicts are above all the emotionally and socially displaced.

Can similar or parallel factors trigger waves of addictive man-eating among societies of lions?

Sudden grand-scale tampering with Simba's established environment, as the railway episodes suggest, may interfere with long-established habits and patterns of movement, while irresponsible hunting of well-behaved prides may so disorganize the survivors—especially if lionesses are killed—that members of the "broken" lion family become profoundly disturbed, emotionally and even mentally. Fully mature lions and, more rarely, lionesses, may seek an emotional substitute in acts of violence and then become addicted to the perverse appetite. Juvenile lions, like our own delinquents, will succumb with greater frequency than the more stable adults.

This very rudimentary theory might seem inconsistent with another kind of aberrent lion behavior occurring in so-called undisturbed environments such as game preserves—most notably the Kruger National Park—where lions will sometimes murder and cannibalize each other rather than attack and eat men. Here it may be that social factors, such as overcrowding within artificial boundaries, may prevent normal pride formation and adjustments, spurring the lions to make some rather brutal adjustments of their own.

Whatever the full explanation, the fact and paradox remains that a highly social animal such as Simba may turn against the society he needs or war ferociously with an alien society that he commonly respects. Perhaps, when we understand our own motivations, we may understand his.

In normal mating battles, where boss or bachelor are only rarely killed, the outcome makes relatively little difference to the mainstays of society—the ladies of the harem. Each member, as she becomes pregnant, continues working for her former or her new gentleman until the last weeks of her 105- to 110-day gestation period. When her heaviness becomes too oppressive, she stops hunting. The pride will now support her, as they support aged females, by giving her a free lunch at their kills. During the final days of her pregnancy, she leaves the pride and searches for a suitable cave or den among the rocks or in a dense thicket, as close to water as possible. Then she tries to keep under cover; if overtaken by labor pains while in the open, hyenas may attack even as she lays on her side giving birth.

If all goes well, the den-hidden lioness usually gives birth to three or four cubs, although she sometimes has only one and rarely may have five or six. Since her body is equipped with only four teats, the weaker surplus cubs will perish very quickly. The ratio of male to female births is just about even —remarkably so, unlike mankind's substantially higher ratio of male births.

About a foot long and weighing less than a pound, the cubs are born with open blue eyes, unlike domestic kittens who are blind for ten days (although an occasional cub may be born with eyes closed and open them within a day or two). Their woolly coats are marked with atavistic spots that rarely fade completely for the first three or four years; their tails are short and have no terminal adult tuft; their mouths are toothless for some three weeks; and they sprawl foolishly on back, side, or belly, unable to walk until their second month.

To feed this helpless heap of little lions, Simba Jike must give milk, and to keep up her milk she must go hunting. That means leaving the infant cubs back in the den, where they may be found and devoured by hyenas—the lion's one natural enemy who preys only on the very young, the very old, those badly wounded in hunting the larger game, or those

54

who may have been crippled by a hunter's badly aimed bullet. For these last the end may come as a mercy; for the cubs —although it may affront lovers of nature films where the fluffy baby animal is never eaten by the big bad predator—it is simply nature's unsentimental method of population control. What keeps the infant mortality rate to a reasonable percentage is probably the intervention of the lion "aunt," a lioness without current cubs of her own, who sometimes comes to baby-sit when Simba Jike leaves her den for nocturnal hunts and continues to help out after she brings her babies to the pride, at age four to six weeks, just as soon as they can walk.

Lionesses and older cubs welcome the babies with enthusiastic affection; their father, or at least the reigning male, is more reserved, but treats them with an attitude of kindly tolerance. They may tumble all around him, even catching their claws in his mane, but his only open rebuke is to rise and walk away.

Subsisting on milk alone during their first months, the cubs will suckle from their mother or from any nearby lioness. Simba Jike will accept one and all impartially, only pushing older cubs aside or even nipping them harmlessly when they crowd her smaller babies from the milk bar. Weaning starts when the cubs are three to four months old; then she brings them chunks of bloody meat and if they show no interest, she regurgitates some half-digested meat as baby food to tempt their still uneducated appetites. The cubs soon learn to take meat in any form, then to love it, and are weaned completely by their fifth month. At this age, when they have reached the size of large dogs, their real education starts: Simba Jike takes them hunting.

For their first nocturnal expeditions—and a lioness will never hunt with very young cubs during the daylight hours —she may hide them in a patch of tall grass or stash them away in a gully while she does the actual stalking. They sometimes wander off but usually will stay where they are put, especially when guarded by a lion aunt. The aunt's underlying motives have been criticized by some naturalists; in fact, she has been pictured as a self-seeking harpy who merely loiters by the cubs in hopes of sharing their meat. That she does get some meat is beyond argument, but so long as human baby-sitters charge an hourly fee for their services, it seems a little harsh to criticize the motives of a baby-sitting lion.

As the cubs grow older, stronger, and more capable of

keeping up the pace, Simba Jike teaches them to stalk and kill, actions which they perform with bumbling, often clownish inefficiency. Meanwhile, she still has a husband to support. He helps at times, but more often he merely supervises from the background, looking on as his wife or harem makes the kill and then moving forward to drive his family away from the meat. Compounding the injustice, any bachelors of the pride can come to eat beside him while lioness providers and hungry cubs are shouldered aside or even swatted if they persist.

If the kill is a small one, nothing may be left. If there is more than enough to sate the male appetite, the lionesses eat next, by now frantic with hunger. Half-grown cubs, fed with scrupulous care during their infancy, are now batted aside if they try to dart in and feed beside their mothers. They must wait their turn, and only get enough to eat if the kill is a fairly substantial one. When the hunting is poor, they become emaciated or even die of starvation.

This eating pattern follows another classic African tradition, and a most unfortunate one. Among bush natives, most of whom can never get enough meat to satisfy their bodies' natural needs, the man of the family eats first and usually eats his fill regardless of the household hunger. Women rarely get any meat. Children, who get virtually none, may develop *kwashiorkor,* a protein-deficiency disease that leads to death or mental retardation. Only the Bambuti Pygmies, allegedly primitive in their ways, allow equal rights at table, distributing fair shares of meat to women, children, and the aged.

If lion cubs survive the early threat of hyenas, diseases such as rickets, and the constant threat of starvation, the close bond between cubs and mother gradually weakens until they are fully independent by age two. Female cubs often stay with the pride, becoming official harem members when they reach sexual maturity, which occurs sometime between their third and fourth year. Males, who usually leave to form their own bachelor prides, mature at the same age, when their regal-looking manes begin to grow, but it takes a couple of more years before they are strong enough to rule a harem.

Considering his ways, it seems obvious that Simba makes a less than satisfying king. But, since lion-lovers may be mourning over their shattered legend, I can at least extend a gesture of consolation by nominating the species for a new and more appropriate title—Queen of Beasts.

Lazy, good-natured, sociable, and even loving as they are,

lions are still predators, and the largest predatory animals in Africa. The ladies, lighter and more agile, average eight feet in length and weigh in at 275 to 300 pounds, while the full-grown males may exceed a length of nine feet and a weight of 400 pounds, standing seven feet tall if they rise on their hind legs. Living free and eating only one to three times per week, Simba will rarely attain the 500-pound weight of some zoo lions who are fed every day, but he is quite capable of hauling away the half-ton carcass of a stolen cow.

Beyond size and brute strength, lions have been shaped by evolutionary forces—and shaped superbly—to perform certain well-defined functions: to find, observe, stalk, spring, seize, kill, and eat an ever-wary prey. For each of these functions they have developed corresponding powers and equipment, impressive in the young lion and lioness but gradually deteriorating in the pampered lioness-supplied pasha.

Splendid eyesight, excellent hearing, and a sense of smell much keener than is commonly believed, enable them to spot and observe the movements of their prey by day or night. Intelligence and great cooperation, approaching at times a kind of lion mental telepathy, make it possible for them to stalk successfully the speedy antelope and zebra who can easily outrun them. But they often make mistakes and go hungry, most commonly by trying to trap their quarry in a crescent rather than a full circle and by persistently setting the ambush from the rear when a flank attack from cover would be more effective.

After the slow stalk, belly close to the ground, brings him fifty yards or so from the quarry's unsuspecting rear, the lion charges. He makes his sprint at a far slower speed than the cheetah—about thirty miles per hour versus seventy—but launches himself at the end in a longer spring than either cheetah or leopard, covering up to thirty or thirty-five feet. He lands with stunning impact, extending forepaws up to eight inches in diameter, each of them edged by four massive claws and a short curving dewclaw that can alone disembowel a man.

With smaller antelopes, already bowled over and partially stunned, he may clamp the neck between his four huge fangs and snap it with a single twisting bite. When dealing with larger prey, he will usually seize and twist the nose to the side with one forepaw, trying to trip the animal forward so that it will fall and by its very weight break its own neck. If his bulldogging maneuver fails, he may be in for trouble: zebra, roan and sable antelopes, or even young giraffes can hit a

57

tender or a vital spot with flailing hoofs and badly injure or even kick a lion to death.

That risk, although a very real one, seems minor when compared to what he faces when attacking his largest and most dangerous prey—the wary, powerful, and very tenacious Cape buffalo, who may outweigh him five or six to one.

Because of the discrepancy in size, a single lion or even a pair will rarely attack a full-grown buffalo unless severely pressed by hunger. Generally, three or four lionesses will work in concert, aided by their lazy pasha and, if they are lucky, by a bachelor colleague as well. In making the attack, the lead lion—often one of the clumsier but more powerful males—will charge and spring from behind, seizing the buffalo's massive neck in his jaws while he tries to execute the bulldogging or nose-twisting maneuver with a forepaw. For greater leverage, he keeps his hindlegs on the ground, but one of his companions may take a flying leap onto the buffalo's flank. The rest will harry like a pack of giant terriers, biting and clawing wherever they can to wound, weaken, and confuse their huge opponent.

The buffalo may rear, buck, swerve, and run in circles, trying to shake the lead lion off his neck. He may roll over and over on his back, desperate to free himself, while the pack of lions harries and the leader tries to hang on, maintaining steady pressure on the nose. If bulldogging fails to bring results, he may try another favorite maneuver, shifting his jaws to the buffalo's throat and trying to kill him, as a cheetah sometimes kills its prey, by slow strangulation.

The outcome of such a battle depends in large part on the number of attacking lions. Although a single lion has been known to kill a full-grown buffalo, he will usually be trampled, gored, and trampled again until his remains are hardly recognizable. Two attacking lions have a better chance while three, four, or more will usually wear the buffalo down and, despite their own casualties, make the kill.

The surviving lions have a three-quarter-ton or even one-ton carcass to console them. As usual the males will pitch in first, but for once there will be more than enough for lionesses and cubs. All the banqueters will slice off flesh with jaws that cannot move sideways like our own but function like a giant vertical scissor edged on either side with a pair of knife-edged cutting teeth. They will lick flesh from bone with the highly modified rasplike tastebuds of their rough cat tongues, but will not try to crack or chew the bones; their molars are weak, even degenerate compared to the fine grinding teeth of bears and dogs.

After eating twenty to forty pounds of meat and skin apiece, they will doze with bulging bellies near the kill, rising from time to time to drive away vultures, hyenas, and jackals. They will eat again in a day or two, then again, until the ravaged carcass is a mass of writhing maggots. Then they will keep on eating, maggots and all, with equal relish.

A lion-style buffalo hunt isn't a pretty picture from start to finish, but I know a really ugly one: a pack of hunting tourists, eager for trophies rather than meat, who butcher the buffalo just as bloodily although they fight with superior weapons. Describing one such pack, Alexander Lake, a professional hunter who cherished no illusions about his clients or his trade, wrote the following in his book *Killers in Africa—The Truth About Animals Lying in Wait and Hunters Lying in Print:*

> I once saw three sportsmen pour four .450 slugs and one .510 into the side of a five-year-old bull. He'd been trotting broadside to the hunters about eighty yards away. When the fifth bullet hit, he turned toward the shooters and broke into a raging gallop, grunting with each jump. Two of the men fell pants-seat over kettle as they bumped each other in their rush to get away. The third ran a few steps, stopped, dropped to a knee, put gun to shoulder, but held fire until the beast was within twenty yards.
>
> Thirty yards farther back, I cut loose with my .303 at the same instant. Both bullets took the bull at the base of the throat. He turned a somersault, coming to rest on his belly, neck stretched out, all four legs doubled under him. With all that lead in him, he wasn't quite dead. . . .

Considering the buffalo's raw stamina and power, it's quite a triumph for a pack to kill him—but only if they fight as Simba does, with teeth and fingernails.

Hunting Simba himself, the butchering tourists have equally heroic adventures, or think they do. Often their guide will stage a farcical lion hunt, even more nakedly obscene than the so-called leopard hunt, leading his stumbling clients to a pride of lions which has been trained by a week or so of conditioned reflex therapy to come to a certain spot when called. If this statement sounds like a conservationist's fairy tale, then listen to ex-hunter Alexander Lake's candid description of the method:

Feed a pride of lions until they get used to finding an antelope or zebra at the same place every other day. Feed them until they quit hunting for themselves. As you throw down the bleeding carcass at the feeding spot, you blow the Galton whistle. The lions soon associate the sound of the whistle with food and come a-galloping.

The stage is set, but when the White Hunter picks up his pack at their posh Nairobi hotel, he has to steer his picturesque Land Rover along a somewhat circuitous route, just to make it look good. When he comes within a few miles of the predestined goal, he sights or pretends to sight vultures circling in the distant sky. "Very likely a lion kill in the area," he tells the pack. "We may have a chance!" Then he drives hell-for-leather toward the "salted" lions (my expression, not his, for game previously conditioned or driven to a spot where it is subsequently "discovered," just as gold may be discovered in a salted mine).

Arriving in the vicinity, daring sportsmen dismount from Land Rover and the White Hunter leads them through a mock reconnoitering. After he considers them sufficiently impressed by the procedure, he signals to a native tracker hidden in the bush to blow the supersonic Galton whistle, or dog whistle, as it is sometimes called. The men hear nothing, but Simba does. Like Pavlov's laboratory dogs, conditioned to salivate when the scientist rang his dinner bell, the lions come a-galloping.

Sometimes the tourist pack fires twenty bullets or more into the body of a single lion. Then they like to pose for victory photos—documentary proof that they have really faced and foiled a charging lion. Believing absolutely in the spontaneity and danger of the hunt, they talk about their "moment of truth," their "proof of manhood." The White Hunter, trained Thespian that he is, agrees enthusiastically but jibes in private. I remember well how one professional told me, at the Thorntree Terrace bar of Nairobi's New Stanley Hotel, that his boastful client of the week before "might have proved as much by staying at home, loading his rifle, hiding behind the Frig, and gunning down the household cat while she headed toward her saucer."

If the tourist pack are willing to do without the picturesque Land Rover and the other classic trappings of an old-fashioned safari, they can take advantage of the latest technological improvement: they can hunt lions from a helicopter. That sort of thing used to be absolutely illegal under the former colonial governments of the Congo and East Africa, but now that the new independent nations have relaxed hunting regulations, it's quick, safe, and comfortable to chase Simba and his ladies with the copter until their muzzles are flecked with foam, then to land in a strategic spot, and wait with guns cocked until the copter herds the panting lions toward you.

Besides, all the celebrities are doing it. Take a look at the handsome color photograph on page twenty-seven, top right, of LIFE Nature Library's excellent publication, *The Land and Wildlife of Africa.* Its caption reads: "HUNTER OF THE NEW SCHOOL. Arthur Godfrey disembarks from a helicopter used to spot game and herd it toward rifles—and to shorten an elephant kill from a week to two hours."

Aslo examine a series of victory photos on that same page and the preceding one. They show movie cowboy Roy Rogers (who hunted by land rather than air, accompanied by an un-named fellow client, two White Hunters, two Land Rovers and twenty-five natives, plus hot water and a refrigerator) triumphantly seated astride a dead waterbuck, squatting over the corpse of a warthog, and caressing the horns of kudu and sable antelope cadavers. In one photo he is posing proudly with his rifle beside the carcass of a ten- or fifteen-pound porcu-pine. I wonder if it charged him. At any rate, it's a fascinat-ing picture of a wild animal.

Lions, for all of their power and intelligence, have little better chance than a porcupine when they are herded by heli-copters, trained to gallop toward Galton whistles, run down on horseback, and shot while being harried with lion-hounds (a very popular method of the past), or, only a little less ob-scenely, when they are actually discovered and attacked on the open savannah by a large pack of White Hunters, tour-ists, gun-bearers, and beaters. Real sport can only take place between man and lion when the lion *has a chance to win.*

Considering the average tourist's level of marksmanship, I would call it a fair fight if he took his high-powered rifle and faced the lion alone, unaided by his White Hunters, compan-ions, and bearers. Then he would quickly find that he was dealing with Africa's "second most dangerous animal," and possibly find it out a little too late. Even if the experienced professional hunter or any cool-headed expert with a gun faces the lion alone, there is at least some chance that he may fail to place his bullet in a vital spot. But I can't consider the latter a really sporting proposition—not when a dead-shot uses a weapon that can kill an elephant against a 400-pound lion.

Carl Akeley once gave his own opinion on the only sportsmanlike way to hunt lions. "It is spearing," he wrote in his book *In Brightest Africa*, "and spearing takes a black man." He went on to describe the Nandi, an East African tribe whose warriors make a collective spear attack. The Nandi are brave, very brave, but they cannot compare with the Masai —a somewhat Egyptian-looking tribe of Nilo-Hamitic cattlemen whose warriors will take a spear in hand and go to face a full-grown lion in deliberate single combat.

When I describe the Masai lion-hunters, I speak from more than academic knowledge or casual acquaintance, for I have lived with the Masai, drunk the warm blood of cattle with them, loved their women, danced their traditional dances to the foghorn-sounding music of a blown kudu horn, and been accepted as an initiated warrior of the tribe. There is only one way for a white man to achieve that acceptance: armed with a spear, he must challenge a full-grown lion in single combat. I made that challenge, and the lion who answered it was and remains the one and only animal that I have ever hunted.

It was autumn of 1951, four years before the dynamite explosion took my right hand. I had left Burundi on a six-month vacation, driving my pickup to Kenya and turning off the road itself to drive across the stony savannahs of the huge Masai reservation that stretches to the Tanganyika border and beyond. I was very young, only twenty-four, and very self-assured. Then I met a Swahili-speaking Masai elder named Masaka—a stocky, middle-aged man, naked under his flapping calico robe, his face and body smeared with rancid red-ochred sheep fat, who lived in a cow-dung plastered hut, dined on milk, meat, and blood, washed his drinking gourds in cow's urine, and explained to me why he and his fellow Masai were civilized and I was not.

"We are the only people who really know how to live," he said with unshakeable pride. "We are not like the Kikuyu or the Wakamba, who plant things in the ground: they are not warriors and they know nothing about cattle or God. We have one word for all of those ignorant people—*Ol-Meeki*. That means the 'savages' or 'natives.' As for you white men, you know a little more than the natives—but you are not Masai."

"What's the big difference?" I asked.

He smiled. "Sometimes I work for white men who come to

hunt in Masailand. They kill lions with guns, many guns. Sometimes they even let a woman shoot one of the guns. Can a gun make a woman into a man?"

"Can a spear?" I countered.

"Yes. Maybe once in every three duels, the warrior will kill the lion. The rest of the time the lion wins. That is why the white men put our warriors in jail when they catch them going out to duel with lions. They worry that too many young men will be killed, but they never try to understand why the young men are willing to die. That is because the whites know nothing about *empijan* and *olwuasa*—courage and pride."

Hearing those words I felt momentary resentment of what is usually called the "insufferable arrogance" of the Masai. But thinking it over by the flickering campfire, just outside Masaka's thorn-fenced village, I began to feel a certain sense of shame for my race . . . shame for the so-called hunters who come to Masailand blasting away with guns and barking orders to "boys" and bearers, some of whom are *real* hunters . . . and shame for the rest of us who live our "civilized" lives out of tune with deeper realities, sometimes plodding on from birth to death without facing a single real challenge, a gamble with pain or death for what the Masai call *engisisata* —the glory.

"Masaka, I am going to kill a lion," I said suddenly, "single-handed, with a spear."

He laughed openly. Then, seeing I was serious, he begged me to forget it. *Nkirisa*—the English authorities—would jail his entire village, he explained, if they were mixed up in a white man's death. *"Nkirisa* will never know," I insisted. "Even my own government doesn't know that I am here. If the lion wins, let him eat me. If he doesn't like the taste of white man's meat, then the hyenas can have a good time."

"My people will never believe this," Masaka protested, "and even if they do, they will think that you are *pumbavu* —just plain crazy."

That was apparently his own opinion when we parted for the night. Next morning he was even more upset when he volunteered to help with breakfast and I said, "Good, I'd like to drink some fresh blood." Then he rolled his eyes upward and said a little Masai prayer, *"Na-Ai! Na-Ai!,"* asking advice and consolation from the Sky God. But I persisted, eager to prove my good faith by respecting Masai custom, and at last drank a pint of warm blood drawn by a little wooden arrow from the jugular vein of Kerete, his favorite cow, quaffing from the same gourd as Masaka.

The strongly flavored cow's blood had a curious after-taste derived from the good old Masai custom of doing the dishes in cow's urine. But it wasn't too bad, and my slightly over-acted gratitude—I smacked my lips like a happy vampire—apparently convinced Masaka that I was either incurably serious or incurably *pumbavu*. So, still muttering occasional prayers, he promised to take me to the warrior's *manyata*, a separate village rather like the gladiator schools of the ancient Roman empire.

Side by side in the cab of my pickup, we bounced across the stony savannah for a good two hours before reaching the *manyata*, a circle of thornbush surrounding some fifteen huts and a big cattle kraal, situated somewhere east of Lake Natron near the border of Kenya and Tanganyika.

There were women and children there and many young girls—to entertain the warriors, as I later discovered—plus a few visiting elders. But overshadowing the rest were the *muran* or warriors themselves. Ranging in age from sixteen to thirty and averaging about five foot eight, all were smeared with red-ochred sheep fat from the tops of their pigtail hairdos to the tips of their sandaled toes. Each carried a long-blade spear, and to a man they stared at me with magnificent hauteur, looking more like American Indians than any Africans I had ever seen.

I was elated at the idea of joining such a superb company of men, then deflated when Masaka refused to translate my *"pumbavu"* intentions to the non-Swahili-speaking warriors, then flabbergasted as he secured permission for my stay at the *manyata* by presenting me as a candidate for court jester rather than colleague-at-arms, telling the *muran* how "strange" I was and "how much fun it would be" to watch me.

Watching the Masai themselves during that first day, I looked on wistfully as the warriors practiced swordplay and spear-thrusts while the old women patched the huts with *imodiok* or fresh cattle dung. My dinner was a quart of rich milk and next morning's breakfast was another pint of fresh blood. I tossed it off like an old hand while the warriors looked on astonished.

When they questioned Masaka, I insisted that he tell all. Very reluctantly, he did. The warriors burst out laughing. One, a tall man with a terribly scarred belly, made a brief comment and they laughed even louder. Masaka explained

The real king never travels, hunts, or feeds in a pride, pack, or herd. He stands or dies alone, as a king has to. He has no real friends, even among his own kind, and will not settle for a banal family life. Pound for pound, he is the strongest animal on earth, a creature seemingly assembled out of steel muscles and tendons. He is also one of the most intelligent: coolly calculating, patient, and immensely wary.

Copyright by Bill Wilson Wild Life Photography—Nairobi, Kenya

Hailed as the "King of Beasts" since the days of Aesop, the lion is an easy-going loafer who rarely strikes regal poses. After washing himself and yawning like an oversized house cat, he will probably roll over and fall asleep on his back with all four feet raised in the air. Lionesses and younger lions will sometimes climb a tree, draping themselves over the limbs with utter disregard for the popular belief that no lion ever climbs aloft.

Left: Maurice A. Machris

Above: Photo Satour

Arising from his slumbers, the so-called King of Beasts meanders about the savannah, sometimes pausing to squabble with another male. Meanwhile his unsung mate, who richly deserves the title Queen of Beasts, is either hunting up his dinner for him or zealously attending to the growing cubs.

Top: Copyright by Bill Wilson Wild Life Photography—Nairobi, Kenya

Right: J. Verschuren, Coll. Institut Parcs Nationaux Congo

Hunted by man, Mbogo has also had to fight off lions and to protect his young from raids by lions, leopards, and hyenas. Simply to survive he has become rather shrewd, learning from experience to be wary where wariness is needed and to attack before he is himself attacked and slaughtered.

Copyright by Bill Wilson Wild Life Photography—Nairobi, Kenya

Elephants require at least fifty gallons of water per day, and whenever possible they will trek to rivers, lakes, or swamps so that they can also swim and frolic in the water. To expedite this never-ending round of eating, drinking, and bathing, a herd will probably walk at least twenty miles per day, all the while enjoying social and family diversions.

Above: J. Verschuren, Coll. Institut Parcs Nationaux Congo
Below: Photo Satour

Hippopotamuses, or "river horses," as the Greeks called them, love to play in rivers, lakes, shallow pools, and evil-smelling mudholes—grunting, rumbling, snorting, blowing, bellowing, and burping, or sleeping in the shallows with their heads pillowed on each other's backs. These hippos are in the Kibirizi River, Rwindi Valley, Congo.

The timid disposition of the rhino makes him fear, and fear deeply, the very objects that he wants to examine. He hesitates, agonized, while the two conflicting instincts boil within him. Usually he runs away, spooked like a giant cat, but sometimes rushes forward to investigate with the world's most farcical display of bluff, noise, wasted energy, and sheer ineptitude: the notorious rhino charge.

Photo Satour

Kifaru's only real enemy is, of course, man. His only real friend is the tick-bird. When the busy birds spot approaching hunters, they flap about and squawk to alert the nearsighted rhino.

Copyright by Bill Wilson Wild Life Photography—Nairobi, Kenya

Designed by nature as a fish-eating, crab-eating, garbage-eating scavenger, this decrepit hobo of the riverbanks and lakesides has become, despite himself, Africa's Public Enemy Number One.

Top and left:

Copyright by Bill Wilson Wild Life Photography—Nairobi, Kenya

with an embarrassed but-I-told-you-so expression: "The tall man is named Konoko. He said, 'You'd better load your gun. That is the only way a white man can kill a lion.' The other *muran* believe him. He is the only man at this *manyata* who has faced a lion single-handed. Others have tried it and died. But *ol-ngatuny*—the lion—didn't beat Konoko; he just tore out a few loops of gut while Konoko killed him with the spear. We stuffed the gut back into his belly, poured some sheep fat in the hole and sewed him up with oxhide. Then he got up and walked home."

That report was somewhat unsettling. But I replied stubbornly, "Tell him that I don't even own a gun, that I will fight with a spear as he did, and that I will not leave this place until the fight is finished."

Konoko answered, "You are young and very tall. You look strong and you talk strong. But you are not a Masai." Then, to my surprise, he offered to train me himself. But I soon realized his motive: to prove for his own, and for the other warriors' complete satisfaction, that I was just a white man "talking strong."

For my proposed duel with Simba, Konoko presented me with the three traditional tools of the Masai warrior: the *elongo,* or shield, made of buffalo hide stretched on a wooden frame and painted with brilliant heraldric designs; the *olalem,* or shortsword, worn at the right side; and the *arem,* or spear, a thin and flexible three-foot blade of badly tempered iron connected by a six-inch wooden shaft to an iron butt about three feet long. Since my new weapon and I were just about the same length, Konoko decided to give me a new name—Arem.

During the next three weeks, "The Spear" threw his heavy iron spear more than two thousand times, holding the twenty-pound shield in his left hand. The target was a bundle of dry grass tied to one end of a six-foot wooden stick which Konoko held some eight feet away, leaping to the side as he let it fall forward. Masaka squatted nearby, lecturing on strategy and tactics while he kept an oral score of the mock battles.

If my spear nicked the edge of the grass bundle, I was credited with wounding Simba—just enough to enrage him and ensure my prompt death. If it struck the wooden core, the soft spear-blade bent badly—and Simba killed me while I was trying to pull it out and straighten it for a desperate jab. Only if the blade neatly bisected the six-inch radius of dry grass surrounding the core would Masaka announce that I had speared Simba through the heart. Then he added, invariably, "But he killed you before he died."

Nothing I said or did could change Masaka's attitude. I was going to die and that was that. In fact, on the very eve of the Simba-Arem duel, he would talk of nothing but the splendid funeral rites the Masai were planning, not for Simba but for Arem.

"We will not let the lion eat you," he informed me gravely, "until the proper ceremonies have been performed. We will chase him away for a while—we will even kill him if he will not go! Then we will place you on your left side with your legs drawn up, your head to the north and your face turned to the east. We will bend your left arm under your head as a cushion and fold your right arm over your chest with the hand on the heart. Then we will take a last look at your body and return to the *manyata* in single file, singing sad songs in honor of your courage. Soon, all of Masailand will know the wonderful story of Arem, the first white man to duel with a lion! As a final tribute to your memory, we will taste neither meat nor milk for three days. We will drink only blood, in honor of our dead fellow warrior."

"Masaka," I protested, "I'm not dead yet."

"You will be," he kept repeating mournfully.

On the morning of the duel, the men of my warrior escort belted their calico robes at the waist and applied a fresh coating of red-ochred sheep fat to their naked chests and faces. Konoko solemnly donned his *olowuaru,* a magnificent headdress made from the mane of his conquered lion, and three other warriors put on their own *olowuaru.* During separate collective hunts, each of these men had won the mane by being the first to throw the spear. The rest of the warriors wore ostrich-feather headdresses that framed their faces in a circular black mane. I was bare-headed and dressed in rumpled khaki shorts and shirt.

Leaving the *manyata* in single file, Konoko led, I followed, Masaka trotted behind me, and a long file of seventeen warriors marched behind him. We must have trekked for four or five hours, passing herds of zebras, gnus, and Thomson's gazelles, before we spotted two fair-sized lions in the distance, lying near a clump of thornbushes.

We advanced and spread out, trying to make a ring around the pair of bachelors. As soon as we got within three hundred feet they retreated. We followed, and as we approached again, they again retreated. Their attitude was entirely different from that of the fearless, confident lions in the national parks of the Congo, Uganda, and Kenya who were aware of their complete security: these animals obviously knew and feared the Masai.

We walked and ran for a few more hours, trying to trap one or the other in a circle formed by bodies and shields—a human arena for the duel—but had to give up at sundown and make a temporary camp, carving a clear space in a big clump of thornbush with our shortswords. I was terribly tired after trying to keep up with the Masai, whose physical endurance is unequalled, but I slept very poorly.

At dawn Konoko sent out two scouting parties; a couple of hours later one returned, very excited. They had spotted another group of lions—three bachelors holed up in a big clump of bushes. Two of the cats were small, but one was full-grown with a beautiful mane. "We are very lucky," said Masaka. "If the big one had wives instead of friends, we could never drive away the females. The lion will run if you attack the lioness, but she will always stay to defend him."

When the second scouting party returned, we left on a double-time march, reaching the lions' hide-out an hour later. Konoko sent ten warriors to beat the back of the bush and the rest of us waited, shields upraised, attempting to block the lions' escape route. Almost at once, the three cats burst out of the thornbush. Two made it to freedom; the third was trapped within the circle of bodies and shields. He stood almost at the center, a maneless young lion who couldn't have weighed more than 250 pounds, turning his head from side to side in nervous confusion.

Konoko pointed with his spear. *"Tara!"* "Kill him!"

I hesitated. If I fought this animal and won, I could almost hear the Masai murmuring to themselves, "Well, it was just a little lion . . ." I pointed my spear at the 400-pounder who had come to a halt about a hundred yards away. *"Kitok!"* I answered. "The big one!"

Konoko stared at me angrily. Skeptical as he was, he probably thought that I was trying to delay the inevitable. But he called an order and our circle broke into two files. The small lion bolted across the savannah and we set out to trap the big one. We chased him for almost an hour; then, exasperated, he sat down to take a breather in the shade of a cassia tree, giving us a chance to surround him. Realizing he was trapped, the huge lion sprang to his feet snarling, furious, and ready to charge the circle. Nineteen Masai warriors answered him, yelling like Apaches.

He drew back, obviously frightened. His head swayed

slowly as he looked for a gap in the ring of howling Masai and padded nervously around the cassia tree. Quickly the circle grew tighter and tighter until the nineteen men stood only two or three feet apart, forming a perfect human arena roughly thirty-five feet in diameter.

I knew that from any point in the circle the lion could reach me in two giant springs as I entered. I watched him for a moment while I wiped away the sweat streaming into my eyes and rubbed my sweaty palms in the dirt. Then, with my buffalo-hide shield gripped in my left hand and the spear in my right, I leaped into the arena. "Simba!" I shouted. "Simba, come here!"

The lion ran back and forth nervously about ten feet away. The Masai slowly raised their spears to protect the circle as I waited for the lion to charge. He refused. I took a step forward and shouted again. Immediately he sprang in the opposite direction—a twelve-foot leap that toppled my friend Masaka like an ochre-colored tenpin—and streaked across the savannah. I was sick with apprehension; then Masaka rose, displaying his shield ecstatically. The marks of the lion's claws were deeply engraved upon the painted buffalo hide, but not upon his own.

In two parallel rows, we pursued the big lion. He was growing more and more wary; this time it took nearly two hours to trap him. Again the circle tightened around him and the Masai screamed with excitement. Then, just as I had the first time, I leaped into the human arena, intent on making the lion charge me. He retreated, threatening to spring at the other side of the circle. The Masai brandished their shields and shouted a chorus of abuse. He backed up and looked around uneasily. He was about twenty-five feet away and still refused to charge me.

I waited, nearly exhausted by hours of violent exertion. My shirt and shorts were soaked with sweat, my breath came in gasps, my heart pounded against my ribs with terrible force. I balanced the spear in my right hand, vibrating it slightly in the Masai warrior's style, but the lion still refused to charge. Shifting the spear to my left hand for an instant, I picked up a pebble and tossed it at his head. It struck just below the left eye. That did it. Simba grunted, turned, and started toward me.

He stopped about ten feet away, staring with baffled but furious eyes. I felt a moment of infinite pity for the great golden beauty I was about to destroy. Then I took a step forward with my left foot and crouched, drawing back my spear arm all the way. His hindquarters trembled and his tail twitched. The warriors stopped screaming and there was utter silence.

Like a cat springing on a mouse, the lion sprang toward me. I looked for the spot, found it, and threw the spear with all of my strength. Then, as Simba and spear met in mid-air, I leaped wildly aside. He completed his arc, the heavy butt of the spear struck the ground, and the impact drove the blade even deeper, ripping it across his already transfixed heart.

He rolled over, howling with pain and rage, then crawled and staggered toward me. I backed off, unsheathing my short-sword. He swiped at it, and once his claws clicked against the metal as he pursued me. The protruding spearbutt swung from side to side under his great head. He followed me for nearly thirty feet while the circle moved with us. Then he fell on his side, his head stiffened, his mouth lolled open, his eyes dulled, and he died.

The Masai burst into a wild orgy of joy. They shrieked, sang, and jumped high into the air like men released from a catapult. Two of the warriors started to shake violently and foam at the mouth, caught up in the strange hysterical fits that the Masai call *apush*. One barked like a dog while the saliva dripped from his chin, and both at last fell to the ground in a stupor. I stood next to the dead lion, watching. Then Konoko, skeptical no longer, stepped toward me with a broad, wonderful smile and gathered me into his arms. *"Ira ol-Maasani,"* my new brother said. "You are a Masai."

In *Congo Kitabu*, I described in detail the continuing celebration over the lion's body: the triumphal trip home, running all the way while we sang, laughed, and shouted; the amazing welcome I received at the *manyata*—nine gourds of milk ritually poured over my head; the dances and the songs that followed; and the two young girls who gave Arem a Masai conqueror's reward . . . but that has little to do with Simba.

Simba lay dead on the savannah, somewhere east of Lake Natron. Two Masai stayed behind to deal with his body: they cut out his heart, to be eaten by the warriors with ceremonial relish; they cut off his massive claws for distribution among the members of my escort; and they cut away his skin, mane and all, brought it back to the *manyata* and presented it to me.

The rest of Simba waited, as dead lions always wait, for the vultures and hyenas.

MBOGO

The Vigilant Warrior

In his book, *In Brightest Africa,* Carl Akeley remarked:

> While the lion is usually satisfied with giving his victim a knock-out blow or bite, the buffalo, when once on the trail of man, will not only persist in his efforts to find him but, when he has once come up with him, will not leave while there is a vestige of life remaining in the victim. . . .

A hunter I met once told me of an experience he had with a buffalo which shows in rather a terrible way these characteristics of the animal. He and a companion wounded a buffalo and followed it into the long grass. It was lurking where they did not expect it and with a sudden charge it was upon them before they had a chance to shoot. The buffalo knocked down the man who told me the story and then rushed after his companion. The first victim managed to climb a tree although without his gun. By that time the other man was dead. But the buffalo was not satisfied. For two hours he stamped and tossed the remains while the wounded man in the tree sat helplessly watching. When the buffalo left, my informant told me, the only evidence of his friend was the trampled place on the ground where the tragedy had taken place. There is nothing in Africa more vindictive than this.

If Carl Akeley, a top-ranking naturalist and the conservationist largely responsible for the founding of the Congo's national parks, could condemn as vindictive any animal that had been attacked, wounded, and pursued, what can we expect from ordinary men?

Professional hunters usually agree that the Cape buffalo, called Mbogo in Swahili, is Africa's most dangerous animal, Number One killer of that infamous killer syndicate, the Big Five. As reason they usually cite the fact that he will attack unprovoked—while he is being stalked rather than shot at—and that he is vindictive—fighting on when wounded until horns and hoofs have cut, trampled, and ground his blundering opponent into earth-colored tapioca.

Amateur hunters parrot that judgment while vying with each other to display the most impressive buffalo trophies, most of them shot by the White Hunter after his client's panic-stricken bullets wounded or even missed the huge target. Sometimes in their fevered urge to show their prowess with "Number One," they don't even bother to go through the motions. Alexander Lake reported in *Killers in Africa:*

> If you want to make a nice piece of change get yourself a buffalo head with horns fifty-seven or more inches in spread. There are always a hundred or so phony sportsmen hanging around bars of Nairobi and Johannesburg who will pay you one thousand dollars for record buff horns. Last I heard, the record was fifty-six-and-one-half inches. Those wealthy bar-fly sportsmen really pay for trophies that prove them mighty hunters.

The general public, dazzled and misled by hunters' legends, puts absolute credence in Mbogo's bad reputation, but almost always calls this alleged arch killer "the water buffalo," confusing him with India's good-natured, even friendly beast of burden. The only real water buffalo in Africa are former Indian animals exported to the Nile Valley, where they pull ploughs or toil at irrigation ditches and wells. But the public can't be blamed, not with movies and television constantly spreading the error, both on the screen and by their advertising and promotion. Even some of the better films faithfully follow suit, as evidenced by a widely distributed brochure publicizing *Hatari!* It contained a photo of a handsome Cape buffalo captioned by the painfully familiar words, "Water buffalo, one of the most dangerous animals in Africa . . ."

Surrounded as he is by hunting and Hollywood folktales, Mbogo's character and habits have been libeled to the point where his image—to borrow a public relations term—now resembles that of an animal Al Capone dedicated to a life of massacre and murder. "What animals does the water buffalo prey on?" I have sometimes been asked during lecture tours from California to New England. I have even been queried about the habits of the "African man-eating buffalo." Aroused by hunting propaganda, I suppose, the eager questioners had never paused to explore the problems that a predatory, meat-eating, man-eating life would bring about for any animal closely related to the common cow.

Domesticated cattle, buffaloes, water buffaloes, yaks, bisons, the many species of antelopes, and even sheep and goats are all members of a single huge family, the *Bovidae* or hollow-horned ruminants. As such, they graze or browse for a living, using jaws that have a horny pad in place of upper incisors and canines, then digest their vegetable dinner in complex four-chambered stomachs. If left in peace they chew their cuds with a vegetative expression, but strictly for defensive purposes they are equipped with paired, unbranched horns composed of keratin that grow slowly and continually from bony cores on the front of the skull. With a few exceptions, male and female both are horned; the bull's horns are usually stouter, longer, and, in the Cape buffalo, are surrounded at the base by a massive helmet-like boss that can actually turn a soft-nosed bullet.

What has made Mbogo a "super-cow," if I may call him that, has been the differing treatment accorded to these two bovine species. Protected by men, cattle have been bred for beef and milk production, becoming, like all domesticated animals, complacent and rather simple-minded when compared to their free-living relatives. Hunted by men, Mbogo has also had to fight off lions—the only other predator who fights a full-grown Cape buffalo—and to protect his young from raids by lions, leopards, and hyenas. Simply to survive he has become rather shrewd, but he is not diabolically clever as hunters claim: he has simply learned from experience to be wary where wariness is needed, and to a greater extent than most animals, to attack before he is himself attacked and slaughtered.

In game preserves and national parks throughout Central, East, and South Africa, the confident Cape buffaloes spend their daylight hours grazing on open savannah and wallowing blissfully in mudholes or swimming in rivers and lakes—as fond of water as the true wáter buffalo. Although their vision, hearing, and sense of smell are all extremely keen, they disregard or blandly tolerate any humans who watch them.

But man has created a second Cape buffalo—a nervous, ever-watchful beast who hides in the densest thickets he can find, coming forth to graze, drink, and swim by night, but always staying close to cover in the daytime. Some have taken refuge in remote papyrus swamps or moved to high strongholds such as Ruwenzori's Mountains of the Moon and the bamboo-forested Virunga Volcanoes of the Central Rift Valley. There, fleeing from human savagery, they find a haven among the peaceful gorillas and elephants, sometimes roving to altitudes of over ten thousand feet. This second Mbogo may attack a man on sight, wisely suspecting his motives, and if wounded he may charge and fight with all the incoherent fury of our own historic "berserkers."

A week or even a few days of persecution may convert the placid buffalo of unhunted territory into the short-tempered, vigilant, and even aggressive warrior. Yet most of them—like "fighting" bulls in a bull ring, goaded on by the torturing pain of *banderillas*—have to be provoked, and provoked persistently, before they will attack armed hunters.

When shot at and missed, Mbogo usually beats a hasty retreat. Sometimes he will circle back upon his trail, ready to make his own attack, but rarely makes it unless further pressed. When he receives a flesh wound he will still retreat more often than he charges, but when the heavy-caliber bullet smashes into solid bone, his pain and fury mount. Then he sometimes charges, but may still flee and circle back upon his trail to lie in hiding rather than in wait.

When he does decide to charge, as he may at any stage of the hunter's game, he thunders forward with his massive neck outstretched and horns laid back over his shoulders, watching his target keenly and, unlike the inept rhino, only lowering his head at the last moment. But if bullets fail to stop him, the man can still jump aside like a matador—providing he doesn't panic and head for the nearest tree. Mbogo's charge will carry him far enough beyond so that the hunter can set himself for another aimed shot by the time the buffalo turns.

If his charge succeeds, Mbogo tosses first and then tramples. When wounded, he will sometimes grind his enemy into a mere stain on the grass . . . but I hardly feel it stains his reputation. It seems a natural reaction to expect from a giant hoofed animal crazed by pain; in fact, America's own moose, elk, and even deer will sometimes do the same and with far less provocation. As Ernest Thompson Seton once reported, concerning bouts between deer and men, "If, however, the deer is the conqueror, he never ceases to batter, spear, and trample his victim as long as it shows signs of life." During their rutting season, deer will even chase, with lascivious intent, human females—a buck in full season once treed two women just a few miles from San Francisco; but they are never known as America's vindictive or immoral deer, perhaps because they look so well on ribbon-trimmed Christmas cards.

Buffalo attacks without apparent provocation may be made by an aging so-called rogue, hunted before and justly fearing or hating all humans; by a cow cut off from her calf, who will charge through hell itself to reach the frightened baby; by a diseased animal, maddened by rinderpest but still strong enough to move; or by any buffalo suffering from old wounds, whether caused by lions' jaws, white men's bullets, native arrow-points and spear-points, or the nails, stones, and other trash that natives cram into their antique muzzle-loading guns.

The herd itself will never charge at humans, or at anything else. Their only violent group reaction, often from a trivial cause, will be a wild stampede *away* from actual or fancied danger.

Alone, on foot and quite unarmed, I have charged at herds of more than a hundred Cape buffaloes, stampeding them in the opposite direction. When I suddenly bolted forward, shouting "Boo! Get lost!" or its Swahili equivalent *"Toka!"*, a hundred tons or so of startled bovine herd prudently, or so they thought, decamped. Once, when a large herd stampeded *toward* me—probably panicked by a prowling lion—there was far more danger. Had I tried to run away across that stretch of open savannah near Rutshuru, south of the Albert National Park's Rwindi Plains, I certainly would have been overtaken, trampled, and crushed beneath four or five hundred thundering hoofs—buffaloes can travel at a speed of thirty-five miles per hour versus twenty for the fastest man alive (which I am not). So instead of taking suicidal flight, I waited quietly for the oncoming herd with arms outstretched, trying to look like a new species of baobab tree.

Fleeing as they were from some kind of danger, there was no good reason for the panic-stricken animals to waste their time investigating an immobile object that presented no real menace, even a bearded, very phony-looking tree. The buffalo stampede split into two, streaming by on either side of me. There was a great deal of noise and dust, plus a strong, sweet, bovine scent, far more powerful than that of native cattle—but that was all.

In the past, herds of several hundred buffaloes were fairly common; today the average herd probably numbers from thirty to sixty cows, calves, and young bulls, usually led by a bossy old matriarch. When they decide to face a danger rather than stampede, as they occasionally may do when one or more are shot and killed by hunters, they array themselves with the bulls in front shielding the cows and calves. After a while, however, they invariably retreat. Mature bulls will often run in bands of two to six, roving from the herd, and they are easier to approach than the worrisome baby-tending cows. Older bulls will sometimes lead a solitary recluse-type existence, but they are not necessarily morose or savage; like aging male humans, they probably have little patience with the fussiness of family life or the competitive antics of bachelor males.

Bulls may fight at any time of the year—apparently for status in the herd rather than female favors. I watched such a contest once, crouching at the edge of a thicket near the Malemba Nkulu swamps of Katanga. The two bulls faced each other with lowered heads, then charged with all of their force, their sable-colored horns crashing together. The horns locked and neither tried to free himself but instead attempted to force the other backwards. Each strained with all the massive muscle of his quarters, but before long the older bull began to yield, moving backward step by step and at last dropping to his knees. The challenger twisted his horns free and gored his enemy in the neck. At that the old buffalo fled without making any obvious sign of official surrender.

Since there is no definite mating season, calves of varying ages are usually present in the herd, born after matings that differ little from the barnyard amours of domesticated bull and cow. Often, however, Mbogo breeds during the African summer, with his lady giving birth to her single calf somewhere between January and March. The cow will usually hide her woolly little baby, sorrel-colored like herself, in tall

84

grass and remain near its side somewhat separated from the herd for the ten days or so that it is still a trifle wobbly on the legs. The calf follows his mother for about six months before achieving semi-independence.

As he grows older, the bull calf gradually turns to an almost coal-black color, reaching sexual maturity during his third year. His full span of life may conceivably encompass thirty years, but bulls older than twelve or so usually start to gray, shed most of their hair and gradually lose their fine hearing, sense of smell, and keen eyesight. They may even go blind, unlike the dim-sighted elephant whose vision rarely grows appreciably worse whatever age he may achieve. These aged bulls, crowned with large and impressive-looking horns, are usually the easiest buffalo to approach; they cannot hear, see, or even smell distant hunters and may be unaware of danger until the first bullets hit them.

Recluse bulls have learned to like the Indian corn and millet grown in native fields, although bands of roving bulls and the herd itself rarely come close to human habitations. They dine on grass for the most part, sometimes browsing on tender shoots of shrubs or trees, and never go far from water, living by choice near rivers or lakes where they can drink their fill, cool themselves with a brisk swim, and soothe their tick-bitten and gadfly-tortured hides by wallowing up to the neck if they can, in sticky black mud. But wallowing doesn't *rid* them of the ticks; to solve this painful and annoying problem, Mbogo relies on a faithful valet-companion, the "tick-bird," or oxpecker. This extraordinary member of the starling family also functions as a burglar alarm, warning Mbogo of approaching danger—an especially vital service for the aged, near-blind bulls.

How the buffalo and tick-bird first got together is explained in a Batutsi legend from the Kagera River region of northeastern Rwanda. The tall Batutsi—or "Watusi" as they are usually called in movies and travel literature—claim that God, like a Belgian district commissioner, decided to take a census of his grazing and browsing children. What happened next is absolutely typical of native life in Rwanda, where every man plots incessantly to bolster his social status, and even "boys" will hire "boys" of their own who in turn hire "boys" to demonstrate their status and prestige.

God told the animals to line up in two files, one for those with cloven hoofs, the other for the rest, with the strongest member of each tribe standing at the head. The many varied antelopes and the tall giraffe obediently trotted into place behind the mighty buffalo in a long, long line that stretched across the savannah. The second line was much shorter: the zebra stood at the end, the rhino in the middle, and the elephant at the head, forming a compact (but zoologically improper) tribe.

While God was busy checking them off, the two tribes started a big *palabre* about their respective rights to the grass and shrubbery. Annoyed by their snorting, bleating, and mooing, God decided that they needed a little more discipline and organization. In future, He told the buffalo and elephant, each of them would be a chief and function as His personal deputy, divinely authorized to judge, mediate, or mete out needed punishments. "Can you handle the job?" God inquired anxiously. "Is there any way I can help you?"

The elephant, confident and self-assured, declined to ask advice or aid from the deity. But the buffalo mooed, "I won't look like a real chief unless I have a deputy of my own. Besides, with so many subjects to rule, I really need someone to report on tribal affairs, pass along my orders, and keep an eye on the elephant's tribe. In his spare time he can help me with my ticks."

God nodded, considering it a reasonable demand. Then He called together all the birds who dwell upon the savannah, telling the buffalo to look them over and select his new deputy. Inspecting each and every one, the buffalo listened briefly to its song, then tested out its tick-picking ability. He settled at last on a brownish bird with a red-tipped beak who said "Chirrr," picked ticks very efficiently, and seemed to have an alert but friendly disposition.

"You are now the buffalo's official deputy," God informed the bird. "I order you to ride on the buffalo's back, take care of all the ticks that trouble him, relay his orders and decisions, and sound an instant alarm in time of danger."

"That's a very important job," answered the tick-bird. "I really need a deputy."

God told him to take his pick. The tick-bird then pretended to inspect the other birds, but he knew all along that he was going to choose his best friend, the buff-backed snowy-winged egret: the egret would take orders but he wouldn't try to take over since he picks and eats no ticks, preferring flies.

Ever since that day, fulfilling God's commands, tick-bird and egret have been Mbogo's constant companions. Whenever you see them attending to giraffes or antelopes, the Batutsi explain, they are only passing along the bosses' orders.

When they seemingly defect to zebra herds or rhinos, they are actually engaged in spying for Mbogo. But the clever tick-bird never takes the risk of spying on the elephant chief himself; he delegates that dangerous job to his egret deputy —an ingenious twist of legend to explain why tick-ridden elephants, for reasons of their own, will not tolerate tick-birds but permit egrets to strut along their broad heads and backs or follow in their tracks snapping up flies.

Playing his role of chief deputy and sentinel, the tick-bird is remarkably devoted. His frantic call of "Chirrr, Chirrr," is not a mere cry of general distress but a true warning to the buffalo and an urgent plea for action. I have witnessed with my own eyes how a frantic tick-bird—his cries ignored by a sleeping bull, a gray, bald, and probably deaf animal—dashed himself repeatedly against the massive head. Even when the buffalo lies dead, felled by hunters' bullets, the faithful tick-bird still may try to rouse him. But the bird shows wonderful discrimination: when he tends native cattle he ignores approaching men, knowing that they do not come as hunters.

Playing his own role of deputy's deputy, the egret, or cattle heron, is hardly a true or dedicated sentinel. His undirected cry of alarm or actual flight from danger may alert Mbogo, but the bird doesn't wait to find out. In fact, his presence sometimes gives the buffalo away, since flocks of egrets will fly in circles over the herd, snowy wings flashing in the sunlight like heliographic signals to distant hunters white and black.

The white men, bent on thrills and trophies, take Mbogo's head as their chief prize. Hoofs are saved for transformation into ashtrays, and the bull's scrotum may be carefully cut away, cured, trimmed, and stitched into a sportsman-favored tobacco pouch—just the sort of thing that really wows the boys back at the office or the lodge. But guides and amateurs may also satisfy a far more natural instinct with the buffalo's remains: unlike the fibrous, rank-tasting flesh of carrion-loving leopards and lions, the meat of grass-eating buffalo tastes as sweet as that of any Texas steer. Since it is somewhat tough unless properly aged or marinated, white gourmets prefer to eat the tongue, kidneys, and the succulent paté-like marrow of the leg bones. Their bearers and "boys" will dine heartily on less popular cuts, cooking the meat in rich stews and soups; but the major part of the carcass is discarded, left to animal scavengers in a land where people die for lack of meat.

Black hunters of the past, driven by that valid need for

meat but unequipped with firearms, made only minor inroads on the buffalo population. Most Africans trapped rather than hunted the formidable Mbogo, relying on snares and pits whose construction took far more time and effort than to-day's up-to-date poaching methods. Both snares and pits were employed by the Pygmy-like Batwa of Rwanda; this tough, resourceful little people used to fashion highly intricate traps from green wood and woven lianas, or dig enormous trenches twelve feet long and ten feet deep with leafy branches covering the top and sharpened stakes waiting on the bottom.

The true Pygmies of the Congo forest never dig pits or lay snares for any animal, but sometimes make a collective spear-hunt, pitting their wits and strength against the red forest buffaloes of the Ituri. Members of this smaller species, warier than the wary Cape buffalo himself, are by reason of their less unwieldy size more dangerous opponents, especially for spear-wielding men who average only four feet six inches and usually weigh less than a hundred pounds. The red forest buffalo kills many who try to spear him; knowing this, the brave but never foolish Pygmies rarely undertake such a buffalo hunt unless goaded on by the forest's meat-craving Negro tribes who have reduced many former Pygmy nomads to a state of fixed feudal dependence.

A different kind of spear-hunt, for a vastly different motive, was formerly practiced by Rwanda's status-conscious Watusi. The movie-going public may adore them for their glamorous appearance and their height—grossly exaggerated, since they average a little under six feet tall—but the Watusi are in all respects a far less decent, fair-thinking people than the often-maligned Pygmies. Forbidden by their Nilo-Hamitic customs and religion to eat game, Watusi aristocrats hunted buffalo for sport, sallying forth with packs of brave, barkless basenji dogs which they spurred with hunting horns to harry the buffalo while they themselves threw spears in relative safety. I once watched, and with great disgust, one of those so-called buffalo hunts, conducted by Rudahigwa Mutara, the former King of Rwanda. For all the real sport involved, the Watusi might as well have been White Hunters or, even worse, a pack of fox-hunting socialites in blackface, unhorsed but following their prey with hounds and horns. The dead buffalo's meat was, of course, given to the dogs.

My own Masai brothers of East Africa, while related to the Watusi by their shared Nilo-Hamitic origin, would have laughed in derision. Some of them still go forth to hunt the animal they call *il-osowani,* but they fight on decent terms, spearing their prey or dying without hiding behind a pack of harrying dogs. Like the Watusi they eat no wild game, but they have a somewhat practical purpose: cured buffalo hides make fine warriors' shields. Horns are usually given to the medicine men, who use them for grinding healing herbs or holding magic talismans and stones; but once again the enormous heap of meat is wasted.

All of these black hunters belong, however, to Africa's rich and fascinating past. They may have killed the Cape buffalo bravely like the Masai or absurdly like the Watusi, but they killed very few. Today's native hunters and poachers, corrupted by the ever-widening influence of Western tradegoods, money, and the safari curio racket, slaughter buffalo with high-powered rifles and they slaughter on a grand scale. They sell hides, horns, and some meat for a profit, but the great bulk of meat is still wasted. For every buffalo they kill, butcher, and haul away, they probably wound four or five that escape and die in hiding. Without refrigeration much of the remaining meat may putrefy before the butchers find moneyed customers to buy.

Human hunger for meat, endemic throughout protein-starved Africa, is often used as a pretext for continuing game slaughters. But the buffalo population, along with the rest of the game, probably cut by 90 per cent during the past century, is now diminishing at an even faster rate while the Africans remain hungry. If they continue to kill irresponsibly, while opening former game preserves to irresponsible whites, they will be even hungrier when the last buffalo dies.

Other closely related members of Mbogo's family from other parts of the world seem headed for that irrevocable fate: in Celebes the few surviving anoas, or "pygmy buffaloes," are hiding out in the mountainous interior, hunted to near-extinction for hide, horns, and meat; in the Philippines less than a hundred pygmy buffaloes survive, persecuted by ranchers and Manila "sportsmen"; in Malaya the giant gaur, or "Indian bison," the earth's largest bovine animal, has been reduced to a mere three hundred survivors; in Tibet the wild yaks are being slaughtered by natives armed with European rifles and ammunition; and in Cambodia, the oxlike kouprey, a rare animal unknown to science until 1937, has already been reduced to a population of about two hundred, apparently headed for extinction before scientists even reach agreement on its exact classification.

Free-living European "buffaloes," who actually were bison, survived into the twentieth century. A herd of over seven hundred roamed through Poland's Bialowieza Forest until 1914, but all were slaughtered during World War I. Since World War II, through the efforts of Polish authorities, a captive herd has been built up from isolated animals surviving in zoos or private collections where they breed fairly well. A few have been released from captivity, and some sixty semi-feral bison now live free in the Bialowieza Forest. With luck they may survive until World War III.

The North American bison, once the most abundant large animal upon the earth, probably numbered at least sixty million strong when the United States entered its post-Civil War period of expansion toward the West. By 1889 there were a mere *thousand* left, and most of them were hiding out in Canada. What killed America's own "buffalo" in such fantastic hordes were modern firearms—.44 Remingtons and .40 Sharps, which permitted mass slaughters; and modern railways—the Union Pacific and others, which allowed men to haul away a small fraction of the carnage.

Bison tongues were shipped east to New York and even to London, and bison hides rolled eastward on the railroad cars for use as stylish "buffalo robes." As for the meat itself, a ton or so was probably wasted for each pound that was actually eaten. Millions of tons rotted away on America's rolling prairies, tainting the air with effluvium, while replete coyotes, wolves, and buzzards turned away from the feast.

Profit was of course the prime consideration. But another motivating factor was involved, and one which clearly demonstrates how humans sometimes suffer from the slaughter of "mere animals." As Dr. Webb B. Garrison candidly described in his book *Strange Bonds Between Animals and Men:*

Later analysts have concluded that the all-out war upon the bison was not wholly motivated by economic factors. For though records of the time include few direct references to support such a view, it is clear that some whites killed buffalo in order to sabotage the red man's war effort. . . .

. . . Resisting an 1875 political move that would have led to protection of those bison remaining in Texas, General Phil Sheridan warned: "The buffalo hunters have done more in a few months to bring about peace with the Indians than the whole Army could do in thirty years!"

Late in life, old-time hunter Frank Mayer admitted that army posts usually issued free ammunition to buffalo killers. For many a man in uniform subscribed to the view that there was no choice: in order to subdue the Indians, it was necessary to wipe out the animals on whom they were dependent.

Reduced as they were to one thousand survivors, Mbogo's shaggy Yankee cousins seemed to be headed for unavoidable extinction. But American conservationists, fighting a grand fight, at last obtained legislation to protect the bison. Since then the animals themselves, reproducing rather quickly as bovines usually do, have staged a miraculous comeback: the present population now stands at a safe 25,000 and the herds, restricted to limited areas, have to be thinned periodically.

Looking backward at our own "civilized" record both in Europe and America, it hardly seems realistic to expect any more intelligence, sympathy, or foresight from the unsophisticated Africans. We are just beginning to understand what animals mean to our environment, even to grasp the moral fact that they may have their own right to live. The Africans are very far from either concept but, unlike ourselves, they really need their buffalo and other game as a direct source of life-giving food.

The answer to this desperate animal-human dilemma may possibly be found, if some effort is made, in the Cape buffalo's domestication.

White Hunters and their fans will certainly be appalled at the thought of their much-publicized Number One killer being worked, milked, and herded like a common ox or cow, but the Indians have proved rather conclusively that such a feat can be accomplished. Their *bainsha,* or domesticated water buffalo, is physically much the same as their very scarce *arna,* or free-living water buffalo—a wary, short-tempered animal much like Mbogo in character and habits, who sometimes bowls over elephants during his panic-stricken stampedes. If the Africans can match the Indian example, they will have a major natural resource: Cape buffaloes are far meatier than scrawny native cattle, give plentiful and very tasty milk, can pull twice the load of any working ox, and are easier on the pasturage.

That Mbogo can be tamed, trained, and actually domesticated is beyond doubt. At the Albert National Park's Rwindi Plains and other game preserves, formerly elusive buffalo herds became fairly tolerant of men and rather placid in their ways after the first ten or twenty years of absolute protection. Individual animals, when caught young and treated with some kindliness and patience, are no more dangerous than common cattle, who must, after all, be handled with respect.

When abused, either in the barnyard or the bull ring, cows and bulls have both gored and trampled men.

I had such a tame buffalo of my own, purchased at the tender age of eight or nine days from a native hunter who had shot its mother, and I kept that small Mbogo at my private game preserve near Mugwata, in the Congo's Kivu province, some twenty miles or so from the border of Rwanda. He was a little shy at first but soon became as affable as any Hereford calf, friendly with his native keepers, and forever nudging at my rear to beg for the coarse salt I kept in a back pocket. His nudges grew a little trying as he got bigger, but he never showed a trace of bad temper. Then, when he was barely half-grown, he charged playfully toward a passing Bahunde native. The man threw his spear—although my young Mbogo was confined within a kraal—ripping open the buffalo's big flaplike ear. From that time on, although he still trusted his keepers and played with me like a friendly dog, he charged furiously at any unfamiliar native who came near him.

If the Black Africans, who have never made a systematic effort to domesticate their animals, can show some patience, understanding, and good will, they can live in peaceful partnership with the Cape buffalo. He is really more cow than killer—even his Swahili name, Mbogo, sounds like a deep, plaintive moo—and his needs are very simple: good pasturage, plenty of water to splash in, and above all, decent treatment from his human neighbors. Up to now he has received the opposite from black and white alike.

Mbogo's actions have been correspondingly "vindictive" but only in the sense of Voltaire's classic axiom, perhaps more fitting for the Cape buffalo than any other so-called wild beast: "This animal is very vicious; when you attack him he defends himself."

TEMBO

The Solid Citizen

There is an animal who laughs, weeps, gets drunk, plays practical jokes, falls in love, gets married, goes on honeymoons, doses himself with laxatives, poultices his wounds, pulls his aching teeth, and sometimes earns his living as lumberman, teamster, builder, postman, hunter, soldier, actor, acrobat, or even clever smuggler.

Although he is not a man, he is recognized and treated as another kind of human being throughout India, Ceylon, Burma, Thailand, and the other countries of the Orient. India's Brahmans even believe that the *hathi*, as they call him, prays at dawn and sunset when he stands in silence watching the sky with contemplative devotion. Buddhists and other Asiatics agree that this unique animal has a primitive religion of his own and thus treat him with respect and reverence. But in Africa, where he is often called Tembo—a Swahili name that sounds like a vast, throbbing drumbeat—he is simply *nyama,* or "meat," to the hunting natives and "the big tusker" or "ivory" to the hunting whites.

To explain this discrepancy, people usually maintain that African elephants cannot be tamed. The Indian elephant is docile and intelligent, they say, but they call the African species a fierce, unapproachable, untrainable, or even murderous beast. This cherished view of our Western civilization merely holds the mirror up to man: the history of human-Tembo relations demonstrates with stark clarity how this "untrainable" animal has, for more than five thousand years, behaved *exactly as we have taught him to behave.*

Back in 3500 B.C., the highly civilized Egyptians, history's first and ablest animal-teachers, trained African elephants as riding mounts and servants. Between the second and third centuries B.C., the Carthaginians trained African elephants for war (including Hannibal's famed thirty-seven-elephant corps that marched to the distant Alps and waiting Rome), armoring them with iron plates, loading their backs with javelin-throwing soldiers, and marching them to battle. A few hundred years later, the dissolute Imperial Romans trained African elephants as gladiators, acrobats, tightrope-walkers, or even burlesque comedians who acted out suggestive charades and lumbered through obscene Pyrrhic dances. During modern times, gourmet-minded seventeenth-century Frenchmen trained their country's first African elephant, at the Versailles menagerie, to dip its bread in soup and drink twelve pints of wine per day; respectable-minded nineteenth-century Englishmen trained their own country's first African elephant, the beloved Jumbo, to eat currant buns and carry frolicking children on his back; and practical-minded twentieth-century Belgians trained the Congo's bush elephants to haul logs or pull a plow.

Beginning in 1899, as a pet project of Belgium's King Léopold II, elephant-training stations were established at Kira Vunga, Api, Gangala na Bodio, and Epulu in the northeast Congo's elephant-rich Ituri Forest. Top-notch *cornacs*—experienced Indian mahouts or trainers—were imported to educate the first animals and, hopefully, to impart the secrets of their art to crews of Congolese natives.

The art requires more patience than many African novices could muster: Indian *cornacs* used the elephant-goad (*hawkus*) to tap their charges lightly as a signal or to make gestures, but they never really struck a blow. Using force to discipline any animal, they well knew, leads that animal sooner or later to use his own and often greater force to discipline the trainer. The graves of six native student trainers at the Api station are mute testimony to the folly of trying to beat or bully an animal who outweighs a man seventy to one. But some Congolese persisted, learning to respect their elephant partners and continuing the Indian *cornacs'* methods and traditions until the last days of the former Belgian Congo.

To capture a few promising young Tembos, herds were stampeded by firing shots into the air. Four- or five-year-old calves were then roped or netted, brought to the station, tethered to trees, and accustomed to the sight, sound, smell, and manners of men over a ten-month taming period: their *cornacs* talked to them, sang traditional Hindu songs, and plied them with sugar cane, sweet potatoes, pineapples, and bananas while bathing, brushing, or rubbing them down.

The songs were all-important. Emotional as they are, elephants show extreme sensitivity to music. Circus elephants still display the same reactions as the first elephants tested during recent ages—Hans and Parkie, a young couple brought to Paris' *Jardin des Plantes* in 1798, who swayed in time to marches, trumpeted excitedly when trumpets blew, and showed their wonderful discernment by falling asleep during symphonies (even as I do). Many elephants reach a state resembling true hypnotic trance when soothing music is played; martial airs, on the other hand, were probably of prime importance in training elephants for war.

Asiatic elephants have, of course, enjoyed a broader professional range: they work as postal messengers, carrying a human mailman and some five hundred pounds of mail; perform as hunting steeds, bearing howdahs full of sportsmen in India's famed *shikars*—elaborate staged hunts almost as phony as present East African safaris; or dabble in the ancient art of smuggling like some Siamese elephants who, laden with leather pouches full of contraband, have sneaked across the border into Cambodia, guided by whistled signals from their distant keepers. Albino Asiatics, such as the famed white elephants of Thailand, can even play the role of earthly god. In the past they were suckled by human wet-nurses, massaged with priceless oils, regaled with jessamine-flavored drinks, crowned with diadems of beaten gold, ringed with gold around the tusks, hung with golden chains around the neck, robed in purple velvet fringed with gold and scarlet, and sheltered from the sun by gold and crimson umbrellas. More recently, they have been provided with special trains, shower-baths, and electric fans—which they probably enjoyed much more.

The Congo's trained elephants, although they never attained the status of postman or god, proved conclusively within a brief quarter of a century that they are just as docile and intelligent as their Oriental cousins. They may in fact be more intelligent, if given a chance to prove it. Zoo and circus experts sometimes call them nervous and high-strung because they are more alert and apprehensive than the Asiatic elephants who have lived in close, continuous partnership with civilized man for four or five thousand years. But it seems entirely natural considering the troubled history of their species. Aside from Belgian efforts in the Congo, the elephants of Equatorial Africa received a very different training at the hands of man; they were taught to fear, evade, or even fight humans who pursued, killed, and butchered them for meat or ivory.

Before Arabs and Europeans arrived, the natives had little interest in the elephant's tusks. Only a few tribes, such as the eastern Congo's Balega, took the trouble to carve some of their best masks and figurines from the very tough but durable ivory; most craftsmen preferred easily whittled but quickly decaying wood. Tusks were sometimes used to prop up the sagging roof of a hut or to build ornamental stockades, and the Pygmies employed small ivory mallets to beat out tree bark for their loincloths. But there was plenty of "dead ivory" lying around in the bush—tusks from elephants who had died naturally—so the living animals weren't hunted for such trivial purposes. Sometimes natives made an effort to trap or hunt elephants who raided their fields and banana groves but, for the most part, they looked at the elephant and saw a walking mountain of meat.

Most native trappers relied on huge pitfalls, fourteen feet deep and covered with light wood, reeds, and grass, which they dug along the paths leading to the elephants' watering places. The pits had smoothly sloping sides tapering down to a very narrow bottom so that the trapped elephant's legs were pinned together, making it very difficult for him to move. Since he was helpless when the trappers came, they butchered him with spears, hatchets, and machetes, hacking off meat without first bothering to kill him.

In East Africa the Wakamba and Wanderobo tribes set harpoon traps over the elephant paths. Iron spears were set in twelve-foot logs, weighing in all some four hundred pounds, and the whole contraption was raised to a height of twenty feet. When the elephant brushed against the triggering device —a liana or a light bar of wood—the weighted harpoon was supposed to plummet downward into his neck and sever the spinal cord. More often it struck a glancing blow, permitting him to escape and either die slowly or recover.

Hunting, if you can call it that, was usually practiced by the most barbaric method known to man—the ring of fire. Between rainy seasons, when the twelve-foot-tall *matete,* or "elephant grass," is tinder-dry, savannah-dwelling tribesmen used to set a flaming circle up to two miles in diameter around an unsuspecting elephant herd. Detecting the distant smoke with their extremely keen sense of smell, the elephants often managed to escape but were sometimes trapped within the closing ring. Many were burned to death in the roaring flames or asphyxiated by the suffocating smoke. Others, driven by desperation, charged through the fire. Half-charred and blinded, they were easy prey for waiting hordes of spearmen. Those who burst through at unguarded points along the flaming circle met a far more tragic fate: with most of the thick hide burned away from their bodies, they were sentenced to slow agony. Sometimes native villagers heard them in the nearby bush, groaning and sobbing day and night until they died.

Some native hunters, such as East Africa's Wanderobo and Waliangulu or the South African Bushmen, shot poison arrows from an ambush or stalked the elephant, smeared from head to foot with their quarry's own dung, to jab him with a poison-tipped spear. But contrary to popular belief, no African ever used a blow-gun, a weapon employed by South and Central American Indians and by some Melanesian and Malayan peoples. The elephant sometimes died within a few hours if the toxic substance was a potent one, such as acocanthera, the famed "Bushman's poison," and fresh enough to take its full effect. If the poison had been kept too long, it sometimes took days or even months for the escaping elephant to die. Sections of meat surrounding the poisoned wounds were, of course, discarded; the great bulk of flesh remained edible.

To the north, Abyssinians and half-breed Arabs of the White Nile hunted on horseback, armed with huge broadswords. Three or four mounted hunters cut an elephant out of the herd and ran him down until he stopped, ready to charge. As he tried to attack the main body of hunters at the front, a single man attacked him from the rear, leaping from his horse and trying to hamstring the animal by slashing his

Achilles' tendon. When successful, this maneuver left the elephant virtually helpless. Tembo has what is literally an Achilles' heel: due to his anatomical construction and his pacing gait, an elephant with one disabled leg cannot walk at all. It was now an easy task to slash the arteries and tendons of his other leg and to stand by, watching, while he bled to death.

To the south, in Mashonaland, hamstringing hunters went on foot, stalking sleeping elephants with broad-bladed axes. But in Equatorial Africa, where the hunter's traditional weapon is either a spear or bow, hamstringing was never practiced.

The Masai and other warrior tribes of East Africa have never made a practice of spearing elephants. These pastoral people eat no wild game, raise no crops that elephants may raid or trample, and satisfy their initiation requirements by hunting lions, the enemies of their cattle. Other tribes, who craved and ate the elephant's flesh, rarely used their spears until their prey had first been trapped, weakened by poison arrows, or burned to near-death in rings of fire. There were a few Africans who faced uncrippled elephants with spears alone, but the only people who still attempt to do so, who confront the world's largest land mammal, are the smallest men on earth—the Congo Pygmies.

Travel books and hunters' tales repeat endlessly the legend that the Pygmies hamstring elephants. They never pause to wonder how a ninety-pound man can strike a single blow, slicing through the tough hide and tough tendon with his *ipe*, a five-foot-long wooden spear capped by an eighteen-inch blade. I have taken one of those little spears and tested it on the hind leg of a dead elephant, but although I stand two feet taller than a Pygmy and outweigh him nearly three to one, I could barely nick the tendon. Even with the longer, iron-butted Masai spear, it is impossible to hamstring an elephant: a spear simply doesn't have a stout enough blade or the proper weight and balance.

Knowing the dangers involved, as with their buffalo hunts, the Pygmies rarely try to spear the forest elephant until pressured into it by their meat-hungry Negro overlords. The Negroes coax and threaten, bribing them with *pombe* or native beer and bananas. Sometimes they even give the Pygmies *bangi*, locally grown narcotic hemp that the hunters smoke like hashish before leaving camp.

In *Congo Kitabu* I described a Pygmy elephant hunt in full detail—the only such hunt, to my knowledge, that has ever been witnessed from start to finish by a white man. Keeping up with the agile Pygmies, who can pass swiftly and silently through the most tangled bush, was the major problem during the four or five hours that they tracked the elephant down. Then, as they prepared for the final stalk, they masked their human odor by smearing themselves from head to foot with the elephant's fresh droppings; I too was given a liberal coating of the sticky dung, which wasn't particularly pleasant.

During that slow, silent stalk, the twelve Pygmy hunters moved in crescent formation through the dense bush, closing from the rear on the unsuspecting elephant—an old bull with small tusks who was browsing on an uprooted mimosa tree. The lead hunter, whom the Pygmies call the *tebe,* detached himself from the center of the crescent and covered the final fifty or sixty feet alone. At the very last, when the *tebe* crept up behind him as soundlessly as a Red Indian, the elephant somehow took alarm and started to turn. Simultaneously the Pygmy heaved his spear into the elephant's bladder.

Shrieking with rage and pain, the elephant whipped around, thrusting with his tusks. The *tebe* leaped to the side and four Pygmies rushed forward, sinking their own spears into the animal's belly and flanks; seconds later, the main body of hunters closed in like a swarm of angry bees. The elephant stampeded through the undergrowth, lashing from side to side with trunk and tusks. Caught up in the passion of the kill, the hunters followed, hurling spear after spear. Soon the elephant found it almost impossible to move: with every step protruding spear-shafts caught on bushes or trees, twisting the weapons in his entrails. Agonized and utterly confused, he stood for a moment, motionless. Then a Pygmy hurled his spear into the upper part of the elephant's sensitive trunk.

He tried to lunge forward but the spear-butts slowed him down, permitting the Pygmy to escape. Meanwhile the hunters, now weaponless, pulled at the loops of bowel hanging from his belly. He fell to his knees, convulsed with maniacal spasms; his legs flailed, his bowels emptied, he rolled over onto his side, and his great head rose and smashed to the ground. Then, thank God, he died.

For once, none of the hunters had been killed or seriously wounded, so all twelve of them performed the Pygmies' traditional victory dance around the mountainous corpse. They danced for over an hour, piping a shrill tuneless song on their wooden hunting whistles as they circled, stamping their feet, around the dead elephant or marched in single file on top of the carcass, leaving bloody little footprints from the croup to the head. Then the dancing stopped. The Negro masters had arrived, at least a hundred of them, bringing empty wicker baskets to carry away the meat.

The Negro chief gave a signal. The intrepid Pygmy who had acted as the lead hunter climbed to the top of the elephant's bloated belly and plunged in his spear. Stomach juices spurted out in a six-foot geyser, driven by pressure of the methane gas that had been building up in the dead elephant's intestines. Then the Pygmies gathered up the spears they had used for the hunt and returned them to the Negro masters. The Negroes doled out a dozen machetes. When the work was finished, they too would have to be returned.

The Pygmies carved a huge hole and two of them walked into the elephant's belly, hacking as they went. Others crouched on the flanks, carving off chunks of meat and heaving them toward the waiting baskets. A seemingly endless file of Negroes carried away basket after dripping basket. Chief and tribal dignitaries would share the prized trunk, heart, and liver, but all would eat ten or even twelve pounds of meat before they slept, perhaps for an entire day. The twelve hunters who had killed the elephant received a spindly stalk of bananas, a big pot of beer, and some pieces of skin which could be boiled for soup. That was the Pygmies' share.

Despite the agony they brought to individual elephants, none of the native hunters and trappers made a substantial dent in the elephant population. Their methods, from pits and snares to Pygmy spear hunts, took tremendous time and effort and yielded as their prize a single elephant. The only real exception—ringing an entire herd with fire—was a sporadically held affair which the smoke-sniffing elephants often managed to evade.

The real carnage started at the beginning of the nineteenth century when Arabs and the Arab-Negro half-breeds called "Swahilis" began moving westward from Zanzibar and other coastal strongholds. They came in search of ivory—white ivory torn from Tembo's jaws and "black ivory" (slaves) to carry the tusks back to the coast, then to be sold in the slave markets.

Native chieftains traded tusks and men for the Arabs' shiny glass beads, brass and copper wire, iron chains and "fire tubes," as they called the antiquated muzzle-loading guns. The chiefs, at first, had no trouble procuring ample stocks of their own tradegoods: they set their people to gathering vast quantities of dead ivory from the bush, and sold the slaves they had already taken in intertribal wars. But supplies of both quickly dwindled. Now the chiefs started to sell their own people, while urging the rest to hunt and keep hunting elephants, using all of their traditional methods plus the new muzzle-loading guns.

Wielded by the Arabs, the guns had some effectiveness. The Arab marksmen usually aimed for the knee, attempting to cripple the elephants. Wielded by the natives, the guns were almost laughably ineffective. Their ammunition painfully wounded but seldom killed, especially when they employed nails, chain-links, and other dross instead of bullets; and the hunters themselves had little or no idea of what they were doing. Most of them crammed in too much powder and ammunition, after having it "charmed" by the local *nganga,* or medicine man, and simply pointed the gun at the elephant rather than aiming it at any significant part of his anatomy. When they fired, the deafening blast and huge cloud of black smoke scared them out of their wits. Many used to drop their guns as soon as they pulled the trigger, high-tailing it for cover and only returning when the smoke had cleared away.

The elephants, who had never seen or heard anything like it, usually rushed in the opposite direction. Some escaped unwounded, but others carried a bullet or a load of chain-links in the flank or belly. Some were actually killed by the muzzle-loaders, more by chance than marksmanship, but these were probably very few compared to the numbers who were now falling prey to increasing hunts by more traditional methods.

Arab inroads against white and black ivory lasted until 1892, when twelve hundred troops of the newly formed Congo Free State, led by a handful of Belgian officers, went to battle against the thirty thousand armed Arabs of Tipoo Tip, Rumaliza the Ravager, and the other arch despots, entrenched by now in the Congo itself as well as in bases formed earlier along the shores of Lake Tanganyika. That war, one of the most daring struggles against fantastic odds in history, ended on Steptember 22, 1894, when the last Arab slaver had either surrendered or fled eastward to Zanzibar. Peace had now come to the natives of Equatorial Africa, but the elephant population, seriously depleted by the Arab-inspired pogroms, was at war again in less than three years.

The enemy's advance guard consisted, amazingly enough, of a single man: W. D. H. Bell, an Englishman who came, in 1897, to what is now Kenya, carrying his favorite book, a worn copy of Dickens' *Pickwick Papers,* and his high-powered rifles. He was, according to his own description, the "first man of any sort to devote himself exclusively to hunting elephant, and the first to demonstrate the extreme deadliness of modern firearms."

Comparing himself to native hunters, Bell explained in his book, *Karamojo Safari:*

> I possessed and carried to the hunt the result of centuries of intelligent application of nature's laws to the problem of causing death. My rifle was a weapon streets ahead of anything the black man could produce, ingenious as he is in his use of poisons and traps, spears and arrows. And moreover, my mind was more capable of appreciating the necessity of introducing my tiny death-dealing bullet into such parts of the pachydermatous anatomy as to produce the desired result in the quickest and least fuss-producing manner. . . .

"Karamojo" Bell, nicknamed after his favorite hunting grounds, was indeed a crack shot, rarely missing with his "tiny death-dealing bullet," a round-nosed projectile weighing from 215 to 250 grains, fired from .256-, .275-, or .303-caliber rifles; but his greatest asset was the elephants' almost absolute ignorance of civilized hunting tactics.

Herd by herd, he proceeded to enlighten them:

> If the ground is clear enough, what you do is this. Say, for example, you have closed with three bull elephants tree-browsing gently along. You range alongside without difficulty. You kill the first one with an easy shot to the brain. You get a fast one into a head that turns inquiringly toward the sound of the shot, and he goes down. But the third one flees, you after him. . . . There is nothing more satisfying than the complete flop of a running elephant shot in the brain.

As with the Arabs, Karamojo Bell's object wasn't meat, although some of his countrymen were fond of baked elephant's foot, cooked in the skin and scooped out like a Stilton cheese; he was after what he called "the big stuff."

On a single afternoon in the Lado Enclave, he killed nineteen bulls bearing 1,440 pounds of ivory. At the Pibor Flats he bagged ten bulls bearing "mighty big stuff," as he described it—1,463 pounds of ivory that later brought him £900 at Hale's Auction Rooms in London. Two other fifteen-elephant bags each produced roughly 1,400 pounds of ivory for conversion into billiard balls, piano keys, crucifixes, and curios. The entire bag of his fourth safari into Karamojo country, a fourteen-month affair comprising six months of actual hunting, was 354 tusks taken from the jaws of 180 elephants and totalling 18,762 pounds of ivory, "all first-rate stuff, salable on the spot to the Indian merchants at seven rupees per pound, say ten shillings per pound." His profit from that one safari was, as he reported, £6,000.

Karamojo Bell was, indeed, the first and most coolly efficient man ever to devote his skill with modern weapons to the "problem of causing death" for the elephants of Equatorial Africa. He was the first, but hordes of white elephant hunters and poachers followed in his tracks. They slaughtered herd after herd, while automatically training the survivors to become ever more wary, fearful, resentful, and even defensively ferocious.

When stalked, elephants sometimes stalk the hunter, becoming to outward appearances a perfect reflection of men. Some of them, especially those who carry heavy-caliber slugs lodged in their abscessed skulls, even become vindictive, stamping the life out of a new tormentor and then dismembering his corpse. No African elephant has, however, attained the moral standards of allegedly civilized men who killed elephants, and still kill them, to sell or keep their teeth as trophies.

In that sense and that sense alone, the African elephant remains absolutely "untrainable."

Despite the hunters' record, our Western world has always been impressed and intrigued by elephants. The "ponderous pachyderms," as showmen like to call them, have been the favorite zoo and circus spectacles from classic times to modern, provoking endless curiosity about their habits and inspiring the kind of tolerant affection, even love, which is rarely given to large and potentially dangerous animals. Most of it has been directed toward the Asiatic elephant, partly because the public sees him much more often, partly because his physical appearance is so wonderfully absurd.

Baggy-skinned, with a bulging forehead, droopy little ears and a downward-sloping behind, Tembo's poor relation looks like a wistful old lady who has scrubbed too many floors. The Asiatic cows have no tusks, only "tushes" level with their jaws, and the bulls' tusks are rarely more than four or five feet long, often curving erratically. Some only grow a single tusk, and almost all of Ceylon's bulls are *muknas*—full-grown tuskless males. The Asiatic elephant is hairier and has a single finger-like projection at the tip of his trunk which is mainly used for gathering grass; while Tembo, who does much more browsing, has two beautifully adapted little "fingers" which grip a branch and slide along it, stripping off a neat bundle of leaves.

Tighter-skinned, with a smoothly sloping forehead, ears like vast spreading sails, and hindquarters higher than the midpoint of his back, Tembo is a larger and more powerful animal: bulls average ten-and-a-half feet at the shoulder and weigh five-and-a-half tons, but may reach heights exceeding twelve feet and weights of over seven tons. The patriarch of all modern elephants, a giant among giants, was the bull elephant from Angola, shot in 1955, whose body is now preserved at the Smithsonian Museum in Washington, D.C. He measures thirteen feet, two inches at the shoulder and weighed at the time of his death all of *twelve* tons.

If extinct elephants are considered, the Angola patriarch is himself overshadowed. America's own Imperial Mammoth, who ranged through the southwestern United States and Mexico during Ice Age times, was over fifteen feet tall, probably weighed at least twenty tons, and was built like a shaggy double-decker bus equipped with fourteen- to sixteen-foot tusks instead of front bumpers. This fantastic creature's only serious rival for the title of world's all-time largest land mammal was the baluchithere, a rhino-relative from Mongolia who was taller and longer but probably lighter since he was constructed like an overweight giraffe. Both of the great mammals were, however, far exceeded by the largest dinosaurs, who reached weights of fifty to sixty tons; and all past or present giants of the land are dwarfed by the serene immensity of the world's largest animal: the 100-foot, 150-ton blue whale.

Tembo himself comes in two distinct sizes, races, or subspecies: the large or bush elephant of the savannahs, averaging from five to six tons, and the smaller forest elephant—the kind my Pygmy friends hunted in the Ituri—who is darker-skinned, hairier, rounder-eared, and rarely exceeds five tons or eight feet at the shoulder. Cows of either race usually weigh at least a ton less.

The so-called pygmy elephant of the Ituri is, I feel, a myth. Various authorities, probably judging from immature forest elephants, have long vouched for its existence, given it a Latin name, and even issued licenses to shoot it, but no one has ever produced a specimen, alive or dead, of an adult "pygmy elephant." While living in the Ituri, I questioned many Pygmies on the subject. None of them had seen or heard of a dwarf *uku,* as they call the forest elephant, and no such creature could be found in their legends. On the contrary, their only mythical elephant is a character called "Piobo," a giant monster who can crush a whole camp beneath a single foot. But despite his fearsome reputation, no one ever worries about meeting up with Piobo: he is just a character in Pygmy fairy tales.

An African "water elephant," alleged to inhabit swamps near the Central Congo's Lake Léopold II, appears to be a white man's myth. This unlikely creature is said to have a sleek skin like the hippo, a long narrow neck, no tusks, and an abbreviated two-foot trunk. Several European "observers" claim to have seen it, but I suspect very strongly that they were hoaxsters bent on giving the Congo a tourist-attracting Loch Ness Monster of its own. Their accounts are no more credible, in my opinion, than the wacky little legends of the wonderful *Elephant Book* that swept America in 1963. I have in mind the one that went, "Why do elephants float down the river on their backs?" The answer was, of course, "So that they won't get their pink tennis shoes wet."

The real Tembo, whether dwelling in forest or savannah, is blessed with intriguing enough anatomy. Trunk, ears, skull, legs, feet, and soft parts have all been highly modified by natural selection to the elephant's present mode of life. So have his giant "tusks," which are not true tusks in the classic sense, like the canine teeth of hippos, warthogs, walruses, and narwhales, all of whom have been slaughtered for their ivory. Elephants have no canine teeth: their tusks are actually two upper incisors, the only incisor teeth they have, which are enamel-capped at the tip and solid ivory on the outside, with a large nerve-core running through the interior. They grow continuously during the elephant's lifetime, but only two-thirds of any living tusk is actually visible; the rest, above the jaw level, is solidly rooted in the skull.

As for the maximum length of the Africans' tusks, at least one bull may have exceeded the sixteen-foot record of the mighty Imperial Mammoth. Gordon Cumming, a nineteenth-century authority, mentioned a tusk as long as twenty-one feet, nine inches, while others of that era claimed lengths of over fourteen feet and weights of 250, 300, or even 400 pounds for a single tusk. Such fantastic reports cannot be entirely discounted. As Clive A. Spinage commented in his authoritative work *The Animals of East Africa:* "The size to which an Elephant's tusks will grow seems to be largely due to inheritance, and it is a definite fact that Elephants in East Africa today bear smaller tusks on the whole than they did fifty years ago, owing to the persistent shooting of those with the largest ones."

Thus, men have not only trained African elephants to behave like wild animals; hunters, by their choice of quarry, have actually influenced their physical evolution.

The longest tusks on "official" record are a pair from Kenya, one eleven feet, five-and-a-half inches, and the other eleven feet long; while the heaviest pair, whose owner dwelt on the slopes of Mount Kilimanjaro before his incisors came to rest in the British Museum, weigh 226 and 214 pounds. The two tusks of any pair always differ slightly in length and weight, for the elephant habitually favors one for digging and rooting about with. Most elephants are "right-handed," just as we are, which is why the Arabs call the right-hand tusk *el hadām,* or "the servant."

I once saw an elephant in the Congo's Albert National Park who was equipped with two small tusks on either side of his head. He may have been a freak of nature, but most freakish tusks are created by man: when the hunter's clumsily placed bullet damages the tusk, abscess usually results, but the injured socket sometimes sprouts as many as six or even more small and very useless tusks.

Tondo, or tuskless African elephants, the equivalent of Ceylon's *muknas,* are usually under-endowed females. Very rarely, however, a full-grown bull may lack any external sign of tusks. These aberrant bulls have been persecuted by some East African tribesmen—even by whites—solely on the strength of a bizarre native legend, the story of the so-called Elephant Stone.

According to one old-time elephant hunter, John Albert Jordan, who described himself as "the worst ivory poacher in East Africa," the tusks of a *tondo* grow inward instead of outward to form the Elephant Stone, "just as an oyster grows a pearl." The stone is "larger than the Koh-i-noor and glitters more wondrously," he claimed, although the Koh-i-noor itself or any other diamond is a dull-looking lump of carbon until cut and faceted.

In his book, *Elephants and Ivory,* Jordan recounts:

> I once shot a tuskless bull when I was with the Wanderobo, a great bull that lay all night in the forest, and I sweated as I waited for the morning when the skull could be cleft open. In the morning the Wanderobo cut into the skull with their axes

and there, at the right side of the skull, where the tusk should start, was a large ball of ivory about the size and shape of a cocoanut. I hacked at it with a hatchet, believing it to be the shell of the Stone, and in the end I had nothing but splinters and shavings of ivory, for there was no Stone. But it is my fancy to believe that it exists.

Fortunately, there are no such legendary beliefs, native or white—no mystique at all!—about the elephant's molars. No one hunts the six-ton giants, reducing them to trophy tusks or ivory splinters for their back teeth, each an eight- or nine-pound mass of flattened dentine plates, the very substance of ivory, lamellated by the bony tissue called cementum.

At any one time, Tembo has only four of these immense molars in actual use, two in each upper and lower jaw. As he grinds away at hardwood twigs the crown of each tooth is gradually reduced to a mere shell and the root itself resorbed, but a new set of four molars has been growing in the gum behind the four in use. As the new set pushes its way forward, the shells of worn-out teeth are shed without trouble. The elephant may even swallow them without knowing it, contrasting sharply with the grief he faces when he has to pull an abscessed tusk.

Because the molar-shedding process is so easy, scientists have had their troubles trying to figure out how many molar teeth an elephant may have. According to some authorities, he goes through six or seven sets during the course of his lifetime; according to others, he may have up to fourteen successive sets of milk teeth and permanent molar teeth. All seem to agree, however, that the number of available molar teeth is related to a far more fascinating number: the number of years an elephant can live.

Estimates of sixty to seventy years have been made by those authorities who grant the elephant six or seven sets of molars. Those who credit him with a full-fourteen-set supply feel that he can reach an age of 120 or even older. Others, who have tried to guess Tembo's age from his tusks rather than his molars, reach even higher figures, since the tusk of a living elephant gains on the average only three-quarters of a pound each year. Computing on the basis of that growth-rate, the 226-pound tusk enshrined at the British Museum represents an elephant who may have lived for three hundred years. The unauthenticated 300- and 400-pound tusks suggest elephants who may have lived for half of a millennium.

Yet, paradoxically, no elephant has survived in captivity for more than sixty-seven years.

That fact, undisputed as it is, has frequently been offered as conclusive evidence that *all* elephants are limited to a human-style seventy years. I don't agree. The life-span of free-living elephants cannot be judged from that of zoo specimens who have had, in some antiquated zoos of past and present, little opportunity to get sufficient exercise and to eat the kind of food or the quantity of food they need for long-term survival.

In African forests or savannahs, elephants browse on a wide variety of leaves, grasses, twigs, fruit, and roots. Because their huge stomachs and intestines digest only 40-45 per cent of the food they receive, cows may eat 800 pounds of food daily and bulls may actually consume half a ton. Yet they fast periodically, while purging themselves of intestinal worms by digging with their tusks for laxative earths—decomposed limestone or clays—and gulping down heroic doses. They may also dig for water, since they require at least fifty gallons per day, but whenever possible they will trek to rivers, lakes, or swamps so that they can also swim and frolic. To expedite this never-ending round of eating, drinking, and bathing, a herd will probably walk at least twenty miles per day, all the while enjoying social and family diversions. Zoo elephants, in contrast, have little chance to move about and are fed accordingly. They usually receive 100 pounds of alfalfa hay per day, supplemented by bread, fruit, and vegetables, plus peanuts, crackerjacks, chocolate, or whatever else they can cadge from their adoring public. No one knows what dietary deficiencies they may suffer from, or to what extent their normal life-span may be shortened and their character affected for the worse.

Nothing but an utterly deranged physiology could ever inspire an elephant to turn man-eater, but it has actually happened—not in Africa but in Zurich, Switzerland. The incident was described by W. K. Teppler of Des Moines, Iowa, in a letter published in the October, 1958, issue of *True* magazine:

Chang, a pampered 8-year-old bull, was punished for unruliness by being deprived of his daily walk through the zoo and confined to the elephant pit. To console her favorite zoo animal, a young office girl left her home after dinner one night with bread for Chang and did not return. In the morning, keepers found blood on the pit floor and, among the straw, a human hand and a toe. That Chang had eaten the missing girl was established by evacuation of her undigested clothes, hat, and handbag. Chang was saved from immediate execution by the pleading of his keeper and kept in chains, but three years later he seized the keeper, battered him to death against the bars, and was dispatched with four bullets in his brain—the first and only elephant ever known to have turned carnivorous.

Though none have ever paralleled the Zurich elephant's behavior, bull elephants in captivity suffer from a strange periodic derangement that is known as musth. Two small glands, located just beneath slits in the skin of the temples midway between the eye and the ear, swell and become inflamed; they ooze slowly and stain the face with a dark tarry secretion. The affected animal's behavior may be either manic or morose; he may attempt to rape a female elephant, but he may also try to gore her with his tusks, or he may run amok and trample everything in his path, even his beloved keeper, until the madness subsides. A few females have also shown the same peculiar symptoms.

No one really understands the full implications of musth, but one thing appears to be clear: free-living elephants show the same periodic tarry secretions from their temporal glands, but rarely become disturbed or mentally unbalanced. There is something in their natural environment or way of life that keeps them on an even keel.

Because of musth, bull elephants are rarely kept in zoos or circuses, and that creates a physiological problem for the cows. They rarely have a chance to mate, and when they do mate, under unnatural conditions, they almost never calve. As with childless women who are more prone to uterine cancer and other diseases, barren cow elephants may be susceptible to as yet undiagnosed physical disturbances. Psychological troubles probably follow, especially in zoos of the older type where these intelligent creatures are kept in dismal little enclosures with nothing to do and nothing to amuse them. They may even die of loneliness and frustrated boredom.

In general, I feel, African elephants may live for a hundred years or more in the wild, but because of the factors of confinement, for only sixty to seventy years in captivity. But with elephants, as with lions or people, you always have to bear in mind their individual differences. Most humans live for less than seventy years. There are, however, some two thousand centenarians in the United States, and the oldest human on official record, the French Canadian Pierre Joubert, lived for over 113 years, nearly half again as long as the average life-span.

How long did Angola's twelve-ton patriarch live before he was gunned down in 1955? Two hundred years? More? How many years did it take to grow the 226-pound tusk in the British Museum or the semi-legendary tusks of the nineteenth century? These are fascinating questions but they cannot be resolved while "sportsmen" set their sights relentlessly upon the Big Tuskers—the very elephants who might provide the answers.

Long-term survival may depend upon the molars, but there is another part of Tembo's vast anatomy more vital to his daily life and needs. The elephant's "trunk," as we call it, is actually a nose and upper lip prolonged into a strong, adroit, and very sensitive hand. He uses it to breathe, smell, touch, feel, squeak with pleasure, trumpet with rage, caress or kiss other elephants, siphon up water to transfer to his mouth, or even hold aloft like a snorkel when he crosses rivers by walking on the bottom or swimming underwater. Most important of all, he uses it to get food.

If an elephant should lose the lower half of his trunk, as sometimes happens after wounds and infections, he can still breathe through the stump and drink by entering a river or lake and immersing himself up to the jaws. But there is no way that he can gather food and bring it to his mouth: he cannot use the mouth itself to clip foliage or grass, for it is set too far behind the tusks and the massive base of the trunk. In this predicament all he can do, theoretically, is starve to death within a few days.

I say "theoretically" because I once saw, at the Queen Elizabeth National Park in Uganda, a free-living, perfectly healthy, and even well-fed elephant without a trunk. I had been sitting behind the wheel of my pickup truck, watching a small herd of elephants move through heavy bush about a hundred yards away. There were seven of them, and they seemed like any other elephants until one of the bulls emerged from a thicket of false bamboo, only to vanish at once into another. I gaped in startled disbelief at the living paradox that I had seen; then I jumped out of the pickup to follow the elephants on foot.

As I sneaked from bush to bush pursuing the slowly moving herd, I managed to get a good look at my quarry. His trunk ended in a huge scar just below tusk level: he had probably been stabbed through the trunk while fighting with a rival bull and, following severe infection, the lower part had sloughed away. The scar appeared to be several years old, but the elephant was still very much around.

There was only one logical explanation I could think of, but I had to trail the herd for nearly two hours before they finally confirmed it. As they settled down to browse in a thicket of mimosa, I watched the trunkless elephant stand idly while the herd tore at the trees, gathering twigs and leaves. None of them ate so much as a single leaf but moved instead toward their handicapped companion, bearing bundles of food, as they must have done for several years. He opened his mouth expectantly. Eager to feed him first, two of the elephants jostled each other. The rest waited their turns patiently. In all, they brought their trunkless welfare case so much food that he hardly had time to chew it; he gulped furiously for a while, then closed his mouth tight and shook his head from side to side, rejecting any more leafy bundles. Only then did the other elephants move away and at last start to feed themselves.

The circumstances were unusual, but this kind of affectionate community spirit and cooperation is the rule rather than the exception. Men have often seen two elephants attempt to rescue a wounded companion, supporting his body between their own; and elephants very commonly provide a form of social security for their senior citizens, especially the old bulls whose hearing and sense of smell are growing weaker. One or two younger bulls, called by the East Africans *askari,* or elephant "policemen," will accompany the old duffer, always staying down-wind of him so that they can spot oncoming danger. No elephant, young or old, can see beyond forty yards or so, but those in the prime of life can scent a man if the wind is blowing from the right direction at distances of more than a mile. When the *askari* gets a whiff of something suspect but still distant, he rushes the old gentleman off to safety. If danger comes against the wind and threatens closely, the *askari* fights to protect him.

One such senior citizen, always attended by a youthful bodyguard, was the famed Mohammed or Ghost Elephant of Kenya's Marsabit Mountain Reserve. His tusks were so long and heavy, according to Turkana and Samburu tribesmen, that he couldn't raise his head and had to walk backwards; if he moved forwards, the tusks caught in the ground. That was what the natives told me, late in 1951, when I drove north from the Masai Reservation to Mohammed's favored territory. I tramped around in the bush for several days, trying to get at least a glimpse of him, but the Ghost Elephant lived up

111

to his name. Since then, the grand old bull and his *askari* bodyguard were spotted several times—both of them walking majestically forwards—before Mohammed was finally found, apparently dead of old age, in 1960. Measurements revealed that he had been some twelve feet tall at the shoulder, with a pair of tusks that totaled over 250 pounds.

An elephant may actually walk backwards while traveling through heavy bush, but only when he is grievously afflicted. Should his tusk be broken by a bullet and abscessed at the base, the giant tooth will become so sensitive that any contact with the overgrown foliage alongside elephant trails, even the brush of leaves against his temple, will subject him to excruciating pain. By walking backwards, he can clear a path with his massive rear and spare himself at least some of the pain. Ridden with worms, the putrefying abscess also brings on social ostracism: their keen sense of smell constantly offended by the stink, the other elephants may oust him from the herd.

If the stump of broken tusk is long enough, he will try to pull it: wedging the stump in a tree crotch, he strains backward, wrenching root from socket. It hurts horribly—I once saw a forest elephant weep, shriek, and bellow with the pain —and he may have to try several times before he at last succeeds. If the stump is too short for this technique, he has no real remedy, not even another bullet. Black hunters avoid elephants with broken tusks, knowing their extreme irritability; and white hunters, who pay hundreds of dollars for their licenses to shoot elephants, are eager to get their money's worth of trophies.

Like Mohammed, another famous old bull named Methuselah was constantly guarded by an elephant *askari*. He lived in Uganda's Murchison Falls National Park and always stayed in the same area by the river where the tender green grass was easy on his ancient molar teeth, but he could never be photographed. As soon as anyone approached, Methuselah's young bodyguard would trumpet a furious warning and drive away wardens or visitors. When he died, at an unknown age, the entire herd assembled around his body, mourning, and refused to leave until shots were fired in the air.

Often a herd or individual elephant attempts to bury the dead, piling branches or reeds over the body. Reportedly, tears may run down their faces as they try to drag the huge corpse into a dense thicket in a futile effort to prevent its being found by hyenas or ivory-seeking humans. Sometimes an elephant may give a decent burial, according to his standards, to the hunter he has fought and defeated: he will pile

112

branches over the man's body even while the man's bullet burns within his throbbing flesh. A few hunters, wounded rather than dead, have survived such a Tembo-style burial, later describing the elephant's behavior as "vindictive"—perhaps because he didn't weep.

A ludicrous mock funeral was described by George Adamson, Chief Game Warden of Kenya's Northern Frontier District, and husband of Joy Adamson, the author of *Born Free*. According to Adamson, an old Turkana woman had lost her way and fallen asleep under a tree. She was awakened in the middle of the night by a herd of elephants who had surrounded her. One, a vigorous young bull, was carefully feeling her body with his trunk, apparently trying to satisfy his curiosity about humans. The old lady yelled at him—probably a Turkana version of "Get lost!"—and he backed off but returned moments later. Again she yelled and cursed, and again he retreated. This time, however, the elephant must have decided to rebuke her for rejecting his attentions: he tore off branch after thorny branch from the tree, piled them on top of the noisily protesting old lady, and then urinated on the whole affair. Uninjured but trapped in the dank mess for hours, the indignant victim was extricated next morning by a passing goatherd.

This particular elephant, I think, was playing a macabre kind of practical joke. Another elephant, who was injured rather than insulted, showed the same kind of humor in the bizarre funeral rites he gave to, of all things, a Nile crocodile. The encounter, as described by C. S. Stokes in his book *Sanctuary*, was a remarkable one.

The crocodile must have been very hungry, for even one-ton members of his species will rarely trouble full-grown elephants or even try to snatch a baby when adults are in the neighborhood. At any rate, the giant reptile seized a big bull by the hind legs while he was bathing. The elephant screamed in rage and pain, summoning a companion to the rescue. The second elephant trampled the ambitious crocodile; the first, after a great deal of indignant rumbling, hoisted the dying reptile aloft, waded with his burden to the shore, and wedged the great body into a tree crotch, high above the ground. It was admittedly a rather crude joke, but the elephant may have felt that he was also posting a warning to the entire crocodile population, just as customs officials of the past used to hang condemned smugglers on the beach.

Elephants may have their wakes and funerals, but there are no "elephant graveyards." Despite the well-worn legend, when Tembo feels the burden of advancing age or senses the approach of death, he doesn't set out on a mystic trek toward an African Forest Lawn—he does the logical opposite. Like old Methuselah of the Murchison Park, he sometimes coddles aged legs and jaws by settling down near some convenient source of food and water. More often, he just trundles along behind the herd, trying to take it easy. His bones are seldom found, it is true, but neither are the bones of buffaloes, giraffes, or rhinos, none of whom have been endowed with legendary graveyards. The skeletons of all these huge animals appear indestructible, almost eternal, to those who see them only in museums. In the bush, however, bones of any size disappear very quickly. After being gnawed by hyenas, jackals, porcupines, and rats, they are attacked by smaller, more thorough scavengers such as termites, ants, arachnids, beetles, centipedes, and the other saw-toothed little anthropods. In less time than seems possible, aided by fire, rain, flood, and damprot, nothing at all is left.

The tough ivory of the tusks is more resistant. Although it is often scratched or pocked by the teeth of porcupines and rats, it may last for fifty to a hundred years before rotting away in damp forest. But it seldom has a chance to rot, as proved by the dead ivory which played such a major role in African history. One of the continent's first modern explorers, the eighteenth-century Scotsman Mungo Park, described how the elephants' "scattered teeth are frequently picked up in the woods," and subsequent explorers, travelers, and hunters made similar reports. Even Karamojo Bell himself reported how, at the turn of the twentieth century, the tusks were "still lying about in the bush where they had lain for years." Yet the legend of the elephants' graveyard continues to survive—more indestructible than Tembo's very bones.

An even more bizarre folktale than the West's mossy graveyard story has been concocted in the Orient. According to Indian legend, the lady elephant digs a "love pit," fills it with tempting fruit, and lies upon her back among the sweet-scented goodies, trumpeting coyly to attract passing bulls. When a smitten bull descends into the pit, they make love for an entire month, pausing from time to time to hand each other fruit.

Ludicrous as it sounds, the love-pit myth has some factual basis. There are many things wrong with it: elephants, male or female, fall into pits rather than dig them; they never lie on their backs to copulate *face à face* in the style of whales or beavers; and despite all popular conviction, their actual

114

matings last for a few minutes rather than days, weeks, or an entire month. But their courtship lasts for many months while the doting pair feed each other fruit with their trunks, and mating itself is always instigated by the female. As for the sentimental honeymoon that follows, with the happy couple strolling off together to pick and trade fruit for as long as ten months—well, it might just as well take place within a love pit. Marriage, of the polygamous variety, sometimes lasts for years with savannah elephants, while the smaller forest elephants seem to be monogamous, with a single pair wed for life.

Elephant love affairs have certain well-marked phases: a period of allegedly Platonic friendship, then a courting stage enlivened by gentle head-butting, roguish lip-pinches, and amorously entwined trunks, finally culminating when the cow comes into season. Two bulls, usually weak or immature males, will sometimes have a full-scale homosexual relationship of some duration. But it shouldn't really be surprising, for many other animals aside from man engage in sexual relations with members of the same sex. Male apes and baboons are notorious, as well as barnyard cows and horses, while paired dolphin males become inseparable and even drive female dolphins away.

More normally, two bull elephants will compete for the favors of a cow. She may flirt with both for a time, but usually will give the nod to one and wander off with him, somewhat separated from the herd, to start the serious courtship. If, however, she keeps them both on a string until she comes into season, there is understandably some trouble.

The rival bulls butt heads, kick, and gore with their tusks until one retreats or makes the submission signal by falling to his knees. When leadership of the herd is at stake as well as female favors, neither will submit but fights bitterly until one is badly wounded or, very rarely, killed. The loser may, like a beaten lion pasha, find a place in another herd. If not, he becomes a so-called rogue, although he isn't necessarily bad tempered. The winning bull may now court his lady.

Early in 1957 I saw such a courting pair—and they were well beyond the fruit-picking stage. I was walking through the forest toward a Pygmy camp near Moguda when I heard a storm of monkey chatter well off the trail. Curious, I made my way through more than four hundred feet of vicious thorn bush—it almost seemed to snatch at my legs— then ducked hurriedly behind a huge *Khaya* tree when I discovered what the monkeys were talking about.

115

There was a small clearing about fifty feet ahead, occupied by two amorous elephants. The cow was a svelte little creature, about three tons, with very short tusks, probably only twelve or thirteen years old and just on the threshold of sexual maturity; the bull was enormous for a forest elephant, over five tons, with heavy symmetrical tusks. She swayed sinuously around the edge of the clearing, waggling her plump behind. When he came closer she whisked her tail, turned, rubbed her body along the length of his, and fondled him with her trunk, caressing his ears and flanks and lingering over the lower part of his body. He grunted and lunged, but she retreated. Then, diabolically, she repeated the whole series of erotic maneuvers.

Things went on like that for the next ten minutes. Then, at last, the little cow stopped retreating. The bull approached from behind in the classic style of male quadrupeds, reared up on his hind legs and extended his front feet toward her shoulders. She grunted, squealed, and widened her stance. He trumpeted nervously for the next five minutes while maneuvering toward the goal—the cow elephant's vagina, unlike that of most female mammals, lies considerably forward, almost in the same position as the male's penis. Sinking down upon his hind legs, almost to a sitting position he finally succeeded. The coupled pair maintained that odd posture in unmoving silence for the next few minutes; then the bull rose again, assuming an almost vertical stance with his front feet resting on his partner's rear. Afterwards, he moved off and tried to look casual about the whole thing, while the cow flapped her ears and trumpeted softly.

The honeymoon goes on until the cow elephant begins to feel her pregnancy, usually around the ninth or tenth month. Then she loses interest in romance and grows cold to her lover. He accepts the situation with admirable calm and goes off to find another sweetheart, temporary or permanent. The cow also searches for a female, with a different end in view: her new friend, called the "auntie," keeps her company for the rest of her pregnancy, a total of some twenty-four months for savannah elephants and as little as sixteen months for the forest species.

She gives birth surrounded by the herd. They rank themselves facing outward, like British soldiers in a hollow square, to provide full protection from any predators, animal or human. Her labor is short and usually without complications: twins and breech presentations are both rare. Mother and auntie carefully remove the sheathing membrane from the newborn calf, revealing a three-foot-tall infant weighing from 150 to 200 pounds, covered with thick "gooseberry hair."

The baby can walk in an hour or so, but can do little else. His short, flaccid little trunk is just about useless: like a human infant who cannot control its hands, even to reach for a rattle, during its early months, the baby elephant must learn how to use its trunk to grasp and manipulate objects—a process taking more than six months. At first the trunk is practically a nuisance: he tries to keep it from getting in his way as he stands up leaning on his mother's forelegs to suckle with his mouth. Her single pair of teats, placed between the forelegs, soon swell with milk until they almost seem, because of their position and their shape, like a woman's breasts.

She sometimes carries the newborn baby in her trunk, but soon trains the youngster to walk *beneath* her, spanking with her trunk if he ventures forth from between her legs. She weans him at the age of six months and he is then allowed to walk sedately beside her or between mother and auntie. The auntie—more purely altruistic than the meat-paid lion aunt —usually stays close to mother and child, keeping watch for predators, helping the mother to push her blundering youngster up a steep slope, or assisting her in shepherding the baby past a stream or river.

On the shores of the Semliki River, near Ishango, I once saw a harassed-looking cow cope with such a problem unaided by an auntie. There were six elephants in all: a medium-sized bull, three cows, an elephant teenager of indeterminate sex, and an eight- or nine-month-old baby. The water was rather shallow at this point, so the larger elephants merely walked across, wading up to their shoulders. The baby stayed on shore, eying the water dubiously; he was too small to wade and apparently too afraid to swim. His mother, the last adult to start across the river, gave me the very strong impression that she was steeling herself to ignore him. It was about time, she must have felt, that he attempted it on his own.

The baby elephant took a few steps, then hastily retreated to the shore and cried shrilly, swaying his trunk from side to side. His mother turned and watched for a couple of minutes —hoping perhaps that he might calm down and give it another try—but the baby kept wailing. When she couldn't stand it any more, she waded back. I wondered what she would do, since he was much too big to carry in her trunk, but she soon showed me. Kneeling on her forelegs, she lowered her head and placed her tusks very carefully beneath the squalling baby's belly. He stopped crying immediately. Holding her head high to keep her tusks horizontal, she waded slowly into the water. Ecstatic, the baby smacked at the surface with his trunk, splashing like a human baby in his bath. She reached the shore and, very carefully, she put him down.

I had watched the whole scene, astonished, but what happened next was even more amazing.

Smacking his mother's leg with his trunk, the baby elephant started squalling again. She stared down at him with obvious disgust, then turned and moved away toward the herd. The baby screamed, flinging himself on the ground and rolling on his back, but scrambled to his feet, looking expectant, as soon as she returned. She nudged him with her trunk, pushing him a few steps away from the shore. He screamed and once again started rolling on his back. His mother made a deep throaty rumble—a sort of elephant sigh—and kneeled on her forelegs, lowering her great head. This time the baby didn't wait to be fork-lifted; he simply hopped aboard.

The patient cow waded back into the river and walked in a little circle while he splashed. Then, as she came back to the shore and lowered her head, he started a new bout of caterwauling. She raised her tusks and, for a moment, I thought she was going to dunk him in the river. Instead, she marched in the opposite direction toward the waiting herd, carrying him at least two hundred feet before she put him down, this time a little less gently. He started to cry but she paid no attention, moving away without turning her head. He kept crying, and then, apparently deciding he had pushed her to the limit, he followed quietly.

When a young elephant gets into real trouble, the entire herd may try to rescue him. A very old Pygmy told me of such an incident which he had witnessed some twenty or thirty years before. He had been hunting near the south bank of the Ituri River when he spied and shot with bow and arrow a little potto who was walking along the high branch of a tree adjoining an elephant trail. The tiny lemur—a monkey-relative who looks like a goggle-eyed teddy-bear—didn't fall downward; it clung to the branch with all of its dying force, as pottos often do, in a grip that has to be unlocked after death. The Pygmy shinnied up the tree and was crawling cautiously along the branch toward the potto's body when he heard a distant crackling in the brush. A small herd of elephants was coming down the trail toward the river. Since the brush was rather light, they weren't traveling in single file along the trail but ambling casually on either side and snacking as they went.

The Pygmy saw their broad backs through intervening foliage as they came toward his tree; then there was a sudden sharp explosion of breaking branches and shrill terrified squealing. A young elephant—probably four or five years old from the size of him—had fallen into a pit dug by Bambuba Negroes a week before. The Bambuba had attempted to drive another herd toward the pit, as the Pygmy explained, but their beaters hadn't managed to steer the elephants toward the easily broken cover of light branches and leaves sprinkled with elephant dung. Now, perhaps because the underlying smell of man had fully worn away, the pit had claimed a victim.

Hearing the young elephant's anguished cries, the entire herd rushed toward the pit. He lay at the bottom, squirming helplessly among the broken branches which had fallen with him. He kept crying piteously, and the sound of it drove the other elephants into paroxysms of emotion-charged action. Two cows and a young bull circled through the underbrush, screaming with rage as they smashed at shrubs and small trees. They were trying to frighten away any men who might be lurking in the area, and letting off a lot of steam while doing it. None of them scented the watching Pygmy; clinging to his branch, potto in hand, he was too far overhead.

Another pair of cows, supervised by an old bull who watched them as he rumbled to himself, started to work at one side of the pit, gouging the edge with his tusks and pushing loosened soil inward with their feet. As they worked, they made little throaty sounds to soothe the whimpering captive, but from time to time their indignation toward the pit and its builders burst out in trumpeting shrieks. The young elephant screamed with them, growing hysterical as dirt rained down upon his head. Gouging and pushing repeatedly, the two cows were soon joined by the three elephants who had beaten through the bush, and all of them worked together until they had built a crude earthen ramp leading upward from the slope-walled pit. Then they pulled at the captive's trunk with their own, while the old bull prodded with his long tusks at the youngster's rear. Sobbing and shaking, the terrified youngster half-walked and was half-carried upwards. Then, according to my Pygmy informant, "all the *uku* stood around and talked about it for a long time before they left."

Such an incident might appear unbelievable, but only to

those who aren't familiar with elephants in action. That same intelligence, lively emotion, and ability to cooperate, among themselves or with men, has been demonstrated time and again under widely differing circumstances. Free-living, completely untutored Tembos also build dams, displaying an engineering know-how which is paralleled by that of trained elephants who clearly understand the mechanical principle of the ramp or inclined plane: working with very little human supervision, they haul logs to a slide, carefully position each log at the top, push with their forefeet, then watch with obvious satisfaction as the logs plummet toward the water. Elephant engineers have employed another and even more remarkable approach to a mechanical problem when trapped in mud or quicksand. They have actually taken wide planks, thrown to them by watching humans, and escaped by building a catwalk, moving planks from rear to front as they progressed forward.

Beyond understanding the problem involved, which is astonishing in itself, such a feat requires presence of mind and physical coordination, both traits which indicate high-level intelligence. Circus elephants, trained to perform tricks that free-living elephants would never dream of, show even more impressive coordination for creatures of so vast a bulk: they have been taught to walk on their hind or front legs, to walk atop rows of wooden milk bottles or along heavy-duty tightropes, to stand on their heads, to balance on a single forefoot atop a revolving ball, even to play cricket and ride bicycles. Some of them learn a trick very quickly, others slowly, and others cannot master certain tricks at all—they are individuals, with differing mental, emotional, and physical capacities.

That fact has been ignored, all too often, in statements made concerning Tembo's intellectual capacities. Experiments performed in 1957 by Professor B. Rensch of Munster University in Germany have been cited as conclusive proof that elephants are not overly bright, since the single animal tested in the Rensch experiments required 330 trials before he could solve a puzzle-box problem. That sounds very bad, but an elephant at New York City's Bronx Zoo showed tremendous aptitude with puzzle boxes after an initial fit of temper. As described, very entertainingly, by Vance Packard in his book *Animal IQ:*

Two strings led under a box, which was dark on one side, light on the other. The elephant knew that a lovely apple was attached to one string. But which? She eyed the strings hesitantly, pulled the wrong one. No apple! She became excited, then outraged. She trumpeted and lunged in a terrifying tantrum.

When her IQ testing was resumed, after a considerable cooling-off period, each of the psychologists nervously gripped the fence, prepared to vault it in a flash. To their immense relief, however, she put her mind intently to the problem and managed on the first try to score. It was not long before her pulling average was so favorable that she was eating the psychologists out of apples.

Professor Rensch's blundering elephant appears to have been a moron; the Bronx Zoo's elephant a temperamental genius. That apparent contradiction in itself confirms the high level of intelligence belonging to the species. Only top-ranking members of the animal kingdom, such as men, apes, monkeys, dogs, and the great cats, show such extreme variability. Animals of lesser potential seldom deviate markedly from the dull average. The average elephant, if such a creature really exists, must be ranked near carnivores and even primates, and in fact would excel dog or cat in many separate talents which are lumped together as "intelligence."

But cats, wolves, coyotes, and their like have reached this level of intelligence because they hunt elusive prey, a way of life which favors the survival of the cleverest. Tembo, who browses for a living, is protected from these animal hunters by his great size and power. Ironically, only the earth's very smallest creatures dare attack its heaviest giant: viruses that sicken him with mumps, pneumonia, even common colds; anthrax bacilli, and trypanosomes that cause nagana pest; and external parasites that gall his thick but sensitive hide, such as mosquitoes, ticks, flies, and the dread *siafu* or safari ants that can get into his trunk as it quests through heavy brush or grass, driving him in seemingly demented flight toward the water. Such behavior, misinterpreted, may have given rise to the legend that mice will "run up inside an elephant's trunk to reach and eat his brain." It is, of course, legend and no more: any mouse crazed enough to try it would soon be sent into orbit by the world's longest, loudest, most titanic sneeze. The moving trunk may, however, startle some perturbed cobra, mamba, viper, or any other "snake in the grass" to strike in mistaken self-defense. The bite may kill a calf or sicken an adult.

All of these predicaments are more disease or accident

than any "enemy" who can be coped with. Why, then, should this enormous, unchallenged, six-ton browser have developed such extreme intelligence?

Paradoxically, the answer can be found in that very trunk which gets Tembo into so much trouble. Prehensile, versatile, ever-busy, and equipped with nearly forty thousand separate muscles, it terminates in what I called before a strong, adroit, and extremely sensitive hand. By learning to use that hand—as a race evolving through the ages, and as individuals developing through a prolonged period of infancy—elephants educate their brains to a perception of spatial values and mechanical problems which cannot be reached by animals who have no means of manipulating objects. Monkeys, apes, and men, equipped with far more perfect hands than the elephant's hand-like trunk, are puzzle-box masters; and some animals who lack opposable thumbs but have flexible hand-like paws, such as America's very clever raccoons, score very high on puzzle boxes or other mechanical problems. But handless dogs and cats, who have never developed the corresponding areas in their brains, score abysmally on puzzle boxes and show little or no engineering ability in their natural habitat. Despite their fine intelligence of a different type, any lion or leopard trapped within a pit would be a heap of fossilized bones before other cats conceived of building an escape ramp.

Is mechanical aptitude the basis of human-style intelligence? Humans seem to think so, having long defined man as "the tool-using animal." But that definition has been shaken as men have observed sea-otters using rocks to open shellfish, overweight and rather lazy gorillas pulling at a piece of fruit with a long, crooked branch instead of getting up to fetch it, or enterprising chimpanzees cracking hard-shelled fruit with rocks, gathering termites on a stick and then licking them off like children with candied apples, or even using leaves for toilet paper. The Galapagos finch has long been admitted to the elite company of tool-users, simply because he holds a little twig in his beak to poke insects out of holes, and the Egyptian vulture, formerly despised as a mere scavenger, has even gotten a write-up in *Time* since being photographed by zoologist Jane Goodall in the act of picking up small stones in his beak and throwing them at tough-shelled ostrich eggs. But Tembo isn't "officially" recognized as a tool user, although his ramps, dams, and catwalks rival the accomplishments of chimpanzees and make vultures or finches look like veritable bird-brains.

To build these prodigies, elephants use their hand-like trunks for precision work and their tool-like tusks as picks for digging, levers for uprooting trees, or fork-lifts for raising, holding, and carrying weights. But beyond these "built-in" tools and their great understanding of how to use them, Tembo's still unphotographed use of planks to escape quicksand, or tree-crotch vises for pulling aching tusks, is in the very strictest sense true tool-using. As for merely throwing a projectile like the Egyptian vulture, I have more than once seen forest elephants, extremely drunk after gobbling up vast quantities of fermenting fruit, giggling with delight as they lobbed pieces of squishy fruit at each other's heads and derrières. They were only joking, but the principle was the same. Moreover, trained elephants of classic times threw javelins with force and accuracy; and trained elephants of modern times—John Grindle's amazing crew of the Bertram Mills Circus—have learned to hold bat in trunk and hit cricket balls bowled, fielded, and returned by other elephants. Once they had learned the game, they played it with grand gusto.

Although his mechanical aptitude is seldom mentioned, Tembo's powers of memory are usually exaggerated. The phrase "an elephant never forgets" has become proverbial, but like people, elephants often forget things which have no great personal relevance while remembering those which they have been trained to remember. If they sometimes need much repetition before learning seemingly simple jobs or tricks, we might bear in mind the penmanship exercises that our own children have to repeat, over and over, before they can form the simple letters of the alphabet. In general, however, elephants have excellent memories and are absolutely reliable as show or circus performers, unlike the nervous cats, brooding bears, or unpredictable chimpanzees. But like all their other talents, powers of memory vary from one individual to the next.

The second meaning of the tired phrase "an elephant never forgets" is that elephants invariably hold grudges against humans who have wronged them and scheme constantly to get revenge. This is not only untrue but absurd. If Tembo really carried grudges, half the elephant population of Africa would now be running amok, trying to avenge themselves on the hunters, black and white, who never stop hounding them. Instead, elephants who have been hunted and even elephants who carry bullets in their flesh or bone usually have to be provoked before they will attack men. Some have shorter tempers than others; these crustier types may take the initiative before being bothered again by old or new tormentors. As for zoo and circus elephants, they are very often teased or even tortured on the sly by human sadists. They distrust *anyone* except established friends and keepers.

Most of those friends and keepers, from Siam to the Congo, share the Pygmies' conviction that "the *uku* talk to each other." They believe that elephants' throaty sounds constitute a true if simple language, supplemented by an almost telepathic understanding, and that trained elephants use that same mental telepathy to understand human intentions and desires far more thoroughly than might be implied by their *cornacs'* thirty to forty spoken commands plus hand and *hawkus* signals.

It may be intuition, developed to a phenomenal pitch, rather than true telepathy. Whatever it is, I have often felt it operating while I was handling elephants, and I have heard others describe it, from that fine naturalist Ivan Sanderson, who says "on several occasions elephants who have known me for less than an hour did some of these things *before* I gave my verbal command and when I was at a distance from them" to a Congolese *cornac* named Bodeko, from the Ituri Forest, who liked to say of his elephant partner that "Bella listens harder than people and she knows how to talk without making noise."

Bella was one of two forest elephants I bought in May, 1959, from a privately operated logging station near the government's elephant training camp at Epulu. She was a full-grown four-ton cow with shapely four-foot tusks, while her friend Venus was a trifle shorter and weighed about half a ton less, with stubby foot-long tusks and a slightly petulant expression. While acquiring the elephants, I also hired their *cornacs,* Bodeko and his brother Bokwe. These two remarkable men, trained at the Epulu camp, showed more interest and sympathetic understanding toward their huge charges than most Congolese feel toward their wives and families. They were members of an unimposing tribe, the pygmoid Balese, and before their own training they had looked on elephants as *nyama*—meat—the way Black Africa regards all of its magnificent animal heritage. Now they treated elephants like people.

To describe the two elephants themselves, I should really quote what Bodeko said when he introduced us. "Bella is much smarter than my brother's elephant," he explained. "She tells the little one what to do—you can see how they talk to one another. But Venus! She's always hungry. She eats more than the big one and she still doesn't get enough. She fusses all the time and she always wants to be loved and petted. She lets my Bella do all the hard work, and then she tries to take the credit for it. She's just a child! But Bella has such a big heart that she loves Venus anyway. They are like two sisters—if you ever sold one of them, I think they would both die."

I had no intention of selling either. Instead, like a pipsqueak Hannibal, I planned to march my two elephants and their keepers across the Ituri Forest, past the sawed-off Alps of the Mitumba Mountains and Kabasha Escarpment, toward my prospective game park near the border of Rwanda. Unlike Hannibal, I would accompany the marching elephants in an old pickup truck.

It took us eight days to make that four-hundred-mile journey, with the elephants averaging five or six miles per hour while I drove back and forth, warning each town and village that lay beside our highway route not to panic. They were eight days of wildly varied incidents, fully described in *Congo Kitabu,* but the most consistently intriguing feature of the whole trip was the native population's flabbergasted reaction at the mere sight of Bella and Venus. What happened at Mombasa, the first good-sized town along our route, was repeated everywhere with minor variants.

Both sides of Mombasa's "Main Street" were lined with chattering natives, mostly Balese and Babira. They were wild with impatience. The entire population had turned out and others had come from neighboring villages, summoned by the thunder of the drums. Aside from a few hunters, most had never seen an elephant before. They would find trampled fields and ravaged groves of coffee trees in the morning and cursed the unseen animals who had done the damage. But the elephants gave the cultivated fields a wide berth during the day, preferring to steal sweet potatoes and sugar cane under cover of darkness. So, paradoxically, the people of the forest elephants' homeland were worked up to fever pitch over the elephants' promised coming, while white tourists at the local Hotel des Pygmées waited with rather blasé expressions. All of them had not only seen elephants in the Congo's national parks but were very familiar with them—or thought they were—from zoos, circuses, motion pictures, television, books, and magazines.

Natives clustered in the street, arguing about what an elephant really was, and competed with each other in giving fabulous, almost mythological descriptions. One man, who may have seen a hippopotamus, described Tembo as an enormous pig with long, long legs like four tree trunks and a long, long nose that stretched from the top of his head to the tips of his toenails. Listeners hooted him down, and new native experts came forward with even stranger ideas: elephants were as tall as *Khaya* trees, their ears were big enough to shade all of Mombasa, fire came out of their mouths—and smoke from under their tails.

I began to worry that they might be disappointed by my two refined, medium-sized, non-smoking lady elephants. But when Bella and Venus marched into Mambasa, the natives exploded with excitement. "Tembo!" shouted the men, jumping up and down like Masai. "Tembo!" screamed the women, with big, round, astonished, incredulous eyes. "Tembo!" squeaked the small children, clinging to their mothers' legs in paroxysms of terrified delight. "Tembo! Tembo! *Tembo!*"

The crowd was frenzied; the elephants were calm. Bella looked majestic and a trifle condescending like a dowager empress at a baseball game, but Venus seemed to enjoy the attention—she trumpeted softly and the natives gasped with a thrill of nervous pleasure. Bokwe grinned from his perch in the center of her back, where he sat upon a round cushion of braided leaves, holding his *hawkus* in his right hand and in his left a rope that encircled Venus' massive body just behind the front legs. The crowd gazed up at Bokwe and Bodeko with rapt admiration; they felt that the two *cornacs* were courting death at every minute of the march. I couldn't help but smile. Bodeko had confided the night before that his biggest problem was trying to keep from falling asleep on long rides.

At Mugwata, a rolling tree-clad savannah twenty miles north of the Congo-Rwanda border, Bella and Venus settled down with their *cornac*s as the first residents of my new game park. The eight-day march across the eastern Congo was completed, and it left me with the growing hope that Africans and elephants might learn to live in partnership—if they just got to know each other. The intelligence and sensitivity of the two Balese keepers showed how beneficial the relationship could be for people; and the friendly curiosity of untutored natives all along our route demonstrated that the average "man in the bush" might someday reach the same level of tolerant understanding. That hope was shattered, if not totally destroyed, in July of 1960.

During the first days of the Congo's newly granted freedom, more than a thousand elephants were slaughtered in the Albert National Park alone. Buffaloes, antelopes, and hippos died with them, massacred in such incredible numbers that vulture and hyena scavengers couldn't keep up with the corpses. After thirty-five years of complete protection, the animals had forgotten the very meaning of guns. They watched, trustingly, as hordes of native poachers came to shoot them for their tusks, meat, or horns. Mutinous soldiers of the Congolese army joined in the carnage. Some of them, as one mutineer informed me, machine-gunned elephants or blew them up with hand grenades, "just for the fun of it."

Late in July, after three weeks of the Congo's new freedom to kill, I drove through the Albert National Park, where even rocks and plants had been protected, as in America's own national parks, along with the animals. It was a welter of decomposing corpses. At one point close to the road, in the Rwindi sector, there were six bloated elephant cadavers within two hundred yards: their tusks had been chopped off with an axe and the ivory stubs jutted bleakly out of their fly-covered jaws. Even adolescent cows, whose stubby tusks couldn't have weighed more than ten pounds apiece, had been slain and mutilated.

At Rutshuru, south of the park, a native poacher tried to "make a deal" with me for a huge quantity of ivory. Half of his roadside hut was stacked with it, all fresh tusks from the past three weeks. Trying to get official action, I went to the territorial headquarters of Rutshuru, where I talked with the new native administrator. He was well dressed and well educated, speaking fluent French, but in my opinion he was less civilized than the two unpretentious *cornacs* from the Ituri Forest.

"A new Congo is emerging," he explained, "and its people's needs are more important than the needs of wild animals. You tell me sentimental stories about murdered elephants, but I am more concerned with what their meat and tusks mean to my people. If men sell ivory, it is because they need other things more badly. And if hungry Congolese kill and eat elephants, well-fed Europeans are mere hypocrites to rebuke them for it."

"What will your people eat," I asked, "when the elephants are gone? And the buffaloes? And the antelopes?"

"That will never happen," he replied, smiling. "Who can count the elephants of the forest or the antelope of the savannah?"

Who could have counted the far more numerous bison

who roamed North America's prairies, an estimated sixty million, who teetered on the edge of extinction after being slaughtered for a scant twenty-five years?

Other Congolese and East African administrators share the same naïve belief that there can never be an end to nature's bounty. Looking for quick, short-term income, they have opened up one game preserve after another, luring American tourists with ads that promise "guaranteed kills." Some officials take an even more naïve view. Since leaving Africa, I was stunned to learn of plans to "increase production and the national income," proposed in Uganda's Legislative Council by the Uganda *Argus:* "One of his schemes for increasing production was to scrap the Game Department and shoot off all wild animals outside the National Parks. 'If you are short of money just shoot off all the elephants and sell the tusks,' he said."

The *Argus* also noted:

> Prices at yesterday's Mombasa ivory auction are believed to be the lowest for more than ten years. After the sale merchants gave two reasons—the huge amount of Congo ivory which is flooding into East Africa, and the partial closure of one of the world's biggest markets through stringent import restrictions imposed by the Indian Government. One merchant revealed that at least 200,000 pounds of Congo ivory is stored in private go-downs in Mombasa alone, compared with the 60,201 pounds at yesterday's Government sale . . .

Two-hundred-sixty-thousand pounds of Congolese ivory, and more of it on the way. Judging from the kind of slaughter I have seen, it probably averaged no more than twenty-five pounds per tusk or fifty pounds per pair. According to those figures, the incisor teeth of more than five thousand highly intelligent beings were stacked up in the go-downs— like an African version of Dachau or Buchenwald!—to be sold at ten to twenty shillings per pound. All human or humane considerations aside, the Congo's elephants were worth at best a hundred dollars apiece, while a tamed and trained elephant can be sold to zoos and circuses for five to seven thousand dollars.

As Bokwe liked to say, "I guess that Tembos are smarter than people."

KIBOKO

The Fat Proletarian

Hippopotamuses, or "river horses" as the Greeks called them, love to horse around in rivers, lakes, shallow pools, and evil-smelling mudholes—grunting, rumbling, snorting, blowing, bellowing, and burping, or sleeping in the shallows with their heads pillowed on each other's backs. They can swim at more than ten knots per hour and stay beneath the surface for as long as five to ten minutes, but when darkness falls, they march inland to conduct the second and nocturnal phase of their amphibious operations.

The Jinja Golf Course in Uganda, close to Ripon Falls and Lake Victoria Nyanza, is a favorite hang-out for the local hippo population. They trek from green to green during the night, happily mowing the grass while leaving sets of parallel tracks that look like ruts impressed by broadtired cart wheels. Golfers raved and cursed until Jinja club officials made a new ground-rule: If your ball lands in a hippo's footprint, you may remove the ball and drop it on adjacent turf without being penalized.

At the Rwindi Camp in the Congo's Albert National Park, the hippos sometimes used to come on moonlit nights, walking a full mile from the Rwindi River, just to stand outside the restaurant and watch the tourists eating, drinking, chattering, and playing cards. During the day, the tourists went to the river and watched the hippos.

Other roving "river horses" throughout East, West, Central, and South Africa, invade the natives' cultivated fields of millet, maize, rice, or sugar cane, where they do more damage than Cape buffalo or elephants. The boldest venture into town, where they explore garbage pails and demolish flowerbeds. Once, in the South African city of Durban, a hippo named Huberta raided fruit stands on the main street and came close to entering a theater where a Judy Garland film was playing. Huberta roamed across a thousand miles of Natal Province and the Transvaal, averaging a mile a day while she visited villages, farms, cities, churchyards, Hindu temples, and a Buddhist monastery where she lived for three days, browsing the garden bare of shrubs and flowers.

These reports will come as news to the zoo-going citizens of the Western world. They visit the hippo pool and peer at a vast shadowy form lurking on the bottom. After a few minutes, it surfaces. They catch a glimpse of turreted eyes and slit-like nostrils on a bulging snout. It submerges. Then they leave the hippo pool, convinced that the fat, stodgy-looking animal spends his entire lifetime in the water. At best, they feel, he may creep along the shore. The mere thought of hippos ambling through a golf course or a churchyard strikes them as a Disney-style cartoon or an LSD-inspired hallucination.

Kiboko may be fat, but he is far from stodgy. Aside from his proficiency in water sports, he is surprisingly agile on the land, where he roams from dusk to dawn and even ventures forth on cloudy days. On longer treks, when his skin begins to grow too dry, subcutaneous glands secrete a sort of "suntan lotion," a reddish oily liquid that soothes and lubricates his skin, and has led men to believe ever since Biblical times that hippos "sweat blood."

To explain his odd double life, aquatic by day and terrestrial by night, native story-tellers of the Congo spin a host of legends. Most of them are quite indelicate, but so is fat Kiboko—his thumping, rollicking Swahili name summoning up the real hippo rather than a phony Grecian "river horse."

Once upon a time, according to Azande legend, Kiboko used to live day and night upon the broad savannahs. Then the dry season came, the scorching winds blew, the lightning struck, and the grass burst into crackling flames. Poor Kiboko, singed and terrified, plunged into the nearest lake, landing with a giant splash among the flabbergasted fish. "This is *our* territory," they protested. "Take those gaping jaws and big tusks out of here! You're not going to gulp us down or eat our babies."

"Let me stay," the hippo pleaded. "I swear I won't eat you. I'll go ashore every night and fill my belly up with grass."

"Easily said," scoffed the wary fish. "How do we know you won't cheat?"

The hippo pondered desperately. "There's only one way to prove my good faith," he finally suggested. "Every time I dung, I'll switch my tail back and forth to break up the turds. You can look at all the little pieces but you'll never find a single fish bone."

Kiboko does, indeed, perform this strange ceremony both in water and on land, but hardly for the benefit of skeptical fish. It is the hippo's homely method of staking out territory; and he stakes it out so thoroughly, switching his tail like a frantic pendulum, that zoo hippo pools must be drained and refilled every day. Odder still, if one hippo dares or chances to invade another's territory, the rivals stage a weird duel: they "shoot" each other, not with guns but with bowels, whisking their tails to send the dung flying. The intruder then retreats, but for some obscure reason both parties feel that honor has been satisfied. If a younger bull is, however, bent on issuing a serious challenge to an older one's established territorial rights—especially in overcrowded areas—the two of them will really fight, booming and splashing half the night while they gash each other's hides with their tusks and sharp incisor teeth.

It is an epic battle, for mature hippos may reach twelve or fourteen feet in length, measuring five feet tall at the shoulder and weighing over three tons. Some bulls may even exceed eight thousand pounds, far outweighing the taller and longer white rhino which is usually accepted as the world's second largest land mammal. The question could be argued endlessly, but I don't see any need for it. Let the rhino be second and Koboko can be third largest, with a special consolation prize—the newly created title "world's fattest land mammal."

Both are exceeded by the elephant, but the three giant

131

heavyweights are not related. The lofty elephant has distant ties with dugongs, manatees, extinct sea-cows, and the tiny hyraxes or "conies," while the rhino is allied to horses, and the hippo finds his closest kin among the warthogs, wild swine, and domesticated pigs.

The pygmy hippopotamus is a living testimonial to that relationship. Unlike the "pygmy elephant" he is not legend, and although anatomy relates him much more closely to the full-sized hippo, he resembles wild forest swine in size and habits. Six feet long and three feet tall, he weighs a pig-sized four hundred pounds and wanders through the swamps and forests of West Africa where he neither lives in herds nor dwells in rivers.

Kiboko's place in nature was clearly understood in ancient Egypt where they named the hippo "river swine." Then the Greeks transformed them into "river horses," and the Dutch, arriving ages later, converted them to *seekoei,* or "sea-cows." Meanwhile, the Arabs used a name that means, of all things, "water buffalo," while the Arabs' native converts liked to call the hippo "fish." According to Islamic laws, which parallel the Mosaic Code of Orthodox Hebrews, meat becomes unclean unless the animals' throats are cut while they are still alive. Fish, however, show by their slit-like gills the "knife-marks of the Prophet" and are thus exempt. Cutting the throat of a living three-ton animal presents some problems, but the hippo spends half of his lifetime in the water, so conveniently, he became a kosher-style fish.

Attempting to resolve the contradictions, early nineteenth-century zoologists only made a bad situation worse. They called hippos pachyderms or "thick-skins," lumping them with elephants and rhinos in an artificial family. That error, long ago corrected, still survives among the general public and in circus rings where elephants are introduced, in P. T. Barnum's classic style, as ponderous pachyderms. But another adjective is always used, by all who see him, to portray the good-natured, roly-poly hippo: they cry out in horror and revulsion that Kiboko is, as they describe him, "ugly," if not the ugliest of all animals.

That word, I feel, is rather superficial and misleading. I would rather call the hippo *joli-laid*—a very useful French expression meaning "lovely-ugly," which is sometimes used to describe people so extremely homely that they have a richly human beauty all their own. Fernandel, France's horse-faced comedian, was superbly *joli-laid*. So were George Arliss, Charles Laughton, Wallace Beery, W. C. Fields, and other great actors or comedians of the past. I should like to suggest that hippos, warthogs, rhinos, vultures, crocodiles, hyenas, and all the so-called ugly beasts are instead the animal world's great characters or comics. To know it for a fact, all you have to do is to watch them.

Kiboko looks like an up-ended barrel covered with slate-colored, nearly hairless skin. His girth is nearly equal to his length, so his pinkish belly barely clears the ground while he goes galumphing forward on his stubby little legs. Port and starboard sides move independently in a rather sprightly pacing gait, preceded by his huge box-shaped head and followed by his foolish eighteen-inch tail. His rounded ears, placed at the very summit of his head, are equally minute but never stop twitching. His eyes, close beneath them, are set in periscopic turrets like the eyes of crocodiles and frogs, so that he can watch the passing scene while the rest of him is underneath the water. His squared-off muzzle, two feet broad, is tipped with bristling hairs and crowned at its highest point by two slit-like nostrils; like his ears, they seal completely at his will, enabling him to dive, swim, walk, or even sleep beneath the surface.

To submerge, he has two separate and distinctive styles: if he decides to dive while already in the water, he lets his rear end sink slowly while his front end follows after; but if startled while he is standing on a high bank, he launches himself headlong—like the first-created hippo of Azande legend—landing among the fish with a gargantuan belly-whopping splash. When he surfaces he spouts a column of water, blowing air through his nostrils with a loud snorting noise.

That description fits Kiboko when his mouth is closed. When opened to the widest, whether he is merely yawning or challenging an enemy in water or on land, his entire head appears to split apart. His gaping mouth, some three feet from jaw to jaw, looks like a huge red cavern edged with ivory stalactites and stalagmites.

He has fourteen pairs of molars and premolars, all of them grinding away daily at some two to four hundred pounds of grass and ground forage plus the few water plants he eats as tidbits, mostly lotuses and water lilies. The slightly curved incisors, two pairs of them in either jaw, are long and sharp. The tusks, unlike the elephant's, are really canine teeth and there are four of them, an opposed pair at either angle of his jaws. The curving lower tusks are much longer, growing up to thirty inches or more in a big bull hippo. If either upper

133

tusk should break, the lower one has nothing to oppose it and keeps growing, like the tusks of swine, reaching lengths of four or even five feet.

Tusks and incisors, all composed of fine-quality, extremely hard ivory, are not used in feeding. Hippos clip grass with their heavy lips, trimming it as closely as a flock of sheep. The front teeth are employed for fighting and usually among themselves, since no animal predator will attack a full-grown hippo, not even twenty-foot Nile crocodiles who may weigh a ton.

Bagoma fishermen from Lake Tanganyika, where crocodiles and hippos both abound, have their own way of explaining why an apparent armistice exists between these two enormous animals who share together Africa's rivers and lakes.

"A long time ago," they told me, "the crocodile made a treaty with Kiboko. 'In water you are stronger,' he informed the Fat One. 'But I, and I alone, am master of the shore. If you want to cross the river bank to graze upon the land, I will not let you pass until you promise me a service.' 'What is it?' asked Kiboko. 'Swear that you will watch for fishermen's canoes and always overturn them. Then I can be sure of *my* dinner.' 'Agreed,' the hippo answered. Since that evil day, he has worked as the crocodile's friend and sworn partner, helping him to murder men."

The Bagoma tale states, very simply, the fact that Kiboko and the crocodile do not compete for food, since the herbivorous hippo grazes on the land while the carnivorous crocodile seeks his dinner in the water. For this reason, and because their great bulk makes them very confident, hippos usually ignore or calmly watch their crocodile neighbors unless hippo babies are around. Then the wary mother will attack any crocodile who invades the neighborhood, knowing him for what he is—a would-be baby-snatcher. The crocodiles beat a quick retreat; even a small-brained reptile knows better than to pit his narrow jaws against a huge squared-off barrel of a beast, very much at home in the water, who is quite capable of biting him in half.

Hippo cows, when accompanied by babies, will sometimes launch a furious attack upon canoes, but despite native legend, they are not trying to send *Care* packages to crocodiles. They regard any large object with hysterical suspicion, fearing a possible threat to their young; in fact, they may even mistake the canoe for the basically canoe-like shape of a cruising crocodile. On other occasions, surfacing hippos accidentally collide with canoes and overturn them. Startled and frightened by an unexpected bump on the back, they usually dive like sounding whales for the bottom. But since few native fishermen know how to swim, even those who spend half their lifetimes on the water, passing crocodiles may profit from the collision, dragging poor swimmers underwater or hauling away the bodies of already drowned men.

The natives may be naïve in their interpretation, but early African explorers were very little wiser. Dr. Livingstone, Henry Morton Stanley, Sir Richard Burton, John Speke, Paul Du Chaillu, and Sir Samuel Baker all had boating troubles with devoted hippo mothers, and all described the hippo as a wantonly malicious beast who attacked boats in its boundless lust to kill men.

Baker, one of poor Kiboko's harshest critics, was traveling in a paddle-wheeled steamer on the White Nile when a panic-stricken hippo attacked a whirling paddle, breaking off several floats. Its intentions were, however, far less predatory than his own: Sir Samuel, a passionate gourmet, described with great relish how he ate the flesh and stewed the feet of young hippo calves, then made soup from their skins. It tasted like turtle soup, he claimed, but even better. He was, in fact, so fond of it that he renamed turtle soup itself, calling it, with witty contempt, "mock hippo."

Now I would much rather see a man eat his kill than hang it on the wall, but I don't like to hear animals reviled for not lying down on the platter, and I especially dislike the style of "game gourmets." Sir Samuel at least did some exploring, but many present-day Europeans go to Africa, taking their spice racks with them, for what I call *Cordon Bleu* safaris." They have very little interest in the ordinary game, like bushbuck and impala, which White Hunters shoot for the pot, but insist upon klipspringer, the most delicious-tasting antelope of all. Some lust for baby porcupine, filleted python or even broiled monitor lizard, and all cook the meat themselves, brandishing shakers of oregano or marjoram with ostentatious gestures while their native "boys" watch in wonder. Then they go back to Paris, Rome, or London to compare their latest taste sensations with the other connoisseurs.

Less adventurous types stay at home, receiving from specially hired White Hunters shipments of the most delicious treat that Africa can offer: smoked hundred-pound hippo hams. Steam-fried in sherry with brown sugar, it is praised as peacock tongues were once praised by the Romans.

Meanwhile, the White Hunters who have sold Kiboko's

hams to the game gourmets are probably disposing of his other end to the sportsmen. No one has ever been silly enough to rank the hippopotamus among the Big Five, but a head with two fifty-inch tusks is still worth as much as a thousand dollars to a status-seeking hunter. The motives of a man who secretly buys a Cape buffalo head are at least comprehensible: he wants to advertise a fraudulent triumph over somewhat dangerous prey. But it seems ludicrous that anyone would want to brag about a victory, real or fictitious, over an animal who doesn't have to be tracked or stalked but lies about in shallow water during broad daylight, exposing himself to slaughter.

Native hunters, before the days of modern firearms, used to dig pitfalls or hang weighted spears in the trees bordering hippo trails or "tunnels," the paths that hippos push and beat through dense reeds and tall grass. The bravest hunted with harpoons whose attached lines permitted them to retrieve the carcass after the hippo sank, as dying hippos always do. They ate the meat with real gusto, not with gourmet gestures, especially relishing the fat. No antelope except the eland has any fat to speak of, but a good-sized hippo yields some two hundred pounds of the purest lard. The hide was cut into strips, then dried, trimmed, and hammered into round whips—the murderous, even lethal native *fimbo* or as South Africans later called it, *sjambok*. The finest quality *sjamboks* were, however, made from the dried and stretched penises of buffaloes and rhinos.

Whites who came with guns shot at hippos just to test their sights, potting away from river steamers, or hunted them for sport. Then professionals took over, hunting hippos for their ivory. Besides being very hard, hippo ivory does not yellow like the ivory of the elephant and was thus in great demand for making artificial teeth, fetching as much as six dollars per pound. That market died away as dentistry progressed to porcelain and vinyl plastics, but hippo teeth are still carved into trinkets and remain, even if they fail to reach trophy size, a profit-making sideline for professional hunters.

Hippos learn from experience in heavily hunted areas to be extremely wary. They are no intellectual giants like the elephants, but they have excellent memories and like their smaller relatives, the pigs, they are far from stupid. Where they have been exposed to pits and weighted spears, they will watch suspiciously for hidden traps; where they have learned the meaning of harpoons or guns, they will try to hide their nostrils in a clump of water plants as they surface, taking quick breaths and diving out of sight. But all their wariness serves them little, for their conspicuous size, semi-aquatic habitat and, above all, the need to educate their young, expose them to the gaze and guns of men.

An established hippo herd usually consists of ten to forty individuals, the majority of whom dwell within a territory called the *crèche*—a word that means cradle or day nursery. The herd is a matriarchy run by fussy cows who are utterly obsessed with the care and feeding of their children. Ruling from a central bank or sand bar, they defend the *crèche* of babies from intruders, driving away bull hippos—who are sometimes evilly disposed toward their own offspring. When a boat invades the *crèche*, they look upon it as a group of human mothers might regard a flying saucer landing near a kindergarten. They don't trust it, and they don't wait around to determine whether the boat contains a native fisherman, a Christian missionary like the good Dr. Livingstone, or a hippo-soup addict like Sir Samuel Baker. They attack, and with utter disregard for their own safety.

Older bulls with high social status have their own territories near the outskirts of the *crèche*, while younger bulls have to live in ill-defined, outlying suburbs where they rarely have a chance to meet and mate with nubile cows. All male hippos are thus "rogues" in the sense that they must live outside the main body of the herd, and the usual prattle about embittered rogue hippos is a meaningless generalization based on the conduct of short-tempered individuals.

As the younger bulls grow more powerful and confident, they begin to challenge holders of the choicer real estate, engaging in the dung-shooting duels or the roaring, tusk-slashing battles. Whichever combatants succeed in capturing or holding down the territories near the *crèche* can, from their favorable locations, mate with the cows throughout the year as each comes into season.

Mating takes place in the water, with the bull mounting from the rear. Aside from a little minor foreplay—bobbing about and nuzzling—there is very little real courtship and nothing that at all resembles the elephants' sentimental honeymoons. The pregnant cow simply lives with other cows in the *crèche* and bears, after an eight-month gestation period, a single "calf" which looks more like a hundred-pound, bigheaded, pink-spotted piglet.

Born in the water, in the safety of the *crèche*, the hippo

calf suckles in the water, periodically coming up for air as he nurses. He must learn to hold his breath for longer and longer periods before he can stay beneath the surface as long as his mother. So, to watch over him, she must surface much more often than she needs to, and to protect him from the threat of crocodiles, she usually swims on the surface with the young calf riding on her neck, which he clutches with his little forefeet, or her back as he grows larger. When she takes him on the land, she seldom goes very far and moves with fanatical suspicion. When she naps in the shallows, she usually sprawls on the youngster's body, probably to shield him from unexpected dangers. Whole herds of hippo cows will do the same, seemingly squashing the half-buried babies who sometimes squeal but are never injured.

Maternal care and interest last for about two years; then, as the growing male calves begin to look more like menacing bulls than vulnerable babies, they are kicked out of the *crèche* to find a bachelor existence of their own. By that time, they have reached a size and power which discourages any and all crocodiles—even the twenty-footers—and need fear only man. Bulls and cows become sexually mature at age five, and their full span of life may exceed fifty years. They thrive in captivity despite its limitations, reproducing well and living much more happily than elephants, since their lesser intellect is satisfied with less diversion.

Those who judge Kiboko, Africa's fat, indelicate but immensely good-hearted proletarian, by a quick glance have called him vicious, stupid and, above all, ugly. That attitude was summed up, I suppose, by the famed English essayist, Thomas Babington Macaulay, who declared with self-assured pomposity: "I have seen the hippopotamus, both asleep and awake; and I can assure you that, awake or asleep, he is the ugliest of the works of God."

Such a judgment libels God more than innocent Kiboko, but I don't have to answer it. Sir Thomas Browne did it for me, back in 1642, when he wrote with remarkable understanding: "I cannot tell by what logic we call a toad, a bear, or an elephant ugly; they being created in those outward shapes and figures which best express the actions of their inward forms; and having passed that general visitation of God, who saw that all that He had made was good."

KIFARU

The Frustrated Delinquent

Thundering through a vast cloud of dust, the horned fury charges across the technicolor screen. Will the ruthless prehistoric monster gore and overturn the Land Rover? Will he trample it to scrap iron? Will he eat the White Hunter or the spark plugs?

Open-mouthed, the movie-going public watches the sensational "rhino charge." If the so-called African film is a real stinker, they have already seen savannah-dwelling lions leap out of the steaming, teeming jungle, maddened by the tempting flesh of the White Hunter hero and the heaving-bosomed heroine. Locked in each other's arms, hero and heroine have crouched behind a low rock barrier while unhappy mules, artfully painted with zebra stripes, have been stampeded past them. Inflated rubber hippos, moved by unseen wires, have attacked the couple's boat and dumped them in the water. They have managed to escape from broad-snouted Yankee alligators who have tried to pose as narrow-snouted Nile crocodiles. While struggling onto shore, they have been charged by a troop of well-trained Asiatic elephants wearing fan-shaped plastic ears behind their bulging foreheads. In all, they have been attacked on their brief safari by more animals than any bush native glimpses during his entire lifetime.

These technicolor terrors of the "Dark Continent," from op-art mules to elephants in falsies, have thrilled and chilled the duped audience. Now, as an epic climax, the arch villain of them all thunders toward his classic duel with the Land Rover. How can the watching public doubt what ads, posters, billboards, and brochures all repeat in pictures or in prose— that the black rhino, alias the "horned fury," is Africa's most dangerous and diabolic beast?

No one can deny that black rhinos have attacked Land Rovers, jeeps, trucks, or any other vehicle that has been employed to chase or catch them. Cape buffaloes have done the same. So have zebras, gnus, or even gentle-looking oryx and gazelles. Any animal who normally ignores a car will fight with it, charging pathetically and often suicidally, after being driven to a state of unreasoning hysteria. But the movie-makers can't raise a storm of publicity over a maimed or dead gazelle. It isn't sensational enough, and the public might consider it sadistic. Rhinos, on the other hand, are "ugly monsters" and they have it coming to them: according to their press releases, they will rush to attack any and all passing automobiles.

Africa's black rhino will, on occasion, "charge" a car without apparent provocation. He will also charge at tents, trees, bushes, rats, frogs, men, butterflies, or grasshoppers. Sometimes he will even charge at the sound of his own dung dropping on a leafy shrub behind him. Much more often and for no good reason, he will flee from frogs, butterflies, and all the rest. There is no predictable pattern to his flights or aggressions; the same rhino who retreats in terror from a harmless native woman may gallop moments later toward a group of rifle-bearing white men. If the tourists hold their fire he will, almost invariably, come to a halt some twenty feet away, stare at them briefly, then go trotting off to browse on a thorn bush. But they shoot, and most of them believe sincerely that they shoot and kill in self-defense.

Loud-snorting bluffer and titanic blunderer, more easily stalked and killed than any member of the hunters' Big Five, the black rhino is a rebel without a cause, a chronic but incompetent delinquent. He is, even from the animals' point of view, the bull in Africa's china shop, rushing from one messy disaster to the next.

Attempting to explain his seemingly demented ways, native storytellers of the northeast Congo tell an oddly touching little tale. Long ago, it seems, the first animals were absolutely naked, having neither skin nor fur to cover their tender meat. Seeing their plight, God gave each of them a needle and suggested that they make some clothes. The ancestral leopard, cleverest of beasts, sewed the most beautiful coat. The others did their best, making fine or mediocre coats according to their talent. But Kifaru—the first black rhino and the dumbest animal in all creation—dropped his needle, couldn't see where it was lying, and kicked it into a thicket.

Tortured by ticks and flies, the naked rhino charged back and forth looking for his needle. It was nowhere. Snatching at a thorn, he stitched away with it frantically, then donned his hastily made coat. It hung in deep folds and wrinkles where he hadn't sewed it straight. Seeing it, the other animals began to laugh and taunt him. Snorting with rage, the rhino galloped from thicket to thicket as he searched for his needle. If he could only find it, he would sew himself a rich and glossy coat like the leopard's. Then the other animals would stop laughing. But he couldn't see the needle, even when he galloped over it. Perhaps, he thought, one of those laughing beasts has picked it up and hidden it. So he started charging every living thing he met, as his whole tribe does today, hoping to find the guilty party and retrieve the long-lost rhino needle.

Wild as it sounds, the native legend makes more sense than all of Hollywood's automotive-rhino epics put together. What could be more frantic, more maddened by frustration, more suspicious and aggressive, than a three-thousand-pound animal, nearsighted to the point of blindness, who searches constantly for something he can't see?

Insatiably curious, the black rhino is at the same time extremely timid and equipped with only limited mentality. His hearing and his sense of smell are superb, but his vision is abysmally defective. Each of his tiny eyes, set on opposite sides of his bulky, elongated head, gives him a different picture to look at; each picture is tantalizing in its wide-angle perspective but horribly frustrating in its perpetual fuzziness. An animal Mr. McGoo, nearsighted Kifaru cannot tell a man from a tree at distances of more than thirty feet, cannot see any object distinctly if it is more than twenty or even fifteen feet away, and has to cock his head sideways to see, with one eye at a time, around the bulk of his muzzle and his massive front horn. Moving forward with the horn lowered, he is running blind.

By day as well as night, Kifaru hears and smells a whole world of fascinating objects which he cannot see. His curiosity drives him on to poke and probe among them—to look for the needle, as it were—but his timid disposition makes him fear, and fear deeply, the very objects that he wants to examine. He hesitates, agonized, while the two conflicting instincts boil within him. Usually he runs away but sometimes rushes forward to investigate with the world's most farcical display of bluff, noise, wasted energy, and sheer ineptitude—the notorious rhino "charge."

Once, near the Upemba National Park in Katanga, I watched a typically addlepated rhino stage a typically silly charge. He was busy with a big mouthful of twigs when he heard a frog start to croak about a hundred feet away. He stopped chewing, cocked his head, and listened—with leaves fluttering out of his mouth—then trotted anxiously toward the sound. As he approached, the frog croaked loudly and hopped by chance in his direction. A ton and a half of spooked rhinoceros made an abrupt U-turn, retreating to "safety." He sulked for a few minutes before advancing again. This time the frog jumped in the opposite direction, making him feel more confident: he lowered his horn and charged, smashing the frog under his hoofs without even knowing it. He returned to the spot, sniffing until he found it, and pawed at the little blob of pulp with a puzzled expression.

At the opposite extreme, rhinos have attacked railroad trains. During the early days of the Uganda Railway—while disturbed lions were carrying off the station masters or the signalmen—a frightened and confused rhino charged and jolted a stationary coach, knocking himself down but getting up and trotting away, somewhat dazedly, to brood about the experience. One of the trains was actually derailed when another rhino charged the locomotive, knocking off a steel plate which dropped beneath a wheel. This time the rhino didn't get up.

Such hysterical reactions, whether provoked by a two-ounce frog or a 200-ton train, cannot be blamed on poor eyesight alone. Cursed with equally bad vision, the elephant acts with majestic calm and self-assured determination; his great intelligence enables him to solve the problems that confront him and to keep his warm emotions balanced sanely. Kifaru, commonly and mistakenly believed to be related to the elephant (if elephants could sue, they should sue for slander), behaves very like his real-life relative—the dim-witted, dim-sighted and hysterically skittish horse.

Adored and sentimentalized for his graceful, even noble-looking beauty, the horse has also been acclaimed for his "horse sense," implying practical shrewdness and a sort of rough-hewn wisdom. He is, ironically, the least intelligent domesticated animal of any size or note, while the much-maligned ass, whose name is linked with gross stupidity or folly, is a genius by comparison. Those who handle both are well aware of the horse's mental failings—a lack of basic reasoning power which has been confirmed by extensive scientific testing. Matched against cows in simple association tests, horses proved only half as intelligent; matched against dogs, cats, pigs, monkeys, rodents, and other animals in multiple-choice tests that demanded more sophisticated reasoning, the horse was tied for last place—with the gopher.

Only slightly smarter than Kifaru, timid and terribly nervous, deprived of binocular vision and fuzzily nearsighted, the horse shies away from a fluttering bit of paper just as the rhino shies away from a butterfly. Although he is far more accustomed to cars, even a well-trained horse may sometimes bolt when suddenly confronted, as he will bolt at any startling sight or sound. To work at all, most horses need blinders on their eyes; they must be shielded from the nerve-racking provocation of the dimly seen objects and imagined terrors of the world around them. In case of fire in a stable, when the terror is a real one, they must actually be blindfolded before they can be led to safety. Then, if left untied, they may rush in uncontrollable hysteria back into the very flames they fear.

Free-living horses, zebras, and wild asses are all, in varying degrees, nervous, timid, unpredictable, and hard to approach. The related South American and Malayan tapirs—pony-sized, prehensile-lipped creatures who are very close, anatomically, to the primitive ancestral stock from which horse and rhino both evolved—are shy, retiring animals who will flee in panic from a tiny dog but sometimes charge at larger beasts, including humans, in a fit of fear and jangled nerves.

Among Kifaru's closer relatives, the same behavior pattern holds, although he is himself the most aggressive of the five living rhino species. There are three Asiatic representatives: the little Sumatran rhino, who is quite hairy, two-horned and only four feet tall; the smooth-skinned, one-horned Javan rhino, who averages a foot taller; and the Great Indian Rhinoceros, a fantastic-looking creature six feet tall and up to fourteen feet long, with a single short horn and immensely thick skin that is folded into armor-like plates.

Kifaru's fellow African, the white rhinoceros, is even bigger. Measuring up to six foot six at his humped shoulder, fourteen or even fifteen feet in length, and sometimes weighing over two tons, he is the world's second largest land mammal. There are two very similar races: a shorter-horned, flatter-headed type from the northeast Congo and bordering Sudan; and the long-horned white rhino (the record length for a front horn is sixty-two-and-a-half inches) from South Africa's Umfolosi and Hluhluwe Game Reserves. Ironically, neither white rhino race is white but just about the same color as the so-called black rhino—a dark slaty gray. The designation "white" is simply a corruption of the Boer word *weit* (wide) which was used to describe the animal's snout— broad and squared-off unlike the black rhino's rounded muzzle with its tapirlike prehensile upper lip. Less wary than Kifaru, Abu-Garn, as the white rhino is sometimes called in the north, lives in small herds that travel across the open plains, their heads bowed low as they crop the grass.

Kifaru, who is smaller, faster, and more agile, dwells upon the forested savannahs, preferring thorn bush and acacia thickets near a river, stream, or mudhole. He forms no herds but trots along like the prickly loner that he is, head held high as he browses on the shrubbery, using his hooked, prehensile upper lip to strip off leaves and twigs, and sometimes digging with his front horn for tasty roots, salt, or water.

Rare individuals may reach a height of five-and-a-half feet, a length of twelve feet, and a weight of nearly two tons, but the average black rhino is a ton and a half of trouble, five feet tall, and nine to ten feet long. His front horn, which is usually the larger of the pair, rarely exceeds two feet in length, but the record horn measures nearly four feet. His ears are fringed with hair and are somewhat horselike in their shape; his two-foot tail is tufted at the tip and often carried erect; his four feet, like those of all living rhinos, are each equipped with three hoofed toes, the middle one corresponding to the horse's single toe. He can walk, trot, or gallop, sometimes reaching speeds of thirty-five to forty miles per hour, unlike the elephant who cannot really run, even when he is charging at a twenty-mile-per-hour pacing walk.

Asia's three short-horned rhino species fight with their tusks, which are really lower canines, slashing with them like

144

a hippo or a wild boar. Africa's black and white rhinos, who have no front teeth, gore or toss with their longer horns. None of the rhinos, Kifaru included, makes a determined effort to trample an enemy underfoot—as does a furious deer, elephant, or Cape buffalo—but they may run over him, most of the time by accident, while galloping along.

An inept hunter run over by a rhino probably has the same survival chances as a careless California pedestrian. If a hoof or wheel smashes into something delicate and vital, the man expires. If not, he emerges with some broken bones and a galaxy of bruises. Humans who are gored and tossed usually get off much more lightly, as with Californians who are thrown by a fender. A good half of the rhino-tossed hunters get up and walk away to have their cuts and bruises tended. The rest are carried away for more extensive doctoring, and an occasional hunter, probably no more than one in every dozen tossed, is carted away to the graveyard.

Any fighting bull, forced to demonstrate his powers in a Mexican or Spanish bull ring, does more damage when his horns connect with the matador. They are outgrowths of the bovine skull, prolongations of the frontal bones that are covered with an outer sheath of true and very hard horn, and the fighting bull uses them with some intelligence. Kifaru's so-called horns are merely outgrowths from the skin of his snout, without a bony core of any sort and composed of densely matted hairs. The basic substance, keratin, is the same as that of true horn but the structure is much weaker. Free-living rhinos sharpen their front horns on tree trunks or on concretelike termite hills, just as zoo rhinos whet their horns on bricks or bars, but for all their conscientious effort rarely gore a hunter in a vital spot. Charging blind as they do, they sometimes fail to strike with the horn at all, and rather toss with the head or nose.

As a match for human hunters, poor Kifaru is the laughingstock of equatorial Africa, ridiculed in native folk tales and proverbial wisdom. *"Bairinga kipserageta!"* say the Lumbwa tribesmen of East Africa—"May you be killed by a rhino!"—but they only say it to their worst enemies. They cannot think of any more undignified, cowardly, and humiliating death.

It is exactly that, for the great majority of rhino-caused fatalities or severe injuries come when a man turns his back and runs. An inexperienced hunter, white or black, may panic as he sees the huge animal galloping toward him in its classic dust cloud: he shoots in haste, wounds rather than kills, drops his gun, and tries to outrace the dazed or maddened rhino. He can't possibly do it, since Kifaru is at least a third faster, while the very fact that he runs increases the rhino's confidence and the noise he makes while running gives the half-blind animal a chance to use his keen hearing and correct his angle of approach which was, most probably, wrong to begin with. Under these conditions, even a badly wounded and further handicapped rhino may be lucky enough to connect or, rather, collide with his target.

This is not idle theorizing. On foot, alone, unarmed and one-handed, I have faced a full-grown rhino, letting him charge me at his pleasure, and emerged from that experience, repeated scores of times, without so much as a bruise. Those rhino-Hallet matches weren't meant to prove a thing about Hallet, but to demonstrate a few basic facts about the much-misunderstood character and actions of Kifaru.

"What the rhino really needs is a good psychoanalyst," I had long maintained to friends in Africa. "Somewhere, behind the bluff and bluster, the frustrations and neuroses, there's a good-natured animal who would like to make friends."

No one would believe it. Brainwashed by the hunters' propaganda, they looked upon Kifaru as a hardened criminal rather than a scatterbrained delinquent. Hoping to refute that point of view, late in 1959, I purchased a recently captured, full-grown black rhino from the Uganda Public Works Department, christened him Pierrot, turned him loose in a 250-by 200-foot kraal at my Mugwata game park, and walked into the kraal, determined to tame and train him.

Pierrot heard the gate close behind me, and stared nervously in my direction from his position some 150 feet away. He worried about the problem for several minutes before deciding on the traditional rhino answer—charge. Then he trotted toward me, accelerating, his head held horizontally. In that position his already poor vision was blocked by his front horn, so, as he launched himself into a furious gallop, he cocked his head to the side, straining to see with a single eye. When he reached a point about thirty feet away, where he could vaguely distinguish my shape, he adjusted his angle, lowered his horn and thundered toward me—a blind juggernaut committed to a fixed direction.

I had about a second to answer or ignore him. If his aim appeared to be dangerously accurate, I could make a quick sideways jump like a rodeo clown; if not, I could stand my tracks and watch his dust.

On this, his first try, Pierrot's aim looked a little too good. I jumped. He shot past, snorting, with his tasseled tail held high in the air. Decelerating to a stop more than thirty feet beyond, he turned around and peered anxiously, trotting back and forth while he tried to find the target. Since I am somewhat smaller than a railroad train, he failed to locate me. I moved back about twenty feet. He heard me, snorted indignantly, "prrrufff!" and charged again.

This time I didn't have to move. Pierrot misjudged his angle badly, missing by a wide margin. His third attempt was even worse, and after five or six failures he stopped charging. Confused and obviously upset, he snorted, growled, shook his head and pawed at the ground. I let him sulk for ten minutes before I clued him to the target, jumping up and down and hooting like a baboon.

Pierrot raised his head, started to trot in my direction, spotted a small cassia tree at a ninety-degree angle, veered, galloped toward it under full steam, veered again, and wound up 150 feet to my left. He spent the next ten minutes trotting back and forth, head cocked, trying to find me. He was concentrating very hard, but he wasted his energy on two more small trees and a big clump of thorn bush. Then, when he finally spotted me, he charged, missed again, and, of course, missed by an even wider margin.

Disgusted by the whole series of fiascos, a ton and a half of unhappy horned fury sat down on his haunches, grunting. As he did, I charged the rhino, yelling like a Masai. Appalled, he scrambled to his feet and stood, staring, until I got to within twenty feet of him. Then he fled in terror to the far end of the kraal. "The greatest bluffer in all Africa," as Carl Akeley once called him, had been shamelessly outbluffed.

We repeated those absurd maneuvers for the next four days, but I never charged the rhino again. Instead, I simply dodged or stood my ground as Pierrot continued to charge . . . and to miss . . . and to try again. If he became familiar with my appearance, I reasoned, he would be eager to satisfy his curiosity as soon as he decided that I wasn't going to hurt him.

The first signs of understanding came toward the end of the fourth day when I moved to a point within ten feet of the rhino's head and he neither charged nor retreated but watched quietly. After a moment, he started to worry again and backed off. Trying to reassure him, I made a noisy little retreat. That brought him back but he didn't charge: I was well within his field of clear vision and I was becoming a familiar if a somewhat baffling sight. Encouraged, I took a step toward the rhino. He took a step backward. So I took a step to the rear, and he moved forward one step.

We danced that little waltz, with minor variations, for a full month. It was dull work, especially so when compared to the quick, spectacular results that can be obtained with more intelligent animals. Working with my full-grown lion, Simba, in the backyard arena of my place at Kisenyi, I had tamed him in a couple of days and trained him in *less* than a month, to sit, stand, lie down, roll over, mount a series of pedestals, and leap through a hoop of fire. Now, working with Pierrot, the pair of us simply stepped forward, backward, forward, and backward again. Friends and family had predicted my atrocious death beneath the rhino's hoofs, but the way things looked, I was more apt to die of boredom—either that or fallen arches.

The big breakthrough came, one day, as I was standing a couple of feet away from Pierrot's head. He suddenly turned his two-foot front horn toward me, then rubbed his leathery cheek along my arm. I returned the gesture with a hearty slap on the neck, figuring that a rhino would, like an elephant, prefer a firm caress to an irritating little tickle. He nudged me in the ribs with his horn, rubbing it along my body. I took a dozen steps away from him, curious to see his reaction. He came toward me with an accelerating trot. I was in the direct line of charge but I stood my ground as the rhino advanced. He came to a halt with his horn less than two feet from my chest, then cocked his head and ogled me.

I let out my breath, gave him another friendly slap on the neck and led him on a long walk around the edge of the kraal, keeping a position three-quarters forward so that he could see me easily. He followed like a three-thousand-pound lamb, dutifully keeping step—which wasn't at all surprising —turned whenever I turned, and gave me a few playful little nudges in the rear.

Within a week, the horned fury and I were playing ball. We used a three-foot sphere of cattle hide stuffed with straw. I bowled it to Pierrot with my hand and he bowled it back with his horn. John Grindle's cricket-playing elephants would have laughed us off the field, but the rhino found it thrilling sport, smacking the ball enthusiastically but with very poor aim. His physical handicaps made it difficult to teach him more sophisticated games: he was too nearsighted, unable to jump or even to scramble over any kind of barrier, and he lacked grasping equipment comparable to an elephant's adroit trunk.

Training the rhino as a riding mount appeared to be a more promising project. Although he dwarfed an ordinary horse, his dimensions were approached by France's famed Percherons, an equine breed developed by the Crusaders to carry the weight of knights clad in heavy suits of armor. A big Percheron can reach a height of seventeen hands (five foot eight at the shoulder) and a weight of one ton. The largest horse in history, a Percheron gelding named Dr. Le Gear who died in St. Louis, Missouri, in 1919, had in fact been *larger* than my rhino. The great Le Gear had stood seven feet tall at the shoulder (two feet taller than Pierrot), measured sixteen feet from nose to tail (seven feet longer), and weighed just about the same—2,995 pounds.

The first time I mounted, bent on riding him bareback, Pierrot shuddered, heaved, and stamped angrily. Bucking like a bronco was beyond his powers, but he could have rolled on the ground if he had wanted to hurt me. He relapsed instead into cold, motionless disapproval after the storm of protest failed. I sat, spraddled out uncomfortably on his barrel-like back, for at least five minutes while he waited for me to dismount. Then I kicked him in the ribs, hoping to make him go. He went . . . and I bounced several times before coming to rest in the middle of the thorn bush. Unfortunately, I was wearing *kapitula*—baggy tropical shorts—rather than a heavy suit of armor.

The next time I tried it I put a rope halter around his neck and kicked a little more gently. The rhino broke into a fast trot instead of a gallop and I managed to stay aboard by clutching at the rope. There was, however, absolutely no way to make him turn, speed up, slow down, or stop, although I tried every variety of poke, nudge, gesture, and verbal command during the next couple of weeks. Finally, I had to accept the fact that while the rhino might permit me to sit upon his back while he moved about, he would never learn to take directions like his handsome relative, the horse. Less intelligent and even more stubborn, Pierrot was no Percheron.

He was, however, all that I had predicted: a basically good-natured animal who could prove as much if approached with a little understanding rather than a rifle. After making friends with me, he learned to accept the Balese gamekeepers, Bodeko and Bokwe, and the two elephants, Bella and Venus, who lived "next door" in the adjacent kraal. I chaperoned the first five rhino-elephant meetings; then I opened the double doors between their kraals and let them mingle on their own. Venus and Pierrot paired off for a while, going for walks without the shocked and quietly brooding Bella. But the two majestic ladies must have missed each other's conversation; reconciled after a couple of weeks, they afterwards shared the henpecked rhino between them—not as a lover, I hasten to explain, but strictly as a friend.

Free-living black rhinos, unlike my educated pet, have little to do with other animals, elephants included. There is a hoary old legend, left over from classic times, that rhinos and elephants are at war, but in real life the wooded savannah's two largest animals generally avoid each other. The rhino is frightened and uncertain; the elephant, very sensibly, never goes out of his way to look for trouble.

Hysterical rhinos have, however, charged at occasional elephants, just as they have charged at trains. Most of the time, the rhino pulls up and trots off, tail held high, trying to look impressive as he beats a quick retreat. But the huge juggernaut may thunder on, unpredictably, and collide with his even huger target. What happens next depends on whether he merely strikes a glancing blow and ricochets away, terrified, or scores a square hit.

My Masai friend, Masaka, told me of one such incident he had witnessed somewhere on the Tanganyika side of the Masai reservation. According to Masaka, a male rhino with a fair-to-middling horn charged a big bull elephant, holing him in the belly. The elephant replied by seizing the rhino's neck with his trunk and throwing him, as a lion throws a Cape buffalo. Then he double-holed the rhino with his seven-foot tusks and finished him off by stamping on his head. There were no Tembo-style funeral rites for the dead rhino: the elephant moved away, rumbling to himself indignantly and bleeding from the hole in his belly.

Cape buffaloes and other herbivores give the erratic rhino a fairly wide berth; but lions, the only carnivores large enough to try it, are alleged to have fought and even killed full-grown rhinos. Some of those reports may have been inspired by the sight of lions feasting on a poacher-killed rhino, and some may have involved lions caught by a mother rhino while trying to snatch her baby. Even hunting as a pack, lions are just about at their limit when they tackle Cape buffaloes, some of which are only half the weight of black rhinos. Unless really crazed by hunger or the sort of mania that

150

drove the Kimaa lion to attack an iron roof, they are wise enough to seek out smaller prey.

Kifaru's only real enemy is, of course, man. His only real friend is the tick-bird. When the busy birds spot approaching hunters, they flap about and squawk their insistent "Chirrr! Chirrr!" to alert the nearsighted rhino. If he is fast asleep—and rhinos sleep like stone sphinxes—the birds persist frantically. Their egret "assistants," who sit upon the rhino's back looking decorative, or dart about snapping up flies, prudently depart at the first sign of trouble.

The tick-bird's reward consists of warble-fly larvae plucked from suppurating boils which he lances with his beak, drinking off the puss, and ticks the size of kidney beans which he picks interminably from the deep folds and wrinkles of Kifaru's skin. The skin is thick but sensitive, like the elephant's, and the rhino feels the pain of the surgeon's beak. He never protests, preferring it to the constant torture of the parasites, and dimly realizing, perhaps, the safety value of his conscientious sentinels.

The tick-birds may sound off, and rightly, when another rhino is approaching. Hearing the first one's downwind movements, the second one may charge hysterically; the first, suddenly alerted, then may make his own frantic charge at the other. Raising the usual cloud of dust, they gallop toward each other while you grit your teeth, watching and waiting for the horrible collision—but it almost never comes. The furious-looking pair usually gallop past each other, having mutually misjudged their angles, and then go wandering off in opposite directions to browse in the bush. When their aim is better or they make compensating errors, they screech to a halt as soon as they get within twenty feet and go their separate ways, once again trying to look as though nothing at all had happened. Each may have his own marked-off territory, but they stage no serious brawls when territorial borders are invaded.

Attempting to explain Kifaru's strange outlook on real estate, the Azande tribesmen blame it on the same brush fire that sent the first hippo diving into the water. The singed rhinos fled by land, led by the hard-galloping chieftain of their tribe. Once they had made it to safety, the rhino leader advised his warriors to build a wall by depositing their dung at designated sites along their daily routes and wetting it down with urine as termites glue their masonry with saliva. When the next fire came, he explained, the entire tribe could safely hide behind the wall of heaped-up rhino dung.

I hate to spoil a good story, but alas, there is no Great Wall of Africa. The rhino visits and revisits his own droppings, sometimes building sizable mounds to mark out the borders of his territory; but from time to time, he breaks up the droppings with his hind feet, like a dog, and pokes and sniffs among them. Scientists have advanced conflicting explanations—that the rhino is trying to publicize his presence, that the rhino is trying to mask his identity—and observing natives also disagree. Tales of the northern Congo claim that Kifaru is searching through the dung for his long-lost needle, suspecting that he might have swallowed it; while legends of the south maintain that he is checking to determine whether "all the thorns have come out of his brain."

I doubt if anyone will ever figure out Kifaru's exact motive, if he has one, but the native explanations have some special interest of their own. "Needles" or needlelike thorns play a role in most rhino legends because the black rhino actually eats them. While nipping off some three bushels of leaves and twigs every day, he ingests a large number of vicious, flesh-ripping thorns. They never seem to bother him at all. Appallingly, he eats the fat thorny leaves of euphorbia bushes whose acrid, milky-looking sap blisters human skin; and he even dines on fallen branches of the candelabra tree, a species of euphorbia whose juice is used by East African tribesmen to poison arrows which they use to hunt . . . rhinoceroses. While toxic enough if it gets into his bloodstream, Kifaru's cast-iron stomach can digest the poisonous euphorbia; in fact, it forms the major part of his diet in regions where it is used also to kill him.

In lightly hunted areas, game preserves, and national parks, rhinos browse during daylight hours, trotting across fairly open country as they wander in and out of trouble. Where hunting has been very heavy, they feed from late afternoon or evening until early morning, hiding out at other times in special retreats which the natives like to call "rhino houses." Each rhino breaks away or pushes back stems and branches in the denser parts of the thickets, clearing a space some fifteen or twenty feet in diameter with a hollowed place at the center where he rolls during wet weather.

While he is sleeping in his house, an adept stalker can approach close enough to jab Kifaru with a poisoned spear or put the muzzle of a gun to his very ear. But if there are tick-birds present, they sound the alarm, even beating themselves against the sleeping rhino's head if they have to. Kifaru then rushes out of his house, if he awakens in time, to gallop off in terror through the bushes.

If the retreating rhino runs over a hunter, he has allegedly "charged" at his "victim." If a rifle bullet wounds him, he may rush toward the hunter but he still isn't "charging": he is dazed and confused by the shock. If, however, the hunter places a quick-killing shot in eye, ear, or temple, the rhino literally drops in his tracks; he never falls on his side like most dying animals but sinks down with head between his outstretched forelegs, looking as though he had suddenly gone to sleep.

Left undisturbed, the rhino wakes up by dusk or by late evening if the sky is overcast, and goes trotting down a well-worn path to his stream or mudhole, nipping a few thorny tidbits along the way. After a good drink and a soothing roll in the mud, he takes another beaten path to his favorite feeding ground in more exposed country. There he browses, digs for roots with his front horn, and makes his faithful contributions to the rhino tribe's legendary great wall. As morning comes, he sets out toward the water on another of his intersecting paths, takes another drink, and goes home through the thorny labyrinth to sleep away another day.

When he meets a second rhino, they may make a few sham charges; then, if they know each other fairly well, the pair may touch or even rub noses before trotting off in opposite directions. That is just about the limit of Kifaru's normal social life, except when rhino cows come into season.

There is no fixed time of the year, nor any fixed time of night or day, for mating. When nubile cows are anywhere in the neighborhood, ordinary set routines are abandoned: sniffing the cows' love-perfume from distances of more than a mile, bulls sleep and browse less, roaming farther from their customary feeding grounds and, very often, getting into trouble with the native or white population of neighboring settlements. If the cow rhino voices her alluring mating call, a falsetto "Wheeee! Wheeee!" bulls go crashing through the thickets, snorting as they try to find her.

If a bull rhino meets a well-seasoned cow who is strolling all alone, their courtship antics begin. If, however, she is accompanied by her calf—which she cares for devotedly until it is almost as big as she is—the calf, large or small, male or female, shows its own devotion to its mother by attempting to defend her from the would-be lover. The bull retreats repeatedly as the valiant calf charges; he knows that the cow herself will attack, and attack in earnest, if he tries to harm her baby. The comedy continues until the cow manages to calm the calf, or the calf decides on his own that the suitor means no harm.

After accepting the situation, the calf trails along but ignores the subsequent proceedings. Other animals, however, seem to take a special interest in the noisily prolonged rhino courtship demonstrations and matings. Gnus, who are fanatically curious about anything, are the most dedicated animal voyeurs; but elephants, Cape buffaloes, hyenas, baboons, and human hunters may look on from a distance with comically absorbed expressions. The preoccupied rhinos generally ignore them.

The cow rhino walks, walks, and walks, with the bull trotting close behind her. When she urinates, as a rhino cow in estrus does very frequently, he sniffs appreciatively and raises his neck, pointing his front horn toward the heavens while curling his prehensile upper lip in a tough-looking snarl. From time to time, as he follows, he may move up and jab her in the ribs with his horn; frequently they stop and face each other, playfully jousting with their horns or tenderly butting heads.

After a while, the bull advances toward the cow with a curious gait, holding his front legs rigid and dragging his hind legs along the ground, one after the other. Then he defecates and, as a strange accompaniment, swings his head from side to side like a pendulum, scraping his front horn and hooked upper lip against the ground. Since he may perform the same maneuvers when he nears one of his established dung heaps, it appears to be a generalized display of rhinocerous virility.

The cow looks on, presumably with coy approval. But occasionally and for no apparent reason, she may charge, snorting loudly as she beats or gores him with her front horn. The bull, bruised or bloody, gallops away and then returns to circle cautiously, moving with a mincing trot while swinging his head pendulum-style. After several repetitions, she lets him come and maneuver himself into position, standing on his hind legs with his forefeet resting in the middle of her back. But he doesn't try to copulate, although he may have spent several hours trying to attain his present vantage point. He just stands . . . and stands . . . and stands, doing absolutely nothing, with his front horn and tasseled tail pointing toward the sky.

He may stand for all of ten minutes; then the cow moves

away, dislodging him. Sometimes she will charge, belting him with her horn—who can blame her?—but she usually walks off. The sequence now has to start again, and the bull may mount and stand in his bizarre pose up to fifteen or even twenty times during the next few hours.

When he finally decides for reasons of his own that the proper time has come, he lowers his tasseled tail and inches forward. Then he takes the cow and takes her for half an hour or more, while she squeals periodically. Any poachers within earshot can approach at their leisure.

She walks away at last, dislodging the bull, and both browse ravenously. Sometimes she lies down very briefly and the bull lies down beside her. They look like a real married couple, but their paired life may last no more than a few hours, depending on the cow rhino's whims. Unlike the sentimental elephants who engage in long-term marriages, monogamous or polygamous, rhinos seem to favor free love. Although they may accept the same bull for several days or, rarely, several weeks, cows sometimes seek and accept two or three partners during a single day.

If two or more bulls contend at the same time for the rhino cow's favors, the candidates strike pugnacious-looking attitudes—upper lip curled in a snarl and ears flattened—but they rarely strike each other. Instead they engage in sham charges, threaten with half-snorting, half-shrieking cries, drag themselves around with stiffened legs, defecating, and either swing their heads like pendulums or jerk them up and down. Bulls rarely gore each other, as a cow may gore a bull, but they sometimes joust with the front horns, attempting to club the side of the head. One of them eventually decides to retreat, or while the so-called battle goes on between two bulls, the cow may sneak off with a third one.

The result of all these rhino high jinx comes some eighteen months later, after a gestation period longer than that of any animal except elephants. The single black rhino calf, some two-and-a-half feet tall and weighing about seventy pounds, is a playful somewhat coltish little fellow who trots along behind his attentive mother; while the white rhino baby always walks before her, nudged and guided by her front horn.

Whichever species they belong to, rhino babies show the same extraordinary and unique trait: they are the only young animals in Africa who will fight courageously, and fight to the death if they have to, in defense of their mothers. Even a three-foot-high rhino calf will charge repeatedly at a gang of native poachers to protect the arrow-studded body of his dead mother. The baby must be killed or captured before the poachers can approach and cut away the "monster's" coveted horns.

Unlike ivory, rhino horn is apt to crumble when carved and has no real beauty or utility. But, paradoxically, it commands a far higher price—about $15 per pound at African ports of exit. That figure is multiplied many times over in the Orient and Arabia, where dealers may realize between $1500 and $5000 from the sale of a single horn. They usually break it up into gravel-size pieces for sale to superstitious nitwits who believe that it has medical or aphrodisiac powers.

Because the rhino mounts his mate so often and maintains his position for an extended period, wistful Asiatic watchers have believed for ages that ingesting rhino horn—a blatant symbol of the animal's virility—will magically stimulate the user to unparalleled performance with wife or harem. Some aging lechers drink the powdered horn in their wine; others take a piece of horn a square inch in diameter, grind it to a powder, put the powder in a sort of muslin tea bag, and boil it in a cup of water. They drink the wine or dark-brown rhino-horn tea, and many feel a surge of sexual desire, just as nitwits and neurotics of the Western world can obtain relief from imaginary ills by gulping down placebos or sugar pills prescribed to humor them. The effect is purely psychological, for the rhino horn itself has no more aphrodisiac power than ground-up human hair or toenails.

Complete horns with carefully scooped-out centers are purchased by those who are wealthy and fatuous enough to pay several thousand dollars for a "magic drinking cup." According to an old superstition, should an enemy slip some poison into the owner's rice wine or tea, the lethal drink either froths out of the rhino horn or the horn itself flies to pieces. Presumably, disappointed clients don't complain.

Rhino hoofs, hide, hair, bones, blood, viscera, and even urine all have their own pseudo-medical, magical, or religious uses among the varying peoples of southern and eastern Asia. To obtain or profit from the sale of these repulsive medicines and talismans, Orientals have hunted their three native species to the point of near-extinction, beating them out of the bush with lines of howdah-bearing elephants or resorting to their own varieties of poisons, pits, and snares. There are today an estimated 40 Javan rhinos left, at most 170 Sumatrans, and about 600 Great Indian Rhinoceroses in Northeastern India and Nepal. Most of the surviving rhinos dwell in sanctuaries or reserves, but government officials find it very difficult to protect the animals from poachers who will risk life imprisonment or a game warden's bullet to obtain and sell the immensely profitable horn.

Several Asiatic governments, it must be said, set a very poor example to their people. In recent years, with the sanction of official permits from high-level Burmese officials, rhinos have been killed "for medicinal purposes," and although the living animals are "protected by law," the open sale of rhino blood and parts is absolutely and absurdly legal. In Nepal, where less than 200 Great Indian Rhinoceroses dwell in the Rapti Valley region and wardens have orders to shoot poachers on sight, King Mahendra organized a special hunting expedition just a few years ago, so that he might make an offering of rhino blood in memory of his father, King Tribhuvan. Where the king disregards the law, it must be difficult to preach conservation to the people.

To supply the Orient with fake aphrodisiacs and nostrums, and to a much smaller extent for locally used meat and hides, Africa's white rhinos were slaughtered without mercy. They were approached with relative ease on the open grassy plains, and since white rhino cows grow longer horns than the bulls, the cows were singled out for slaughter—a particularly disastrous practice with a slow-reproducing species. In the north, there are probably about 400 white rhinos in the Congo, where they have little chance for long-term survival, and some 600 in Sudan, where they are now fairly well-protected. There are another 1000 in South Africa, where their numbers are increasing due to the very strict conservation laws and meticulous enforcement.

Poor blundering Kifaru, hiding out in his beloved thickets, is seemingly far from extinction: there are an estimated 10,000 to 13,000 black rhinos left, most of them living in national parks and game preserves. That sounds like a safe, even impressive figure, but the rate of attrition keeps increasing as the money-minded poachers swarm into so-called sanctuaries with their rifles, snares, and poison arrows. Even the Masai, tragically corrupted with the rest, are now spearing *e-muny*, as they call the black rhino. They claim "self-defense" but their real motive is the money or, God help them, the illegal drugs they can obtain from the sale of the horns.

Every year poachers kill some 20 per cent of Africa's living black rhinos—and the rhino's birth rate is a scant 5 per cent. The carnage could be reduced if collective fines were imposed on tribesmen living in heavily poached areas and a joint Oriental-African embargo passed against the rhino-horn traffic, forbidding any and all sales. Instead, rhino horn is auctioned off legally in Mombasa and legally imported in the East where, within twenty years or so, Africa's last black rhino will wind up as magic powder in a little muslin bag.

Meanwhile, Western hunters who deplore the Easterners' superstitious follies are attempting to enhance their own virility by killing and decapitating rhinos. Those who fail for some reason or another to obtain the impressive-looking trophy on their own, buy a rhino head in Nairobi or Arusha taxidermists' shops to bring home and palm off as their personal kill. More ambitious hunters—the real "barfly sportsmen"—buy their record or near-record heads on the sly.

Another even more obnoxious token of virility is manufactured from the rhino's penis. Hung in the hot sun with a three-pound weight suspended from the end, it is dried, stretched, trimmed, and polished into a vicious three-foot *sjambok;* a single blow from such a whip will lay a man's flesh open to the bone. Substitutes made from hippo hide are not supposed to be as tough and springy. They also lack, I presume, the same masculine mystique.

Kifaru's thick but soft hide, easily penetrated by a bullet or hunting knife, becomes extremely hard and durable when dried. Worth about ten pence a pound, it has been used for everything from native shields to table tops, sandal soles, and chair seats. The black rhino's flesh has never been too popular with the natives, since he never has any fat and his meat is rather dry. His hams have been praised, however, by some enthusiastic game gourmets; and at least one of them, a certain Dr. Kolb, was fanatically devoted to his liver. Teddy Roosevelt, America's first conservation-minded president, described in his book *African Game Trails* how Dr. Kolb, hunting "north of Kenia," had killed scores of rhinos for their livers and was then charged and killed by a wounded cow who "thrust her horn right through the middle of his body." Hopefully, she got him in the liver.

Teddy himself, who was hunting museum specimens, pronounced the flesh of the white rhino to be "excellent," especially the hump on the withers. African natives agreed, savoring the huge quantities of fat which the white rhino lays on from March through August when his flesh assumes a fine, almost beefy flavor. They ate all of Abu-Garn's meat, especially relishing the hump which was cut out and cooked, skin and all, in an earthen barbecue pit.

To kill black and white rhinos, natives formerly employed

all of their traditional methods: pits, snares, poison arrows, and the rest. Sudan's Hamram Arabs used to hunt rhinos as they hunted elephants—mounted on horses and armed with their two-handed broadswords. Kifaru was, however, much more difficult to hamstring. Smaller and able to maneuver with more agility than the giant elephant, his greater speed rivaled that of their finest horses; and since, unlike the elephant, he can keep on the move with one disabled leg, the tendons of both of his hind legs had to be sliced through. The heavier and slower white rhino—who carried larger and more lucrative horns—was easier to kill.

Early European hunters concentrated on the white rhino for the same reasons. Although mounted on horseback like the half-breed Sudanese Arabs, they needed less skill and daring, since they used modern rifles that killed at a distance. Frederick Courteney Selous, a turn-of-the-century professional who was generally accepted as "the greatest of the world's big-game hunters," described his technique with the vulnerable white rhinos:

> They are, as a rule, very easy to shoot on horseback, as, if one gallops a little in front of and on one side of them, they will hold their course, and come sailing past, offering a magnificent broadside shot, while under similar circumstances a prehensile-lipped rhinoceros will usually swerve away in such a manner as only to present his hind-quarters for a shot.

Despite Kifaru's elementary caution, he was still easy game for rifle-bearing mounted hunters. Selous, the top all-around professional of his era, ranked the black rhino at the bottom of his Big Five, while placing the lion at the top. British East Africa's Lieutenant-Governor Jackson, one of the most proficient contemporary amateurs, also ranked the rhino last, giving his first-place vote to the Cape buffalo. But Sir Samuel Baker—possibly crazed by too many bowls of hippo soup—pronounced the black rhino to be more dangerous than the Cape buffalo or lion.

Even Teddy Roosevelt, a self-admitted novice on the East African savannahs, knew better. He commented tactfully in *African Game Trails* that Sir Samuel had "less experience" than the other big-name, big-game hunters. Then Teddy went on to cast his own first-place ballot for the lion. Sensibly, he judged by results rather than size or appearance. As he explained it:

. . . during the last three or four years, in German and British East Africa and Uganda, over fifty white men have been killed or mauled by lions, buffaloes, elephants, and rhinos; and the lions have much the largest list of victims to their credit. In Nairobi church-yard I was shown the graves of seven men who had been killed by lions, and of one who had been killed by a rhino.

Kifaru improved his score a few years later, when he killed the first American White Hunter, Charles Cottar, a friend of Teddy Roosevelt's. Since then, he has managed to kill an occasional hunter or poacher, while they have managed on their own part to kill some hundred thousand black rhinos. Native poachers armed with modern weapons do the grand-scale killing, as they do with all of Africa's game, while trophy-minded tourists and their guides probably account for no more than two hundred black rhinos every year. But a single white man, the well-known and aptly named professsional, John A. Hunter, killed over a thousand black rhinos in little more than two years—between August, 1944, and December, 1946—with the aid of only three native trackers.

Hunter was far from an old-time profit-minded adventurer. He was a conscientious, responsible veteran in the service of the Kenya Game Department, which had asked him to conduct what he called "the biggest rhino hunt in history" in the Makueni area of the Machakos District. The Wakamba tribe, whose population had already multiplied at least sixfold since the British colonial administration had supplied modern health services and stopped the Masai from killing them, was demanding additional land for settlement.

Hunter, who was not only a crack shot but a fairly astute observer of animal behavior, went into the dense thornbush and acacia thickets where the rhino population had taken refuge. It was far more dangerous work than trophy hunting—almost always practiced where the cover is lighter so that the "sportsmen" can select the finest heads—but he was able, despite the tick-birds whom he called "feathered spies," to carry out his orders. He told the story of that East African pogrom in his popular book *Hunter,* and told it without bravado, comparing Hollywood's so-called horned fury to "an irritable, shortsighted old colonel who suddenly finds a trespasser in his garden."

Afterwards, when thornbush, acacia, and every other living thing was cleared away by labor gangs, the land, "as bare as a polished table," was turned over to the Wakamba for extensive cultivation. By now it is probably worthless, due to the severe soil erosion that usually accompanies such complete destruction of the natural ground cover.

Looking back on his thousand dead rhinos, Hunter himself commented: "Is it worth killing off these strange and marvelous animals just to clear a few more acres for a people that are ever on the increase? I do not know. But I know this. The time will come when there is no more land to be cleared. What will be done then?"

MAMBA

The Handicapped Hobo

Africa's most dangerous animal, judging from a human rather than a hunting point of view, is not the leopard, lion, elephant, Cape buffalo, or rhinoceros. He kills a greater number of men than all of them put together, although he is himself far easier to kill and cannot be compared in speed, agility, or wariness to any member of the Big Five. He is, in fact, so severely handicapped that his very presence in the modern world is a paradox and miracle.

The related dinosaurs, constructed and equipped far more soundly, have been extinct for some 120 million years. Africa's common crocodile, half-crippled by his own anatomy, not only carries on his archaic reptile stock but has long reigned as the continent's most successful man-eater, although he cannot turn his head to seize a man, use his fearful-looking jaws to kill a man, chew a man with his huge battery of teeth, or gulp a man's body down his narrow gullet.

Designed by nature as a fish-eating, crab-eating, garbage-eating scavenger, this decrepit hobo of the river banks and lake sides has become, despite himself, Africa's Public Enemy Number One. Known as Mamba in Swahili—and a far cry from the sleekly efficient serpents known as green or black mambas—he has built his reputation on the folly of his human victims.

Confronted by a single animal species that consistently dines upon men, Africans react with lackadaisical indifference to the hidden threat of his presence, flirting with the danger until it finally catches up with them. Men who would run screaming with terror from an eighty-pound leopard, will take a nap near the shore where flesh-eating animals twenty times larger, less cautious, and more likely to attack may be lurking. Women washing clothes wade in and *face the shore* to beat their laundry on the rocks; children, carried off by the hundreds every year, play in the shallows unattended. No one ever dreams of posting sentinels, and natives scoff or grumble if you try to suggest it. Such an elementary precaution would involve, as they have often told me, "too much trouble."

The solution to this tragic problem cannot be found in killing off the crocodiles. Whenever and wherever the colonial governments tried it, the near or total extermination of the giant reptiles harmed the very people it was supposed to aid: large predatory fish, formerly kept in check by the departed crocodiles, were now free to multiply without restraint and massacre the plant-eating fish population that forms the mainstay of the fishing natives' diet. Some careless individuals were spared a messy death, but entire tribes were soon menaced by starvation or, almost as disastrous, the loss of their traditional way of life.

White men in Africa, who rarely take the same foolish chances and are almost never killed by crocodiles, generally assume an attitude which is even sillier in its own peculiar style. It is almost ritual for them to call the crocodiles "evil," "cruel," "sneaky," "murderous," and "ugly," and to shoot innocently swimming, basking, even sleeping crocodiles with the moral fervor of Crusaders knocking off Saracens or medieval priests burning heretics and witches.

Missionaries and movie stars, poachers and sentimental nature lovers, long-time residents and two-week tourists join in chorus to revile the crocodiles, while trying, wantonly or systematically, to blast them off the map. Amateur hunters take their furious pot shots as they venture forth on credit-card safaris; professionals, who should be more responsible, slaughter crocodiles to indulge their passions while they profit from the sales of hides. Even staunch conservationists succumb—Teddy Roosevelt boasted in *African Game Trails* that he "always shot crocodiles when he got a chance to"—and twentieth-century titans like Sir Winston Churchill have been moved by the same vindictive urge that infects the common man. "I avow, with what regrets may be necessary," wrote Sir Winston after an early journey down the Nile, "an active hatred of these brutes and a desire to kill them. . . ."

Fear and hatred of reptiles, whether dangerous or not, appears to be a built-in part of our evolutionary heritage. Our remote primate ancestors must have had their troubles with the tree snakes, for today's apes and monkeys act as foolishly as most humans; they are frightened out of their wits—filled with almost superstitious terror when confronted by a harmless little garter snake, even a dead one. If equipped with guns and taught to use them, our fellow anthropoids would probably blast away at every reptile on the landscape. Given enough time and evolution, they might even dream up crocodile and serpent horrors to compare with mankind's own reptile "devils": Apep, the wicked night dragon or cloud serpent of the ancient Egyptians who patterned him after the common Nile crocodile; Tiamat, the closely related dragon fiend of Babylon; and the arch villain of the Bible, "the dragon, that old serpent, which is the Devil and Satan."

Crocodiles and snakes have been linked, since the dawn of history, with consummate and even cosmic evil. The animals themselves, hidden away behind their man-made devil masks, are loathed with a passion rarely shown toward any living creature. Snakes, who almost never bother humans when they are left alone, are denounced as "evil" because they sometimes bite in self-defense, usually when stepped upon. Crocodiles are called evil because they sometimes eat men—as they eat any other kind of animal protein that swims, drifts, or blunders into their path, including their own infant offspring. They do not, however, kill for social status, hatred, lust, or superstition, so they cannot qualify as sportsmen.

Designed to prey on smaller, more compact animals than men, Mamba swims with all four legs folded against his body, propelling and steering himself by lateral movements of his long tail while aiming his jaws at fish, crabs, or animal detritus which he tries to catch or engulf. He cannot turn his head sideways, because his cervical vertebrae bear bony ribs that stiffen and immobilize the neck; he has to turn his entire body and his jaws are forced to operate in a strictly horizontal plane. By taking an almost vertical position in the water, human swimmers whom he tries to catch can usually avoid his all-or-nothing lunges. When a cruising crocodile manages to find a human victim, he brings down his upper jaw with tremendous force, pinning the potential dinner against a lower jaw that is fixed and immobile. With most animals there would be no further problem. Mamba is now faced with a new predicament.

Closing his mouth was easy, but the muscles which *open* his mouth, raising the upper jaw, are so ineffectual that he can actually be muzzled with a piece of twine, and his rudimentary tongue, attached completely to his lower jaw, is useless for manipulating food. So, although he has an awesome-looking battery of long, hollow, conical, separately socketed, easily broken, and constantly replaced teeth, the antiquated reptile cannot chew. Using his jaws alone, he cannot even kill a man much less eat him.

The crocodile's mode of solving this dilemma is described, rather charmingly, in a still-current Oriental legend. According to the Malays, whose territorial range is shared by the huge estuarine, or salt-water crocodile, King Solomon himself once forbade Naga Besar—the Big Dragon—to take human life. The crocodile obeys the king in a way that Solomon, for all his wisdom, never dreamed of—by dragging his human victim under water and holding him there until he drowns. Thus he can always claim that the lake or river did it, disclaiming personal responsibility.

The crocodile can then remain below, holding his breath, for nearly an hour. But he cannot swallow while his head is under water, and even if he could, his gullet is too narrow to admit anything larger than a dog or hyena. So he surfaces again, holding his human victim's drowned but still inedible cadaver clamped in his viselike jaws, and then shakes it with tremendous force as he twirls around on the long axis of his body and tail. If he holds it by the arm, arm and body soon separate, leaving him a bite-size piece to toss down his gullet. He can then retrieve the corpse, unless another crocodile tries to steal his hard-earned dinner, and repeat the process with the other limbs and the head. The rest is hauled below and wedged in some convenient underwater cave to putrefy. He visits it from time to time—like a leopard going to his tree-hung carrion—tears off a piece of rotten flesh, brings it to the surface and tosses it down his gullet.

This carrion snack-bar system has undoubtedly provoked more horrified revulsion than any other phase of crocodile activities. Among many comments, one by the late Robert Ruark probably sums up the general feeling. Writing a crocodile profile entitled *The Vulgar Assassin,* he described "the unblinking eyes, the silence of his greasy slide through the water, the utter inexorability of his singleminded purpose, the finality of that steel-trap grip of massive jaw, and the ultimate horror of being drowned and taken to that stinking cave in a mudbank to await the monster's hungry pleasure. . . ."

Is such an end really an "ultimate horror"?

Some African tribes have always put out their dead for carrion-eating hyenas. They are, of course, regarded as primitive, but funeral rites administered by carrion-eating animals have been thought a fitting, proper, even holy way to go by at least one recognized world religion: the Parsees or Indian Zoroastrians place the bodies of their dead on *dakhmas,* or "towers of silence," exposing them to vultures and wild dogs. In recent years, as a concession to the prejudice of other religious groups, some of the Parsees have started to burn their dead by using powerful electric currents or placing the bodies in cement boxes so that they will not contaminate the sacred elements of fire and earth. Frankly, I fail to see why electrocution or being encased in cement—the classic fates of criminals and old-fashioned gangsters—constitute aesthetic or ecclesiastical improvements.

If I seem to lack sympathy for the crocodiles' already drowned victims, I might explain that I have come a good deal closer to the "ultimate horror" of Mamba's underwater pantry than those who talk and write about it with such outraged indignation. Had the crocodiles planned to sell my hide for making pocketbooks and high-heeled pumps, I might still be harboring a grudge. As it was, all they wanted to do was eat me—which seems reasonable enough.

Accompanied by six Bagoma fishermen and fifteen porters, I had gone to a place called Mwekarago Cove, on the eastern shore of Lake Tanganyika near the southern border of Burundi. My six helpers and I were fishing from native dugouts for a herringlike fish the natives call *ndagala,* but we weren't using native methods: we were using dynamite. Under ordinary circumstances, acting as a representative of the former Belgian Colonial Government, I would have brought to justice anyone, black or white, who committed such a flagrant violation of the government's strict conservation laws. Now, clandestinely, I was breaking the law myself, but I had what I considered ample reason: there was grave famine in the drought-stricken Mosso region of Burundi. People were dying of starvation, and there was no other way to feed them.

I had already trucked more than seven tons of fish to the Mosso country, returning to the lake with my helpers on October 24, 1955, to blast and gather a final load. Our four pirogues were grouped in a crude circle about three hundred feet from the shore, and some interested crocodile spectators cruised in the distance, ready to pick off any floating fish that came their way. Standing alone in my pirogue, preparing to drop a charge of dynamite, I held my lighter to the fuse . . . and the flame raced, sizzling, up a foot of the defective Bickford fuse cord. I tried to toss the charge in the water but, before I could get rid of it, two hundred grams of gelatin dynamite went off in my right hand. The rest of me was hurled into Lake Tanganyika.

Fearful of being implicated in a white man's sudden death, the Bagoma fishermen paddled off in a hurry, heading for their village some two miles to the north. But, miraculously, the blast hadn't killed me. Half-deafened, temporarily blinded in the right eye, with my neck and chest lacerated and the stump of my right wrist oozing blood, I found myself instinctively treading water as my dazed mind regained full awareness. I was a seemingly doomed bit of flotsam for the vigilant crocodile spectators, and they probably would have proved it if I had gone into horror-stricken paroxysms at the thought of their table manners or their underwater snack bars.

Two large crocodiles started toward me, their greenish-gray snouts and ridged, scaly backs carving a wrinkled wake through the water. I struck out toward the land, using an awkward left-handed Australian crawl while keeping my mutilated right arm flexed and pressed tightly against my ribs to reduce the blood loss.

I was still a hundred feet from shore when the crocodiles caught up with me. The two big ones I had spotted first were almost at my heels; as I turned my head, I saw five smaller ones approaching from my blind right side. I changed the angle of my body, assuming an almost vertical position as I kept moving toward the shore with a clumsy, one-handed dog paddle, splashing as violently as possible. Two more crocodiles approached on the left, one of them an enormous beast about twenty feet long—almost as large as a native dugout. He shot toward me like a ridged green torpedo; an instant later I heard a hollow *clack* at my rear, like the beat of a big talking drum. It was the sound of his jaws snapping shut. Seconds later, another *clack* sounded near my right shoulder and I felt a crocodile pass behind me, his scutes scraping my back and tearing off the remnants of my blast-tattered shirt. I sped up, swimming the last few yards with a heart that seemed to be bursting, staggered out of the water, and forced myself to walk at least fifty feet from shore, a fairly safe distance, before sitting down to rest.

My escape proved, and more conclusively than most crocodile-human meetings, that the handicapped reptiles have little chance to win if their intended victim simply keeps a little presence of mind. Had I been forced to swim, battered and bleeding as I was, through a school of man-eating oceanic sharks or South American piranha fish, I wouldn't be around to discuss it. My pursuers, luckily for me, were only crocodiles and very badly suited to the job of eating men.

They were, however, far more enterprising and aggressive than their Asiatic or American relatives who are, with one exception, timid and retiring in their ways.

Florida's own American crocodile has been convicted of exactly *one* fatal attack upon a human. It occurred during the 1930's, near Biscayne Bay, when a hunter shot a fifteen-footer and, believing the animal to be dead, kicked his victim. The crocodile lunged, knocked him down, and managed to catch him by the waist, leaving a set of deeply incised teeth-marks that eventually proved fatal. Another American cousin, the alligator—easily distinguished by his broader snout equipped with teeth that are hidden from sight when he closes his jaws—is a much less active, even sluggish animal. According to Ross Allen, the well-known Florida herpetologist, free-living alligators have made exactly one unprovoked attack upon the person of man. It wasn't even fatal.

Judging from these statistics, any American citizen who worries about alligator or crocodile attacks would do better to watch the sky for lightning bolts or even flying saucers. Acknowledging the bland nature of these reptiles, the states of Georgia, Florida, North Carolina, South Carolina, and Louisiana, and the United States Federal Government, have all exacted strict conservation laws to protect alligators from the hunters and hide-selling poachers who, at one time, threatened to wipe them out. In Florida, the only state where the American crocodile is found, eggs, young, and adults are all protected by law from unprovoked attacks by humans.

Mamba's South American relatives, including crocodiles and caimans, are basically inoffensive. Among the Orientals, the little five-foot Chinese alligator is far too small to harbor man-eating ambitions, while the giant slender-nosed gavial is a gentle soul who has never made an unprovoked attack. India's *magar,* or "mugger crocodile," has often been accused, but if he is really guilty of unprovoked attacks, I fail to understand how vast hordes of pious Hindu pilgrims, coming to bathe in the Ganges' sacred waters, fail to achieve instant reincarnation.

The estuarine, or salt-water crocodile, found from Southeast Asia to Australia, has made a very different kind of record. He is the world's largest surviving reptile, an antediluvian patriarch ranging up to thirty feet or more in length; and he is, although equally handicapped, an even more aggressive man-eater than Mamba. Naga Besar—the Big Dragon of the Malays—has, in fact, been guilty of conduct that Mamba never dreamed of: he has committed the reptile world's only recorded *mass* attack on human beings.

It happened during World War II, on Ramree Island in the Bay of Bengal, eighteen miles from the western coast of Burma. British troops, equipped with mortars and machine-guns, had trapped more than a thousand Japanese infantrymen, hemming them up in a coastal mangrove swamp. On the night of February 19, 1945, while both sides were exchanging heavy fire, the Japanese were suddenly assailed from a new quarter; wave after wave of salt-water crocodiles attacked, snatching impartially at dead, wounded, and living. By morning—out of a thousand Japanese—only twenty survived.

This would seem like deliberate, willful, even organized murder. But the waters of the Ramree Island swamp were already scented with blood and man-made carrion, exciting the crocodiles' hunger; while the crash of mortar and machine-gun fire may have driven them to madness. The crocodiles' sense of hearing is extremely keen and easily offended: they will roar in anger at a sudden loud noise, even the sound of an auto engine starting; during mating season they will brawl to the death, roused to fury by each other's booming, bellowing roars. The constant racket of a military barrage probably goaded the offenders to a state of collective hysteria; they may, ironically, have decided that the thundering British-Japanese combat was a kind of super mating battle.

Whatever the exact cause, the crocodile's only mass attack on human beings came as a direct result of World War II—man's own greatest attack upon man. The Big Dragons, inspired to uniquely aberrant behavior, killed hundreds of men on Ramree Island in the Bay of Bengal. Men, who have been at war almost constantly throughout recorded history, killed at least *fifty million* of their fellow humans from the start of World War II to its finish (*Guinness Book of World Records*).

That war, and not the putterings of hungry reptiles in their dens, was and remains the ultimate horror.

Mamba frequently attacks larger, stronger, more imposing animals than men, usually trying to seize them as they come to drink in the evening by river bank or lake side. His night vision is superb, for his eyes are backed on the retina by a layer of rhodopsin that gathers and reflects the light. They glow a brilliant yellow, like a lion's eyes, when light strikes them from the proper angle.

Half-grown buffalo and rhino calves, even a few adults, have been surprised by the keen-sighted crocodiles, swept off their feet by a blow from the thick, immensely powerful tail, jerked down a sloping bank and dragged under the surface to drown. Full-grown hippos are wisely left in peace, but a few wild-eyed crocodiles have actually attacked full-grown elephants. The encounter described by C. S. Stoles in *Sanctuary* ended with the dead crocodile wedged in a tree crotch. An incident I saw near Murchison Falls, in Uganda, was probably more typical of Mamba-Tembo matches. Seizing a female elephant by the trunk as she lowered it into the water, a big bull crocodile pulled at the sensitive trunk for all he was worth. Although it must have been extremely painful, the four-ton elephant pulled in the opposite direction, hauling some 1,500 pounds of stubborn reptile from the river. Then she trampled him to something that resembled filleted crocodile, all the while shrieking her opinion of the outrage.

Only the largest bull crocodiles will attempt to bag such huge and dangerous game. Smaller bulls and cows may try to pick off careless lions, cheetahs, antelopes, warthogs, men, or other fair-sized animals that come to the shore, but rely much more heavily on fish, crabs, mollusks, or whatever else they can catch or dredge in the water.

As a reptile, Mamba is a "cold-blooded" animal whose temperature will rise and fall with that of his environment. To keep it fairly constant, ranging six degrees on either side of 78 degrees Fahrenheit, he follows an endless cycle of alternate basking and bathing. After the nightly quest for food in the heat-retaining waters of river or lake, he comes ashore at dawn to bask on the banks in the gradually warming sunshine. As the temperature rises he may move into the shade for a while, walking or running on his short legs—but never

171

"crawling," as reptiles are commonly supposed to do, on their bellies. When the blaze of noon approaches, he returns to the water where he scrounges for his lunch, or digs up stones and swallows them—not for grinding food but for ballast—or simply lies near the surface like a rough-hewn submarine, revealing himself by the conning tower of his nostrils and the twin periscopes of his turreted eyes. Hitting the beach by mid-afternoon, he basks on the shore again, often with mouth agape to evaporate surplus heat from the moist lining of his jaws. Then, as darkness comes, he returns to the water and the cycle starts again.

During Mamba's time ashore, he is frequently attended by his own version of the rhino's tick-bird: the Egyptian plover, who is friend, valet, and sentinel combined.

Confident and fearless, the plover hops into the crocodile's gaping mouth, plucking leeches from the tongue and picking edible debris from between the teeth. Far from gobbling down the bird or resenting his attentions, Mamba seems to enjoy it. When tsetse flies are present in abundance, the plover runs along the ridged back, snapping up the insect pests. When danger threatens, he reacts instantly, warning his huge partner with an urgent cry that sounds like "Quick, quick, quick!" It is a true warning like the tick-bird's, for the plover will persist frantically, even to the point of dashing himself against a sleeping crocodile's head.

Completing the strange parallel between tick-bird and plover, Mamba's sentinel has his own assistant, the common sandpiper, who scavenges inside the crocodile's mouth but decamps when trouble comes, like the irresponsible egret.

Other birds who socialize with Mamba, on a less intimate level, include skimmers, wagtails, geese, tree ducks, little egrets, great white egrets, sacred ibises, and crowned cranes. All sit or strut along crocodile-crowded shores or sand bars or stroll along the crocodile's back from head to tail, as though he were the very log he much resembles. The peace is rarely broken, but the younger crocodiles, who are much more agile than their elders and less patient with the unspoken law, sometimes snap at diving pelicans or other birds.

There are, predictably, many native legends which attempt to explain these oddly affable relations between crocodiles and birds. Most of the folk tales feature a boastful chicken or francolin who goes to a river bank and hails an astounded crocodile as his brother, explaining that crocodile and chicken wives both lay eggs and their babies both have an egg-tooth, enabling them to pick their way into the outer world. Deeply impressed by the chicken's logic, the crocodile swears off eating birds. Then the chicken leaves triumphantly, finds a python, hails him as another long-lost brother, and delivers the same little lecture on obstetrics. Gravely insulted, the python swallows the chicken whole and does so to this day.

Oddly enough, crocodile and chicken are, in fact as well as legend, closer relatives than crocodile and python. Back in the Lower Triassic Age, some two hundred million years ago, there was a stock of primitive reptiles now called the *Thecodontia,* or "socket-teeth." Small and insignificant-appearing as they were, the thecodonts spawned four highly impressive groups of descendants who are called, collectively, the *Archosauria,* or "ruling reptiles": crocodiles, pterodactyls, and the two zoological orders of fantastically diversified dinosaurs. While they we're at it, the versatile thecodonts also hatched a related group of creatures who are, as T. H. Huxley pointed out, "highly modified reptiles," although we usually distinguish them as birds.

All of the thecodont descendants share some striking physical characteristics over and above their separately socketed teeth, lost in birds since the days of toothed, lizard-tailed *Archaeopteryx* and the later fisherman-diver *Ichthyornis.* The same basic master plan applies in all to vertebrae, ribs, and skull. And, dominating their evolutionary history, there has been an upright, two-legged gait. Obvious among the birds, pterodactyls, and such dinosaurs as *Struthiomimus,* the reptilian mock ostrich, or the notorious predator *Tyrannosaurus rex,* traces of the bipedal gait are evident in the shortened forelimbs of those dinosaurs who reverted, secondarily, to a quadrupedal way of life, even giants like the great swamp-dwelling brontosaurs. All of them show, to a greater or lesser extent, this ancient mark of the thecodonts—two-legged animals who walked upon the earth two hundred million years before the first man was born.

So does the crocodile.

Although it isn't too noticeable, since adaptation to his present way of life has greatly shortened all four of his web-footed limbs, Mamba's hind legs are appreciably longer and stronger than his forepaws. More remarkably, crocodilian behavior still displays vestiges of the past: infant crocodiles paddle vertically like sea horses until they start to swallow stones. Once installed in their stomachs, the ingested stones move the center of gravity forward. Then, and only then, can

173

the young crocodiles assume a horizontal position in the water.

A true son of the old thecodont breed, the ancestrally two-legged crocodile is the only living, and oddly friendly, relative of the two-legged bird. Snakes are members of a very different reptile stock—as the Congolese chicken discovered, to his sorrow—which developed along its own lines during that long two hundred million years. Their only real relatives are lizards and, much more remotely, the lizardlike New Zealand tuatara, a living fossil famed for his vestigial third eye. Even more isolated among existing reptiles are the immensely ancient turtles—plodding conservatives who have survived from the reptile world's pre-Triassic dawn by retreating into heavily armored shells.

Crocodiles have their own armor, different in form but developed in the same basic fashion. Along back and tail, there are pitted bony plates in the deeper layer of the skin, covered by quadrangular horny shields or scales of varying size, arranged in longitudinal rows with furrows of softer skin between. The keeled back is greenish-black in color, while the softer belly skin is lighter, sometimes approaching a murky yellow. There may be 150 scales in all, but imposing as they seem, they are easily penetrated by a soft-nosed bullet. Hide-hunters aim, however, for the brain and never shoot at swimming crocodiles who will dive if wounded and sink if dead. They shoot at the eyes or external ear-openings of those who bask or sleep along the shore; the brain shot kills instantly, preventing the crocodiles from taking to the water.

Mamba's external nostrils, located near the tip of his snout, have valvelike lids and there is a valvelike fold of flesh on the rear part of his tongue which keeps the water from entering his windpipe when he opens his jaws to take swimming prey. His turreted eyes have upper and lower lids, plus special transparent membranes for use, like skin-divers' goggles, under water. The eyes, golden and rather beautiful, are also equipped with lachrymal glands whose natural function has inspired what is probably the silliest of civilized man's animal legends.

Classical, medieval, and post-medieval scholars, sages, and poets—even Sir Francis Bacon, the father of inductive reasoning who constantly deplored fallacies—all repeated the same bizarre tale which is embalmed in current speech as an often-used cliché. They claimed that African waters harbored a supremely evil beast who sobbed in false distress to lure kindly travelers to his aid; then, shedding hypocritical tears, crammed them down his gullet. This fantastic animal, accused of conduct only humans could conceive of, was usually referred to as "the cruell craftie crocodile." His unprincipled behavior was described, of course, as weeping "crocodile tears."

The facts of the matter are a bit less melodramatic. Because the blazing tropical sun causes heavy evaporation, even from his cornified skin and scales, Mamba's blood sometimes becomes excessively saline. Then, since his kidneys cannot excrete all of the excess salt, the rest is eliminated through his eye glands as large but utterly innocent drops of salty water. "Tears, idle tears," Mamba might exclaim with Tennyson, "I know not what they mean. . . ."

Situated just behind his eyes are the small external ear holes and the valvelike flaps that close them when the crocodile submerges. They haven't led to any wild legends, but they were used in the remote past for a wild, wild purpose— to hang golden earrings on.

During three thousand years of Egyptian history, ending after the Roman take-over, pet crocodiles were kept in temple pools by cultists of the crocodile-headed god, Sebek. Tame and affable, the holy crocodiles were hand fed with sacrificial human flesh and decked out with precious ornaments—dainty golden earrings for their flapped ear holes and jeweled bracelets for their webbed forepaws. Their adoring congregations hailed the golden-eyed animals as symbols of the golden sunrise; some of the faithful even identified the crocodile god with Ra, the great sun himself. There were, however, rival sects who denounced Sebek and his holy crocodiles as diabolical night dragons or cloud serpents—the view that was taken over by the Babylonians and Hebrews— and expressed their hatred and contempt by reviling the old dragon-devil as "Stinking Face."

They had, sadly enough, a good reason.

On each side of Mamba's lower jaw, there are highly active musk glands. Aided by another pair in his cloaca, underneath his tail, they exude an amazingly pungent odor whenever the crocodile grows angry, frightened, or excited. The reek of musk, combining with carrion odors arising from the gullet, produces an especially revolting mouth perfume— "ba-a-a-d breath," as it is called in TV commercials, as well as bad body odor, and a bad reputation.

"To my taste," remarked that dedicated game gourmet, Sir Samuel Baker, "nothing can be more disgusting than crocodile flesh. I have eaten almost everything, but although I have

175

tasted crocodile I could never succeed in swallowing it. The combined flavor of bad fish, rotten flesh, and musk is the *carte de dîner* offered to the epicure."

Personally, I don't agree. I, too, have eaten almost everything, dining for many long months on the caterpillars, termites, worms, beetle larvae, mice, and rats which the Congo Pygmies feature on their unpretentious daily menus, plus pottos, aardvarks, pangolins, lizards, snakes, and whatever else they sometimes bag for the pot. So, absolutely free of food prejudice, I offer my opinion: crocodile flesh tastes like indifferent rather than bad fish, slightly flavored with musk. Most natives are more enthusiastic, relishing Mamba's flesh and eating all they can get. We are not, however, "epicures."

Civilized man dislikes the smell of musk unless it is made into flowery perfumes, but crocodiles themselves prefer it in the undiluted form. The musk glands play a much more meaningful role than mere response to fear or rage, reaching their functional peak during the dry season which, for them, is the time of sexual arousal.

Swelling into pinkish-colored balls, the glands of bull crocodiles—and, to a lesser extent, those of cows—exude vast quantities of all-pervading musk. The smell persistently adheres to crocodile paths, even under water, where they skim lake or river bottoms, touching down with the oozing undersides of jaws and tails. Apparently they follow each other's trails of scent, like enormous dogs sniffing at submarine lampposts, until sizable groups congregate. Then, always at night, they carry out their courtship.

It is a brutal affair, unlike the rather placid scenes of alligator mating which have been observed in Florida or Louisiana bayous: the female alligator usually takes the initiative, grunting propositions while she teases a bored-looking male with cumbersome frottage of head and tail. Crocodile cows watch, passively, from the shallows while the bulls stage tremendous Mesozoic-style brawls, demonstrating by sound, smell, and action their virility and power.

Bellowing, roaring, or twirling on the surface of the water with their jaws pointed skyward, the bulls work themselves into a state of ever-mounting passion. With every deep, rumbling, drumlike roar, their swollen glands squirt musk, scenting air and water with the aphrodisiac perfume. Then, apparently maddened by the miasmal aroma and the sound of each other's booming roars, the bulls fight, inflicting terrible or even fatal wounds. They aren't really battling for the favors of one cow or another; instead, the violent melees seem to stimulate all within the area, male and female alike, to the point of actual mating.

When a triumphant bull approaches one of the waiting cows, she usually responds with some minor amorous foreplay, rearing her head and neck out of the water while she emits creaking groans. The pair then copulate, as do whales and dolphins, with their bellies tightly pressed together.

The cow is fertilized by the insertion into her reptilian cloaca of a primitive penislike organ which is extruded from the cloaca of the bull. Similar in structure to the male organ possessed by a few birds such as ducks, geese, ostriches, and bustards, it has no internal tube like a true penis, only a deep groove that runs the length of its surface. But it is capable of true erection, unlike the primitive male organs of lizards and snakes, and the crocodile can actually use it for the act of rape: if a cow is not sufficiently excited, the bull will sometimes throw her on her back in the shallows, performing the sexual act by sheer force of superior weight and strength.

Their mating act completed, bull and cow go their separate ways. Soon she will drive away any and all interested bulls, instinctively aware that they constitute a very real menace to her oncoming brood. Digging in a sandy bank, she makes a hole up to two feet deep and three feet in diameter, then lays sixty or more equal-ended eggs the size of goose eggs, depositing them in three clutches and carefully covering each with a layer of sand.

Her nest is quite primitive compared to that of the cow alligator. The alligator gathers leaves, grass, bark, and twigs to build a cone-shaped heap above the ground, then lays her eggs within the giant bird's-nest. She does not sit upon the eggs and neither does the crocodile. Like those aberrant birds, the Pacific and Australian megapodes and brush turkeys, they let the sun's heat or the heat of fermenting vegetation perform the incubation for them. Both, however, guard their nests with grim maternal fervor, attempting to drive away any intruders bent on stealing eggs. In America, alligator nests are raided by skunks, raccoons, opossums, pigs, and bears; in Africa, crocodile eggs are stolen and devoured by monitor lizards, mongooses, civets, hyenas, jackals, Marabou storks, and even men. Hungry natives discard the musky whites and devour the yolks; Westerners, including Teddy Roosevelt who often ate and praised the dish, prefer the yolks scrambled.

If the harried mother crocodile succeeds in keeping the eggnappers at bay during the two months it takes the eggs to mature, her babies will hatch out—under ground. Using the temporary egg-tooth, the eight-inch-long infants peck their way through the leathery shells and set up a chorus of muffled little croaks. Hearing their cries, even from a distance, the anxious crocodile rushes to her nest and pushes away the sand or hardened earth, freeing her buried brood. Then she shepherds the hatchlings to the water, watching over the flock for several weeks and trying to defend them.

Infant crocodiles are just as tasty as eggs, and are preyed upon by every sizable bird, mammal, or reptile who can catch them. Bull crocodiles are prime offenders, unconscious cannibals gulping their own offspring as though they were mere fish. Even the cows, as time fades their maternal instinct, leave the broods to their own devices and begin to prey, unthinkingly, on the infants they at first defended.

The babies, equipped at hatching time with a full set of teeth, hide away from all of their enemies, parents included, in clumps of papyrus or other sheltering weeds. Paddling upright in gregarious little fleets and yapping at each other sociably while they snap up spiders and insects, they must dodge attacks from eagles and hawks above, catfish and turtles below, and a wide assortment of eager mammals by the shore. Those lucky few who live to be a year old, perhaps no more than one in every hundred, reach a length of eighteen inches and are now ready for other food: shore-dwelling mice and rats, crabs, mollusks, and fish. They now grow some nine to eighteen inches a year, living all the while in hiding, until they reach a length of seven feet. Then the growth-rate slows to an inch or two a year and they emerge to lead adult lives.

Cow crocodiles become sexually mature when they reach the length of eight feet, at age nineteen or twenty. Bulls develop slightly faster and grow to a larger size. As for the maximum size and life-span, no one is certain.

Early explorers of the Nile and Congo rivers and the great African lakes, reported seeing twenty-five- and even thirty-footers; today a twenty-footer is extremely rare. But the crocodiles aren't getting any smaller; men are slaughtering them before they live long enough to reach their former size. I don't use the term maximum size, because there is no real limit to the growth of any crocodile; they have a slow metabolic rate which enables them to hibernate buried in the mud during prolonged dry seasons, a slow growth-rate indefinitely prolonged, and no fixed life span.

Extinct crocodiles from Texas' Big Bend reached estimated

lengths of fifty to sixty feet, perhaps because they lived before the age of hunters, poachers, sportsmen, and their softnosed bullets. The skull of *Phobosuchus,* mounted and displayed at the American Museum of Natural History, is six feet long (the skull alone!). Extinct dinosaur relatives reached lengths of up to a hundred feet; if their growth-rate was at all comparable, how long did it take for them to reach that age? Five hundred years? A millennium?

Man's growth, like that of all mammals, slows after sexual maturity is reached, then stops. His body will die, if violence does not intervene, from old age. Mamba, on the other hand, may be gourmandized while still a hapless egg; picked off as a wary but unlucky infant; bitten in half if he offends a hippo mother; killed in the cause of love by a rival crocodile; or shot in the brain by a man who hates his hide or wants to sell it. He may die in many different ways, but he never really dies a natural death.

Barring accident or assassination, the old devil-dragon is virtually immortal. He may not be wise, beautiful, gentle, loving, chaste, temperate, humble, or generous, but he is patient and enduring. Like the rivers themselves, he "just keeps rolling along."

MAKAKO

The Well-Organized Tribesman

At river's edge, where careless humans face the crocodile-ridden waters with their rears, an alert tribe of so-called subhumans acts with disciplined intelligence.

An advance guard of strong warriors leads the march toward the water. They are fanged and sometimes maned like lions, but their jaws are long and doglike and they walk on four manlike hands. Equipped with keen-sighted, full-color stereoscopic vision, they scan the water and the shore line. Then, if satisfied, they voice the short bark they always use to signal "All Clear!" The entire tribe, from twenty-five to two hundred individuals in all, then comes to drink, relax, gossip, squabble, play, or pick berries on the shady banks while appointed sentinels stand guard on the ground and in the trees. Unlike their human counterparts, the children and diminutive mothers—maneless, short-fanged females less than half the size of the males—are extremely well guarded. If the look-

181

outs spot a pair of turreted eyes and nostrils or a scaly back carving an approaching wake through the water, they give the sharp, shrill bark that means "Danger!". The crocodiles never get a chance to catch and eat baboons.

When the tribe is on the move, foraging for food on rocky plains or lightly timbered savannahs, they march with advance, rear, and flanking guards of junior warriors. The older, more experienced, higher ranking males—a council of monkey chieftains who dominate tribal politics, society, and sex—remain near the center of the group as an inner line of defense for the half-pint mothers, juveniles, and children. They are a sort of baboon Pentagon, seasoned officers who direct group strategy, while the young flankers are the common troops. But when danger threatens, military tactics differ sharply from our own: the generals rush forward to the front lines where they take up more exposed and dangerous positions than their troops. Mothers and children now retreat while the tribal males, united in the common cause, stand their ground to bluff or fight the enemy.

Hyenas, jackals, cheetahs, even leopards, usually decline to meet the challenge. They like to pick off stragglers but they prudently avoid open conflict with the organized troops. The outraged, tusk-baring monkey warriors will not stage their own retreat unless threatened by lions or rifle-armed human hunters.

Brave as they are, baboons realize that bands of fifty- to seventy-five-pound monkeys are no match for three- or four-hundred-pound cats who hunt, unlike leopards, in their own cooperating bands. Whenever possible the baboons try to take refuge in the trees, where they move rather clumsily compared to the lightly built, extremely agile forest monkeys. The lions, who are even less suited to arboreal warfare, rarely try to follow.

When sentinels or flankers spot rifle-armed hunters, the baboons retreat along the ground, keeping a safe thousand yards or so out of rifle range. If the hunters follow, the baboons stay on the move, pausing from time to time to hoot and shriek their righteous indignation. If they hold the high ground (usual baboon strategy) they may shower down a fusillade of stones, sticks, and dirt. If the hunters still persist in following, the baboons may try to stalk and surprise them. They know that some members of the tribe will die, but they also know that the rest can then overwhelm the humans, literally tearing them apart limb from limb. They are even shrewd enough to know that the humans know it.

182

Aside from men and social insects such as ants and termites, they are the only animals on earth who understand and practice organized war.

The hefty, dog-headed, ground-dwelling monkeys are called *nyani* in Swahili. They are known by that name throughout East Africa, but I seldom heard a Congolese native refer to them as anything but Makako. That chattering, tooth-baring word is in fact the baboon's oldest and aptest Central African name, later adapted by the eighteenth-century naturalist Buffon to describe the heavily-built Asiatic monkeys now called macaques, many of whom have taken to the ground and play baboonish roles all the way from China and Japan to their isolated Western outposts at North Africa's Barbary Coast and the opposing Rock of Gibraltar.

The words "makako" and "macaque" were both, however, banned from all usage in the former Belgian Congo and are still banned in today's independent Congolese republic. The baboon's very name is regarded as a gross insult, a near obscene term of abuse. Congolese natives used it for centuries to revile other natives whom they considered inferior, matching our own usage of the epithet "big baboon" to describe someone who is brutal, vulgar, and obnoxious. A few white bigots based in the Congo tried to use the old native insult on their "boys," but they didn't get away with it. The Belgian colonial government punished white offenders with a 500-franc fine, threatening repeated offenders with disciplinary action or expulsion from the Congo.

Ironically, natives kept on using that forbidden word "makako," as well as another they considered even more insulting: they called each other *flamand*, or "Fleming," the designation of a pedestrian Belgian tribe rather than a tribe of monkey pedestrians.

Personally, although I am half Flemish (the other more romantic-minded half is Frenchman-style Walloon) I would just as soon be called Makako. Having watched baboon communities in action and lived, laughed, and suffered through a long series of baboon pets, I have come to realize how much we have in common with these tough-minded monkeys. Baboons, in their broad Rabelaisian way, are just as friendly-mean, altruistic-egotistic, and appealingly obnoxious as their poor relations, present company included. Of all our fellow primates they are indisputably the single type whose temperament and way of life most resemble our own.

Africa's great apes hide away in remote forest strongholds.

The chimpanzee, man's closest living relative and his closest rival in the field of abstract reasoning, never leaves the equatorial forest where he feeds in the fruit-laden trees, spending a scant quarter of his life on the ground. The gorilla, grown too heavy for the trees and only partially adapted to the ground, shuffles along the forest floor, munching bamboo shoots or wild celery. Aside from man, who is seldom met, neither has significant enemies. Snakes and monkey-eating eagles concentrate on smaller prey; leopards have little liking for the manlike taste of chimpanzee flesh and too much good sense to tangle with the huge, immensely powerful gorillas.

Baboons, mere monkeys that they are, have taken a more adventurous path. Like our own ancestors, they have abandoned the sheltering trees—that primate Garden of Eden where everything comes a little too easy—to face the harsh challenge of life upon the savannahs.

Foraging for a living on the open plains, baboons encounter perils that their forest relatives avoid: lions, cheetahs, jackals, and hyenas, all of whom relish baboon flesh as much or more than antelope or zebra meat. They must also deal with the same ancient enemy who prowls through the forest —Chui, the monkey-hunting leopard who considers baboon flesh second only to dog—and deal with him under more exposed conditions. As a final problem, their choice of habitat brings them into frequent contact with another dedicated foe, a gang of fratricidal relatives whose earliest prehistory was grimly intermingled with the trials and tribulations of baboons.

From South Africa to Lake Victoria and Tanganyika's Olduvai Gorge, where Dr. Louis Leakey is still digging up their tell-tale fossil bones, the founders of our human dynasty literally fought their way to manhood on the harsh savannahs. Those ground-dwelling australopithecine "man apes" were impelled by a motivation that was new to the primates, a constant need and craving to devour meat. To satisfy this physiological demand, they developed a psychological style that was also new to the ape and monkey world: they became fanatically, relentlessly aggressive.

Their method was the only one that could have served clawless, short-fanged, less than Pygmy-sized creatures bent on killing for a living: they fought in bands and they employed weapons. Club or rock in hand, the prehuman hunting troops surrounded and attacked the smaller antelopes, then went on to battle with baboons. When they won, smashing Makako over the head with an antelope humerus club, they

Grooming plays a vital role in promoting fairly relaxed relations within the tribe; it is, in fact, the only form of friendly intercourse between social inferiors and superiors. Above left, a West African drill; left, East African yellow baboons. Above right, South Africa's chacma baboon.

Above left and left:

A pygmy chim-
panzee baby (top)
and a fully grown
chimpanzee (right)
of the larger, more
common species.
Below right: a
month-old female
gorilla baby and
her sixteen-year-
old father (below
left), a giant
"silverback."

San Diego Zoo Photo

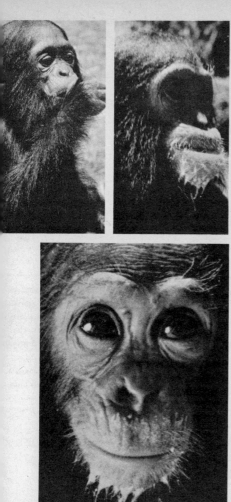

Sophie, a chimpanzee, whose mood obviously improves as she eats. The last picture shows an expression of satisfaction and deep gratitude.

Jean-Pierre Hallet

The author touching noses with a striped hyena. The worst thing about hyenas is their reputation. If well treated, they make playful and extremely affectionate pets.

Julie Macdonald

Right: The hundred-pound hyena has the strongest jaws of any living carnivore and weak, almost crippled hindquarters.

Photo Satour

With their small manes barely visible, the fastest animals on earth lope across their hunting grounds. This picture was taken in South Africa, but cheetahs also range from Sudan to the East African coast. Although they formerly flourished in Arabia and India, wanton hunting by humans has already brought the non-African varieties to near-extinction.

Photo Satour

The gemsbok, who dwells on the southern savannahs below the Zambezi River, is the largest variety of oryx. His northern relative, the Arabian oryx, is said to have been the living model of the fabled unicorn when seen sideways. Both sexes are horned, and both use their unwieldy-looking weapons by tucking their heads far between their forelegs to bring the horn-tips into play. Record horns: bull—38 inches; cow—40 inches.

Photo Satour

Reticulated giraffes at a waterhole, showing four characteristic poses of the world's tallest animal: browsing on loftily placed leaves, scanning the horizon for lions or human hunters, widening their stance to bend, and doing a full "split" in order to drink.

Photo Satour

Waliangulu poachers in eastern Kenya, excited by their kill, are dancing around the body of the fallen elephant. The poachers' total return on the whole operation may not exceed $5—one dollar per ton for the useless, wanton slaughter of the world's largest land mammal.

Impalas, famed for the grace and elegance of their high-bounding gait, in the Kagera National Park, northeast Rwanda.

His dinner seemed impossibly large, but it was within his powers: the bones of a python's upper and lower jaws can move outward and forward and the two halves of the lower jaw are connected at the chin by an elastic ligament alone.

feasted on his brains. It was a rather crude beginning for aggressors who would graduate, a few million years later, to machine-guns and atomic bombs, but it was honest and immensely stimulating: our founding fathers hunted for meat rather than sport, and the hunting life placed an evolutionary premium on the sort of ingenuity that led—as a mere by-product of bigger and better weapons—to primitive cultures and eventually to civilization.

Makako, having survived his early role of monkey Abel to the man ape's fratricidal Cain, was and remains a root-grubbing vegetarian. He snacks on locusts, scorpions, lizards, frogs, eggs, birds, or even small mammals, but sporadically and without the dedicated passion that his human relatives feel for red meat. His physiology does not drive him on incessantly to obtain steaks, chops, cutlets, hamburgers, or hot dogs, so he has not come to share our own predatory turn of mind. His prime problem is defense against predators, especially the great cats who find his flesh so much tastier than our own, and he has learned to stand his ground and fight in furious bands, to wage mass defensive warfare even as we wage mass aggressive wars.

The use of the word "aggressive" to describe baboons strikes me as a serious mistake. Baboons live peacefully and even fraternize at close quarters with antelopes, zebras, giraffes, warthogs, and every other nonpredatory animal they encounter. They will even root around at the base of trees while elephants are busy stripping off the leaves and twigs. But when teased, provoked, or threatened, they explode into paroxysmic fighting rages, telling their enemies to go to hell or attacking their attackers. They have not, however, killed or hunted men for nondefensive reasons and they have never come to depend, as we have, on external weapons.

Baboons possess, like most monkeys and apes, the rudiments of the weapon-using instinct. Aside from angry salvos of sticks, stones, dirt, or even dung, they have reportedly rolled boulders down a mountain side to repel riflemen who opened fire on them. For actions such as these, and others, they must be considered tool-using animals. They are even spur-of-the-moment weapon-users, but they would never dream of *carrying* a stick or stone for constant use, much less manufacturing chipped flints, spears, bows, arrows, rifles, cannons, and bombs. They rely instead on their canine teeth, huge fighting tusks almost as large as a leopard's; on the brute strength of their heavily muscled shoulders and arms, more than twice as strong as a man's although they are only half his size; and on the gang war tactics which guard baboon tribes from the swifter, stronger, better-armed predators.

This is why Makako lives and acts like such a disconcerting parody of man. Baboons left the primate Garden of Eden even as we did, learning to stake out and hold their territories on the open-skied savannah battleground. The less adventure-minded primates stayed behind, picking fruit or foraging beneath the shelter of their comforting ancestral trees. Instead of driving off their enemies, they chose to hide or run away.

That decision has led the forest-dwellers to the prospect of extinction. Of nearly two hundred living forms that comprise our primate order—including tree shrews, tarsiers, lemurs, galagos, marmosets, New World monkeys, Old World monkeys, anthropoid apes, and men—fully forty-seven are by now considered "rare and endangered species" by the Survival Service Commission of the Swiss-based International Union for Conservation of Nature and Natural Resources. The long list of dying primates, as recorded in the IUCN's *Red Data Book,* includes twenty-six lemurs, eight New World monkeys, nine Old World monkeys, and four apes—the dwarf gibbon, orangutan, pygmy chimpanzee, and mountain gorilla. For species after species, the IUCN lists grimly echoing "Reasons for Decline":

> Felling of the forest . . . burning and rooting up of trees . . . clearing of the indigenous forest for settlement . . . reduction of habitat forests by encroachment of agriculture and human occupation . . . heavy cultivation . . . destruction of the habitat by agriculturalists and by the intrusion of large herds of domestic cattle . . . destruction of the forest . . . extensive destruction of the forest . . . uncontrolled destruction of the forest.

They stayed behind in Eden, but the mounting pressure of exploding world population forces men to chop, uproot, and burn more and more of Eden every year. Lemurs, monkeys, and apes die with the dying trees, but in all that long list of "rare and endangered species," you may search in vain for a single species of baboon. The so-called black baboon, or black ape of Celebes, who has made the danger list, is just a large stumpy-tailed macaque who spends most of his time picking fruit in the trees. All eight of Africa's tough-minded pedestrians—the primate clan which faces the widest range of predators in the most exposed habitat, unprotected by any

194

conservation laws—continue literally and metaphorically to "hold their ground."

The gelada baboon of southern Ethiopia, who is probably the connecting link between Asian macaques and African baboons, looks like a big black poodle dog with a flowing lion's mane, a long tufted tail, and a red, naked-skinned breast. He lives in very large troops that favor rocky ravines in the high mountains but descend to plunder cultivated fields. As Darwin recounts in *The Descent of Man,* gelada bands successfully attacked the Duke of Coburg-Gotha's riflemen in the mountain pass of Mensa, rolling down boulder after boulder until the pass itself was blocked. According to other reputable authorities, they sometimes use the same tactics when involved in territorial disagreements with neighboring tribes of hamadryad baboons. Others deny *in toto* that baboons ever employ such tactics in any kind of dispute. Hopefully, Dr. Hans Kummer, a foremost authority on hamadryas geladas, who is now on a one-year Ethiopian field trip, may be able to provide some decisive answers.

The hamadryas baboons, widely spread through the rocky near-desert plains of Ethiopia, Arabia, and Sudan, look like ashen-gray blends of poodle, lion, and sphinx, fully equipped with flowing manes and tufted tails but with longer heads and snouts than the black geladas. They were tamed and trained by the ancient Egyptians, who probably imported them from Sudan, to perform as pets, companions, servants, and even priests. Sacred to Thoth, the god of wisdom, high-class hamadryas baboons presided over morning prayer in temples, facing the sunrise with their upraised hands and barking sanctimonious prayers. Lower-class hamadryas harvested and sorted fruit, weeded gardens, pumped and carried water, swept and cleaned temples and houses, and waited at table, working as butlers and maids.

A little more recently, Julie Macdonald's pet hamadryas female, Abu, whom she described in her well-named and very entertaining book *Almost Human,* lived the life of a true twentieth-century child, becoming addicted to television. Abu's favorite program was the San Diego Zoo's lively show *Zoorama:* she was fascinated by the monkeys, enraged and horrified by the snakes and, predictably, bored and restless during the commercials. But when Julie gave a mop and broom to Abu, hoping that her pet might employ them in the old Egyptian style, the TV-minded baboon neither mopped nor swept the Macdonald's Pasadena dwelling. Instead, she used the wooden handles as levers to topple the furniture. As Cicero once remarked, *"O tempora, o mores!"*

The chacma baboons of Southern Africa's rocky mountain plains are very large, maneless, almost mastiff-sized, and grayish-black with purplish faces, white-ringed eyes and deep black heads, hands, and feet. The Hottentots claim that chacmas can speak but try to keep it quiet for fear that men should make them work for their living. They have good reason, for chacmas have been trained to work as goatherds, watchdogs, water-diviners, oxen-drivers, and even baby-sitters. The most famous working chacma of them all, Jack the "Baboon Signalman of Wietenhage," served a veteran railroad employee, James Wide, who had lost both legs in an accident. Jack pumped and carried water, fetched firewood, cleaned the house, pulled Wide's little wooden platform along the rails, and learned to pull the levers that operated the railroad switches. He started by imitating his master but eventually performed without supervision, pulling the proper lever as approaching trains signaled with a coded number of toots. (Like most baboons, he could count up to five.) During his nine-year career as a railroad man, the baboon never made a single error.

The West African mandrills, more than any other baboon species or perhaps any other animal, are usually described as "ugly," "hideous," or "utterly revolting." People are shocked, embarrassed, but oddly fascinated by the brightly colored callus pads on the rear ends of all baboons—their built-in pillows for sleeping in a sitting position, as baboons do, on an otherwise painful tree branch. With mandrills they are shocked by front as well as rear, for mature males have enormous, sausage-shaped, ribbed and grooved blue-and-violet-striped swellings on either side of their massive scarlet snouts. Female cheek adornments are much smaller and are solid toned in a dull shade of blue. Both sexes have olive-blackish fur and stumpy little tails that are carried jauntily erect like a pug dog's. They are the largest living monkeys—adult males weigh 130 pounds or more and are immensely powerful—but for all their great size or probably because of it, they are less forward in their ways than other baboon species: they stake out territories on the forest floor rather than the open country.

The drills, also West African forest-dwellers, are smaller, more lithely built, brownish-furred, and black-faced with small uncolored cheek adornments. According to Richard Lydekker, one of the most respected naturalists of this century, the drill is "one degree less repulsive than the male mandrill" who is of all living mammals the most "suggestive of the forms imagined during a nightmare." According to me, both of them look like fine robust baboons and the drills have melancholy, rather Lincolnesque faces. (Abe Lincoln's enemies frequently reviled him with the epithet "baboon.") I see no reason why a drill or mandrill should be shaped and colored at either end like the Venus de Milo, and I fail to understand why the standards of a single primate species, no matter how "sapient," should be used to judge some 3,500 species of living mammals, 6,000 reptiles, 3,000 amphibians, 8,600 birds, 25,000 fishes, and an estimated 750,000 to 1,500,000 insects. If baboons had beauty contests—to elect "Miss Savannah," or "Miss Root Grubber"—I doubt that they would cast a single ballot for a smooth-skinned, snoutless redhead or brunette with an uncallused bottom.

There are three types of "true" or savannah baboons, now classified as single species: olive or anubis baboons, brown or guinea baboons, and yellow baboons, who are hardly lemon-colored as the name might suggest but dressed in brownish-yellow fur with naked black face, hands, and feet. Medium-sized, maneless, and with long tails, the savannah dwellers are the real Makakos or McCoys—boisterous hillbilly bands that roam the equatorial plains, galloping on all fours with the babies riding jockey-style on their mothers' backs, grubbing in the ground with their strong hands, lifting up rocks to search for tasty scorpions, raiding native fields, or cussing out their enemies, animal and human.

They may give the casual impression of being rootless nomads, brazen vagabonds mooching from place to place, but they are the very opposite. *Mepwo l-otimite-n-gop enye,* say the Masai, and the old proverb means very simply, "Baboons will not leave their own ground."

Although they travel four or five miles per day, marching back and forth to water holes and feeding grounds, they never pass beyond the limits of their ten- to fifteen-square-mile territory, returning at night to fixed community sleeping places. Depending on local topography, the sleeping place may be a large tree situated near the water, a cave, or a rock pile on the high ground that baboons favor. All such sites serve as natural strongholds where the tribe has its best chance to survive the nightly terror of the prowling cats, and all are defended with the kind of hooting, shrieking, tooth-baring rage which I like to call baboon "patriotism."

"Patriotism is easy to understand in America," Calvin

Coolidge once remarked. "It means looking out for yourself by looking out for your country." It is even easier to understand among Africa's baboons. To a far greater extent than civilized men who live in civilized communities, they cannot survive as individuals and they know it. They not only have to fight their own battles, but they have to watch over and defend tuskless, baby-laden females only half their own size who are not, as with many animals, "more deadly than the male," but are actually unfit to survive without male protection.

A similar relationship exists between male and female humans, or at least existed in the good old days "when men were men and women were glad of it." Female suffrage never would have come, I suspect, if our ladies were a scant three feet high and menaced on every side by leopards and hyenas. As it is, men no longer fight to protect their ladies in the noble style of baboons but hide behind their newspapers to avoid giving up their subway seats to working girls and career women. The ladies look indignant at this and other inconvenient forms of equal treatment, conveniently forgetting that they asked for it.

To protect themselves, their mates, children, and territory, baboon patriots maintain a strictly organized society which has sometimes been compared, and unjustly, to an animal version of Nazi Germany, complete with Gestapo-type police force. It is actually more similar to a socialistic monarchy like present-day England, where an aristocratic upper class lords it over the middle and lower classes but zealously looks out for their welfare. It can even be compared to a democratic republic such as the United States, where the "Establishment," a wealthy, socially dominant class or clique, monopolizes politics, ruling by a combination of social status, education, and self-assured personality which is passed on from one generation to the next as a sort of "hereditary environment," if I may call it that.

Other animals, from barnyard chickens with their well-known pecking orders to gregarious forest monkeys and chimpanzees, organize their social hierarchies strictly on the basis of "every man for himself." An individual chicken or chimp fights his way up the social ladder if he can, then slips down when met and defeated by a chicken or a chimp who is stronger. Only men, baboons, and their close kin, the ground-dwelling macaques, have evolved the *class* society: rule by privileged clique whose members cooperate to protect their joint status and preserve the general status quo while uniting with the lower classes to confront a common enemy.

In coping with domestic problems, as opposed to foreign entanglements, highly placed members of the baboon "establishment" rarely have to use force. A Saltonstall or Cabot Lodge doesn't have to brawl in the streets of Boston to exert his authority; he has the whole apparatus of the state to back him up, and he himself carries an aura of prestige which would certainly be tarnished by such lower-class tactics.

Baboon communities also have their ruling families whose males dominate society from one generation to the next. Far from using force, a socially prominent male seldom has to do more than stare fixedly at a commoner who may crowd him carelessly at a waterhole, reach out to pluck at a choice bit of food, or in any way annoy him. The guilty party—guilty of presumption if nothing else—usually averts his gaze and runs away. If he has sinned against a really top-ranking member of the hierarchy, he may at once make the baboon signal of submission. A defeated lion rolls on his back, an elephant falls to his knees, but a shamed baboon makes a more picturesque gesture of humility. As Konrad Gesner, the sixteenth-century naturalist, described it: ". . . when he is signed to, he presents his arse."

If the insulted socialite is of medium rank, his outraged stare may fail to bring results. In that case, he widens his eyes and lays back his ears to indicate another degree of menace; then, if necessary, rises on his hind legs with his mane flared out impressively, takes a step or two forward, and thumps the ground. By this time, eager subordinates have probably come rushing to his side. They make their own ritual threats, and the culprit either "presents his arse" or gets charged, wrestled to the ground, nipped on the neck, and socially disgraced.

Things seldom come to such a pass, for lower-class males know their place in society; only rare individuals who are endowed with exceptional strength, pugnacity, and self-assurance will attempt to break through the class barrier—and only the rarest will succeed. All-out fights between ranking members of the "establishment" are equally uncommon: they occur in any free-living troop no more than half a dozen times a year. Although individuals may square off in these hierarchic battles, joint challenges are often staged by a pair of allied males seeking to displace another pair who stand higher. The contestants slash with fangs instead of nipping; then losers present to winners and the old or new order is obeyed. It *has* to be if the warriors of the tribe are to fight at all effectively against their common enemies. The human army private may resent the overbearing manner of his sergeant, while the sergeant loathes the snide lieutenant or the captain, who in turn dislikes or hates the colonel, but all of them manage to grin and bear it, or at least to gripe and bear it. So do baboons.

There is far more bickering and intrigue among the females. Depending on his status, each dominant male has a wife, two or three wives, or a five- or six-wife harem. High-ranking males can, moreover, exercise the *droit du seigneur* with the wives of underlings, but underlings cannot reverse the procedure any more than medieval serfs could bed a duchess or a queen. Like their consorts, high-ranking females harry their social inferiors and low-ranking females present their humble rears.

The system is, however, subject to periodic upheavals. As they advance into the estral or sexually attractive phase of the twenty-eight-day menstrual cycle, females of any rank become far more daring and aggressive, challenging social superiors or even attacking them. They are attacked in return, but any male who comes to arbitrate the squabble usually takes the side of the sexually ripening female. Often, he takes more. At the very peak of estrus, when the female is ovulating and her vaginal skin is swollen with retained water into a huge cushionlike protuberance, she is constantly accompanied by dominant males. The other ladies, very prudently, squabble at a distance.

The estral swelling subsides gradually over six or seven days, and the female's mettlesome spirit subsides with it. Pregnant or not, she submits once again to the social order but achieves immunity, if not instant sanctity, by the simple expedient of giving birth. For the nine or ten months that their babies first cling to their bellies, then ride upon their backs, the nursing mothers are allowed to stay near the high-ranking males who threaten to punish anyone, male or female of any rank, who annoys them. When the babies are weaned and move about on their own, their mothers rejoin the common ranks, forfeiting their privileged status.

The dominant males' motive in fostering this arrangement is profoundly meaningful. Unlike forest monkeys or chimpanzees, baboon fathers are extremely fond of their babies. They not only like to hold and fondle infants, whom they indulge shamelessly, but take a tougher-minded interest in the juveniles, age two and older, whom they look after and discipline as needed. This fatherly love and attentiveness, like most phases of baboon behavior, is part and parcel of Makako's life on the open ground. If the tribal males had little interest in the young, they would feel little or no urge to protect both children and females (who are given higher rank as mothers than as objects of sexual desire), and the tribe's reproducing core would soon be wiped out.

Humans feel and behave in much the same fashion if and when they outgrow the happy-go-lucky *"Playboy* Philosophy" view of male-female relations. But they persist in thinking of baboons as the most promiscuous, lascivious, and obscene animals on earth, simply because they have watched zoo baboons and witnessed what is, admittedly, sexually obsessed behavior among bored, restless animals who have neither family responsibilities nor predatory foes to contend with.

The most notorious example was the so-called London Battle of the Apes which took place in 1927 at the London Zoo, when forty females were introduced to an "island" that was populated by one hundred male baboons. The ensuing scenes of assault, murder, and rape took the lives of sixty males and all but seven females. Passed from one brawling suitor to the next, some of the half-pint females died of exhaustion, even starvation. Watching scientists concluded that all baboons are brutal sex fiends, often slaughtering the objects of their passion along with their rivals—and never bothered to speculate, until years later, how such suicidal behavior could possibly permit survival in the wild.

They might just as well have judged human sexual and social relations by sending a boatload of forty buxom chorus girls to an island of a hundred desperate, long-deprived convicts.

Living free in their own social groupings, baboons spend more time grooming each other than they do making love or even quarreling. When they push aside the fur and pick at the skin, they are not searching for vermin to eat or even flakes of salt, as some have claimed. They are merely "pleasuring" each other in a mild and friendly way with a sort of simian scalp massage. Trivial as it may seem, the external grooming plays a vital role in promoting fairly relaxed relations within the tribe; it is, in fact, the only form of friendly intercourse between social inferiors and superiors. Naturally, underlings groom overlords longer and more zealously, but they get a little halfhearted grooming in return.

Unjust as it may seem, baboons themselves are relatively untroubled by the pomp and privilege of the hierarchy. Like civilized men who submit to domination by employers, land-lords, tax collectors, policemen, magistrates, politicians, presidents, lords, and kings, baboons are willing to sacrifice individual freedom for the company of their fellows and the protection of society.

That is the wisdom of Makako, and the only reason why he is still around.

SOKOMUTU

The Man of the Market Place

According to the Congo Forest Pygmies, there is only one real difference between chimpanzees and people. It is not a matter of language, say the Bambuti, for chimpanzees talk as much as people do and make as much sense. It is not intellect or reasoning power, for chimpanzees are smarter than people, excepting only Pygmies. It is not tool-using, tool-making, laughing, weeping, dancing, worshipping a god, having a conscience, or even telling lies. Chimpanzees share all of these human traits, their Bambuti neighbors claim, but there is one human attribute they lack.

"Men have *bali*," the Pygmies explain. "They keep it in their huts and carry it with them wherever they travel. They never let it die. Without bali, there would be no people, only monkeys and chimpanzees."

Bali is the Pygmies' word for fire.

Fire is the hallmark of humanity—feared and avoided by

all animals, except man—and fire is the heart and soul of every Pygmy camp. The big central campfire heats the communal pot of roots, tubers, and greens; it toasts the skewered termites and caterpillars; it cooks the meat when there is any meat to eat; it lights and warms the chill forest nights while the Pygmies dance around it or tell stories. The small smoky fires in the huts warm them while they sleep and comfort them on rain-sodden days. When the nomadic bands break camp, as they do every two or three weeks, the women build new huts in the new clearing, erecting frameworks of interlaced saplings and lianas thatched with broad *mangungu* leaves. But they light no new fires: they carry smouldering brands from the old camp, keeping the same fire as they move from place to place.

Some Pygmy bands who live along the borders of the forest have learned from their Negro neighbors the classic African method of obtaining fire: they rotate a hard round vertical stick (the "male") at high speed against a softer, flat piece of wood (the "female"). In the interior of the forest, where the old ways continue, the Pygmies have no fire-drills or other apparatus. They use, cherish, and revere fire, but they do not know how to make it. An eternal flame burns from one Pygmy camp to the next, like the eternal flames that burned long after men had learned to make fire and forgotten why they once had to keep a flame burning, in Egyptian, Babylonian, Hebrew, Greek, Roman, and Christian shrines, or the eternal flames that flicker today over the hallowed tombs of the Unknown Soldier and President John F. Kennedy.

To explain the origin of their sacred flame, Greek mythmakers told of how a local hero named Prometheus stole fire from heaven, lighting his torch at the sun's flaming chariot. The Pygmies, telling their own version of the story, have an equally daring hero. Like Prometheus, he stole the first fire— but he stole it from the chimpanzees.

Long, long ago, according to the old Pygmy legend, men had no fire. They were forced to eat their food raw, and at night they crouched inside their huts, shivering with cold, fear and misery. They never even danced, for they had no fire to dance around. Then, one day, a wandering Pygmy discovered the village of the chimpanzees. They spoke the language of men, but they were wiser and more civilized: they built huge, elaborate huts, planted banana groves, and danced every night around a blazing campfire. They were generous as well, for they greeted the Pygmy cordially, giving him bananas to eat and inviting him to sit down beside the fire.

When the Pygmy returned to his camp, it seemed darker, damper, and colder than ever. So, remembering the warmth and beauty of the fire, he thought of a clever plan. He made himself a beaten-bark loincloth with a long tail that hung down in the back; then he returned, waited until the grown-up chimpanzees were all busy working in the banana grooves, and entered the village where the chimpanzee children were minding the fire. They made fun of his tail, calling him *makako,* but he didn't get angry. He talked to the children, very sweetly, and all the while he sneaked the fake tail closer and closer to the flames. When the tip caught fire, he ran back to camp just as fast as he could.

Later, when the big chimpanzees came home and their children told them what had happened, they rushed to the Pygmy camp. There was a nice warm fire in every hut, and the entire Pygmy band was dancing around a huge campfire. "Why did you steal the fire instead of buying it from us honestly? What will you pay us now?" demanded the furious chimpanzees. Their only answer was a shower of glowing coals. Singed and terrified, fearing the very fire they had once mastered, the chimpanzees fled into the deep forest, abandoning their huts and groves to live on wild fruit. They have never talked to human beings again, for they remember still the treachery of mankind's ancient crime. Instead, whenever people approach, the chimpanzees shower branches on their heads, trying to get even for that shower of glowing coals.

Very ingeniously, the Pygmy legend attempts to explain the chimpanzee's lack of fire-using know-how, while it comments on his rudimentary primate tendency to greet intruders with a weapon. But even more importantly, it sums up African attitudes toward chimpanzees and gorillas alike. Throughout the forested areas where the great apes are found, legend after legend describes their intelligence and ingenuity, their anger or disgust with humanity, and their subsequent withdrawal from the world of men. Africans look at the apes and see people—men of an aberrant but obviously clever tribe. They feel compelled to explain why chimpanzee or gorilla should have come so close to human status without actually attaining it. And, although the native legends are replete with fanciful details, the explanation they provide is a true one: they place the blame for the apes' failure to attain the cultural level of men on their Eden-style existence in the deep forest.

The chimpanzee's very name, widely used by Swahili-speaking Africans, is a tribute to his almost human nature. They call him Sokomutu, a Japanese-sounding word that means, literally, "the man of the market place." It may seem like a strange title for the natives to confer on forest-dwelling animals they almost never see, but the explanation is a simple one: they *hear* chimpanzees sounding off from their places of concealment in the trees, and the chimps make the forest rock with the near-bedlam noise and excitement of a traditional African market place.

Like a gang of loud-mouthed salesmen haggling with a crowd of housewives over the price of manioc flour and beans, the chimps hoot, bark, screech, and jabber from the moment they awaken to the moment that they fall asleep. Each and every member of the band feels compelled to voice his feelings, talking to himself or to other chimpanzees when he is happy or unhappy, hungry or full, excited or bored, frightened or reassured. And like forest monkeys or like human children ("house apes" as they are sometimes called with mixed affection and despair), chimps not only talk to express their feelings but apparently enjoy for its own sake a quantity of sheer noise which would give an earache to a leopard or a buffalo.

When humans invade the neighborhood, the noise level rises to really epic proportions. The outraged chimps stage a mass protest demonstration by hooting, screeching, stamping, shaking branches, and pounding on hollow tree trunks to produce their own boom-boom-booming imitation of Africa's "talking drums." (Chimpanzees have been known to steal drums from native villages and carry them into the trees, where they pound away with dedicated frenzy.) But when seriously threatened, the hooting, cursing chorus explodes into soloists, with every chimp fleeing on his own. If baboons used the same tactics on the ground, they would have become extinct sometime during the Ice Age. Chimpanzees, who brachiate through the trees, can usually get away with it.

Brachiating, or swinging by the arms, is one of the more significant traits that separate the anthropoids or manlike apes from the lower primates. The smaller, lightly built arboreal monkeys have long narrow torsos that are flattened like a dog's from side to side, and shoulder blades that face each other on either side of the rib-cage, restricting the forelimbs to a back-and-forth type of movement that is suitable for four-legged walking or running along the tree branches. The heavily built baboons do their quadrupedal walking or running on the ground. Anthropoids have shorter torsos that are flattened front to back and shoulder blades that are placed side by side on the upper part of the back. Their forelimbs, free to move through a wide range of lateral and overhead movements, have become differentiated into arms and the hands are used to grasp the branches from beneath as the ape swings from bough to bough.

Our remote arboreal ancestors, the predecessors of the savannah-dwelling man apes, brachiated like the present-day apes but never reached the same level of acrobatic proficiency. They lacked, as we ourselves lack, the apes' marked physical adaptations to the swinging life—the greatly lengthened arms, extremely flexible wrist and elbow joints, hooklike hands, and shortened thumbs. They specialized *the opposite pair of limbs* as they evolved to man apes and beyond, gradually developing the kind of highly modified feet, legs, and pelvis which permit humans to stand and walk erect. Our hands, unspecialized and still equipped with decently long thumbs, were now free to carry clubs, rifles, umbrellas, or baseball bats, and to manipulate stylus, abacus, typewriter, ouija board, and computer.

The gorilla also scrambled down from our mutual family tree, but he waited too long. A confirmed brachiator grown so heavy that the very branches broke beneath his weight, he came to the ground with arms that dangle at the level of mid-shin, a half-developed foot that lacks an instep, and a pelvis-leg anatomy that forces him to crouch and shuffle rather than stand erect and stride. Gorilla babies, who are much more human-looking than the huge adults, are perfectly at home swinging through the trees; when forced by increasing size and clumsiness to spend the major part of their adult lives on the forest floor, they use their long arms like a pair of crutches with the fingers doubled back on the palms. The backs of the fingers are heavily callused and, since their feet bend under as they walk, they even have calluses on the upper surface of the toes.

Ngagi, as he is called in Swahili, has tried to solve the problem of his size by growing even larger: highland gorilla males, who measure up to six foot six and weigh up to 600 pounds or more, are twice the size of females, probably because the biggest males were better able to bluff or defend themselves and their mates against the new enemies they found on terra firma. To support that vast bulk, gorillas chomp away for six to eight hours every day at stalks, stems, and whatever fruit they can get, grinding up the low-energy food with their massive, thickly enameled molars. They are armed with immense canine teeth and immensely powerful chest and shoulder muscles; the strength of a full-grown gorilla has been proven to exceed the combined strength of sixteen men and it may, conceivably, approach that of thirty men (the estimated strength of Bushman, the famed gorilla of Chicago's Lincoln Park Zoo).

Gorillas do not, however, share human and baboonish views on real estate, as described so tellingly by Robert Ardrey in his books *African Genesis* and *The Territorial Imperative*. They have no strong territorial feeling and they are, almost without exception, rather timid and retreating introverts. Their sexual drive and reproductive urge are also very weak—they almost never engage in mating duels and copulate very rarely. Ardrey explains that this "vital discouragement in all but exceptional gorillas has weakened the territorial instinct." I think, however, that the opposite may well be the case.

Without a territory to defend, without a strong central focus for continuing existence, animals of greatly varied species will grow listless and indifferent. It is a well-known fact that many zoo specimens reproduce very poorly even when they are given ample opportunity to meet and mate. The problem is to some extent a matter of diet, but the animals are weakened also, physically and emotionally, by the lack of stimulus and motivation that accompanies the lack of natural territories to acquire and defend.

Humans suffer in today's urbanized societies from that same elementary lack. Since the city dwellers have no real territorial domains, they substitute the acquisition and possession of material goods for the "territorial imperative." But unlike the rich and splendid land their fathers pioneered, cars and color television sets are trivial, unsatisfying motives for a man's existence. So men rebel, knowing only that they feel cheated, against society's "materialistic" values—the only surrogate we have devised as yet for the individual's brutal but profoundly stimulating territorial urge.

This "rebellion of the rootless," if I may call it that, takes extreme forms. Negro city dwellers have expressed their incoherent rage and frustration in anarchic, often self-destructive rioting. Deplorable as they are, the riots show a raw vitality, a fierce will to fight against the unrewarding quality of urban life. Among the "hippies," on the other hand, there is a dull, lethargic, even more self-destructive aura of pathetic futility: a lack of any will to fight or, for that matter, to do anything at all. Retreating from the problems of the real world around him, the dispossessed, unmotivated, melancholy, almost sexless hippie "takes a trip" into his LSD-induced hallucinations, wandering in a daze or sitting in a drugged trance among the unswept litter of his "psychedelic"-decorated hovel . . . and in so doing, he conjures up irresistibly a vision of the dispossessed, unmotivated, melancholy, almost sexless gorilla who shuffles aimlessly along the forest floor or sits, morosely brooding, in his self-befouled nest.

Compared to gorillas, the chatterbox chimpanzee is the ape world's eternal teenager. He is a rampaging extrovert and shameless exhibitionist—inquisitive, exuberant, and hellishly ingenious—and his body does not undergo the profound alterations which make youthful, female, and mature male gorillas seem like members of three different species.

Full-grown male chimpanzees reach a maximum height of about five feet and an average weight of 110 pounds (although exceptional individuals have weighed 180 pounds or more). Adult females average 90 pounds and reach a top height of about three feet eight inches. The difference is appreciable but not extreme: male chimpanzees are roughly 20 per cent heavier and 30 per cent taller than their mates, while human males also average 20 per cent heavier but are only 10 per cent taller. Should humans be transformed according to chimpanzee standards, our ladies would be shrunken down to four-foot height but retain their present weight. (If it ever happens, I would hate to see *Playboy's* center foldout.)

Chimpanzee males never grow the huge bony crests that make the male gorilla's keeled skull appear so very alien. Their canine teeth are of shorter length, and they lack the enormous bony ridges that overhang the male gorilla's eyes. As with men, they are merely somewhat larger, stronger, and more rough-hewn in appearance than their females; their species does not show the marked sexual dimorphism or "two-shapedness" of gorillas, orangutans, or baboons.

Chimpanzees of either sex differ from gorillas, approaching closer to the human, in their smaller molars, less massive jaws, and trimmer bodily proportions, including arms that reach just below the level of the knees. They are the shortest and most manlike arms to be found among the living apes; the arms of Asiatic gibbons and orangutans are even longer than the African gorilla's, dangling at their ankles.

But despite their shorter arms, chimpanzees are far more competent and daring brachiators than orangutans. The Malay's "man of the forest" rarely swings along but hauls himself from branch to branch in slow motion, cautiously releasing a single hand or foot at a time. He looks like a somber, moon-faced old man who has been ordered to reduce and is going through the motions, lethargically and despairingly, in a leafy jungle-gym.

Sokomutu favors instead the grand style of the ape world's real swinger—the lightning-swift, supremely daring gibbon. A chimp will hurtle in the same way from branch to branch, reaching up with alternate hands, but he cannot match the speed or grace of a twenty-pound gibbon; the gibbon has been known to leap forty feet through empty space or to catch a bird with one hand while in transit. Sokomutu's maximum leap is less than half as long—and birds in flight have nothing to worry about—but his volcanic enthusiasm more than makes up for it.

When he comes down to earth, as he very often does, he forages for fallen fruit and palm nuts, raids termite nests to supplement his diet, or wanders about picking the tastier products of low-growing bushes and herbs, especially favoring *Amomum,* a member of the ginger family whose red-husked fruit he carefully peels before eating. He also steals bananas, pineapples, papayas, and other delicacies from cultivated groves and fields, moving about with surprising agility (his feet and legs are even less adapted to walking than the gorilla's, but he has much less weight to carry). He usually walks on all fours, supporting himself on callused knuckles and feet with curling-under toes, but sometimes he will walk very briefly in an almost erect position, throwing his head back and clasping his hands behind it for better balance.

The hands are less humanly shaped and proportioned than those of ground-dwelling macaques or baboons. Sokomutu has the shortened thumb, lengthened palm, and attenuated fingers of the brachiator, who must use his hands as hooks for hanging and swinging. He cannot make his thumb and index finger meet, but he manages to use these overspecialized hands with more skill and savvy than a monkey; equipped with the larger, more complexly convoluted brain of an ape, he has finer hand-mind coordination, longer attention span, better memory, and superior powers of reasoning and concentration.

Living free, Sokomutu gives only minor demonstrations of his latent talent: brandishing and throwing branches, heaving an occasional stone but more often using the stone to crack a hard-shelled fruit, or using leaves as occasional tissue or toilet paper. Once, during a rainstorm in the Ituri, I surprised a chimp who was seated on the forest floor with a big *man-*

gungu leaf placed atop his head. He looked unspeakably funny, but I had no hat and the rain was dripping into my ears. It was not, I suspect, the first time that man has imitated chimpanzee.

Some Pygmy friends maintained that they sometimes saw the *cheko,* as they call the Ituri Forest chimps, "poking around" in termite hills. I never caught the chimps at it and I never knew exactly what was implied. Then, in 1960, Jane Goodall observed and actually photographed chimps of Tanzania's Gombe Stream Game Reserve in the act of "termite fishing": poking in termite hills with grass stems or twigs that they broke off or even trimmed for the purpose, then withdrawing the improvised "fishing pole" and picking off the insects with their lips. They were, as Miss Goodall pointed out, not only using tools but *making* them.

Captive chimpanzees, kept in zoos, circuses, private homes, and research laboratories, have employed a much wider range of tools: they have learned to use hammer and nails, screwdrivers, saws, and pliers; eat with forks and spoons and drink from cups or glasses; drive tricycles, bicycles, motorcycles, automobiles, and even tractors; peck out their names on typewriters; dial telephone numbers and tune television sets. At the Holloman Air Force Base in New Mexico they have been taught to operate simple astronautical equipment as well as a tic-tac-toe playing device—the chimps depress squares on a large board to light up their X's and O's, sometimes beating humans at their own game. Others, kept in a less scientific atmosphere, have taken up the sacred tools of art.

My baby chimp Sophie loved to fool around with crayons and a coloring book. She didn't bother to stay within the lines and she sometimes ate the pages, but more ambitious members of her species have made "genuine oil paintings." According to zoologist Desmond Morris, whose young male chimpanzee, Congo, favored radiating patterns counterpointed with broad horizontal lines, ape artists have an elementary notion of composition, individual style, and a real urge to paint. According to art critics, they are far more talented: the 1964 exhibition of works by a modern master named Pierre Brassau drew high-faluting aesthetic commentaries from the critics. They were, of course, unaware that Monsieur Brassau was a chimp named Pierre who sat before his easel, wielding brush and palette, in a Swedish zoo.

Pierre sold several pictures before his true identity was discovered. I don't know if the purchasers demanded their money back, but it should have been reserved as a "fruit fund": the temperamental artist reportedly eats a banana a minute while he paints. In Sweden, bananas don't grow on trees. As for Pierre's pictures, they are somewhat messy and kindergartenish in style but they show as much genuine originality as the past decade's crop of pop, op, and slop. I may be a "square," but I would rather own an original Brassau than a secondhand Campbell's soup can, a gigantic rubber hamburger, or a dismembered automobile, erotic back seat and all.

Captive chimps also try their hand at a different, more distressing kind of art, at least from their keepers' point of view. They are the animal world's master escape artists, a race of hooting Houdinis who consider any cage an insult to their dignity and a challenge to their ingenuity. It is not so much that they want to run away, for a captive animal regards his enclosure as a territorial domain, deeply distrusting the unknown world that lies beyond it. Many show no interest in leaving, or even have to be driven out if the door or gate is opened wide. But chimpanzees, sensitive as well as smart, grow easily bored, resentful, and restless. Curious as they are, they become intrigued by the *problem* of escaping as well as its results.

To escape, a chimpanzee will untwist wire netting by the hour, working with truly human patience and persistence. He will use a stick or any leverlike object he can get his hands on to pry away at the netting, and he may even try to pick the lock. Like a forest-living chimp with his termite-fishing twig, the caged chimp may waggle a bit of wire back and forth until it breaks, then bend it into shape for keyhole-poking. If the lock is a crude one, he may actually succeed.

This is tool-making of a rather high order, for the locksmith chimp is coping with a problem that he never faces in the wild. He has seen his keeper use a key, but he goes beyond mere imitation when he makes a key of his own. Captive baboons and other highly developed monkeys have learned, by observation and imitation, how to use keys—my pet savannah baboon, Jeune-Homme, once stole the key to his cage from my pocket, released himself, raided the ice-box and feasted on a dozen tomatoes—but no monkey has the intellectual capacity, originality, and initiative to conceive of *making* a key.

Predictably, chimpanzees excel at solving the classic problems that are used to test the primates' ingenuity and mechanical ability: using poles to rake in an orange or a bunch of grapes that lies beyond the bars or stacking boxes to obtain a banana that dangles by a string from the ceiling.

Monkeys rarely understand the possible use of a pole unless fruit and pole are placed in virtual juxtaposition. Chimpanzees, far from needing such a broad hint, will use a short pole to pull a longer one into reach, then use the longer pole to gather in the fruit. If supplied with two bamboo poles, neither of which is long enough, Sokomutu will telescope one of them into the hollow end of the other, making a single adequate tool. In one epic pole-using experiment, the chimpanzee actually devised a better method than the psychologist intended. Confronted by the hanging banana and supplied with a long enough pole, the chimp was supposed to bat away at the banana until he knocked it to the ground. Scorning such a crude solution, he balanced pole beneath banana and swarmed up the pole, hand over hand, as though performing his own version of the Indian Rope Trick. He managed to snatch the banana before he fell, pole over tea kettle, back to earth.

Monkeys will drag a single orange-crate into position beneath the eternally dangling banana, but they will not stack the crates. Chimps have stacked *four* crates into a simian skyscraper; then, finding the fruit was still out of reach, scrambled down to arm themselves with a pole, scrambled up again, and batted away until the banana fell. So far as I know, they have never tried to climb up a pole while balanced on a stack of boxes, but one ingenious chimp named Sultan performed the Indian Pole Trick when he didn't have a pole to work with.

Sultan was supposed to stack some boxes that were scattered on the ground; instead he grabbed the presiding psychologist by the seat of the pants, dragged the astonished man underneath the suspended banana, leaped onto his shoulders, and successfully snagged the fruit.

While performing all these feats of physical and mental acrobatics, chimpanzees are inspired by far more complicated motives than mere hunger or gourmet passion for bananas. They are driven by ego, even as you and I, to compete for attention, to impress an audience, to win approval, admiration, even love. When they blunder and fail to win the reward, they may fly into tantrums, stamping, screeching, and pounding on the walls—partly from frustration and disappointment but as much because they hate to be outwitted, shamed, or one-upped.

Captive gorillas, subjected to similar tests, don't give a hoot what people think of their performances. They act like Buddhist priests forced to attend a football game—aloof and mildly disapproving in a bored and baffled way. Because they take so little interest in box-stacking, pole-using or other mechanical problems, they feel little anger or frustration when they fail. They do not tamper with locks, and they will examine and discard a stick that any self-respecting chimp would use as a cage-wrecking crowbar. But they grow nervous, visibly upset, or even outraged when placed in a test room with equipment that is designed to determine their powers of visual discrimination and learning ability.

At the San Diego Zoo, where the primate collection is under constant study, a fifteen-year-old gorilla named Albert repeatedly smashed the testing apparatus with contemptuous blows of his fists. "It was clear that Albert was not given to making decisions," commented Dr. Duane M. Rumbaugh, the presiding psychologist, "in fact, it appeared that he would rather fight than decide between the square and the circle."

It would be easy to conclude that gorillas are less intelligent than chimpanzees, but more meaningful to say that they are less manlike. The ego-driven chimpanzee exhibitionists actually enjoy the test procedures, basking in their triumphs and moaning over their failures; the inhibited gorilla introverts actively dislike the whole alien ritual of psychological testing. They may, however, do things on their own—when they really *want* to do them—that overturn our hastily drawn conclusions.

Mrs. Belle J. Benchley, former Director of the San Diego Zoo, had just such an experience with Ngagi and Mbongo, two young highland gorilla males who came to the zoo in October, 1931. As Mrs. Benchley recounted in her book *My Life in a Man-Made Jungle:*

> Our gorillas apparently are not interested in anything of a mechanical nature. When we put impediments in the way of their doing what they desire, they appear to lose that desire. At first this deceived us all, but one day when we had left a gorilla shut in for a particular purpose, the other one that was outside walked over to the door, which had confined them for a period of six years without being padlocked or held in place by bars, and, pressing his hollow palms flat against the door, pushed it up to the top and held it there until the other gorilla had walked out. Then, withdrawing his hands quickly, he let the door drop and walked away with no further interest in his feat.

Gorillas simply do not share our own particular set of attitudes and motivations. We cannot judge them by our standards and, in the last analysis, we cannot even evaluate the intelligence of the seemingly human chimpanzees.

Chimps have been compared to two-year-old human children, three-year-olds, or even speech-defective four- and five-year-olds. They are nothing of the sort. Such very young children are poorly coordinated, partly formed creatures lacking judgment and self-sufficiency, while the chimpanzee is superbly coordinated, shrewd, and perfectly competent at dealing with the problems of his society and environment. Motorcycles, cutlery, and tic-tac-toe boards form no part of his tree-swinging, fruit-picking way of life, and the very fact that he can master them is staggering testimony to his mental adaptability—the only valid definition of intelligence.

Anthropologist Irven De Vore, in the LIFE Nature Library's splendid volume *The Primates,* proposed:

Suppose a New Yorker were to be trapped by a group of chimpanzees, shipped to Africa and stuck up in a tree a hundred feet above the ground. Practically all his abilities—his mastery of language, his skill at fixing a disabled fuel pump, his aggressive salesmanship—would be irrelevant to his situation. Hanging on for dear life, frequently confusing edible with poisonous plants and, no doubt, experiencing grave difficulties in distinguishing one chimpanzee from another, he would appear to his captors to be an exceedingly stupid animal. Their judgment, of course, would be unfair, since it would arise from a failure to appreciate that New Yorkers are not used to living in trees.

Many civilized human beings aren't psychologically equipped to survive a week in the forest, much less live in the trees. Tourists and campers who are lost in the woods may die within days of "hunger" and "exposure," although a man can live off his stored fat for several weeks and survive extremes of temperature, even without a campfire, that will kill a 600-pound gorilla. The truth of the matter is, in many cases, that the lost human dies of fear and hysteria: he blunders about in panic-stricken circles; he moans with hunger when surrounded by edible food he either fails to recognize or is too fastidious to swallow; he convinces himself that he is starving rather than hungry, or freezing rather than cold; he runs through the woods, gibbering and screeching, while he strains mind, heart, and blood vessels to the very bursting point.

Chimpanzees, faced by the far less natural problems of life in an alien, chromium-plated jungle, have done more than survive or operate a few gadgets. They have demonstrated the power to understand, use, and even become obsessed by the single human invention—symbolic and absolutely useless in itself—which dominates most of civilized man's activities, ambitions, and desires: Africa's "men of the market place" have acquired the values of humanity's own market place; they have learned to work for money, to spend money, to save, hoard, covet, cheat, steal, and even fight for money.

It happened at the Yale Laboratories of Comparative Psychobiology, where Dr. John Wolfe introduced six young chimpanzees to two "infernal machines." The first, or "Chimp-O-Mat," disgorged a single grape or orange slice when a white poker chip was inserted in the slot, two pieces of fruit for a blue chip, a drink of water for a red chip, and nothing at all for a brass slug. The second, or "Work Machine," was equipped with an eighteen-pound handle; when the handle was lifted—a substantial effort for a young chimpanzee—the chimp could reach in and pull out a single poker chip.

All six chimps learned to operate both machines, hoot at slugs and discard them, unfailingly favor the two-grape blue chips over the pallid one-grapers, choose a red chip when water was withheld and they grew thirsty, and to labor at the Work Machine for chips they couldn't always spend at once.

What happened next depended on their individual characters. Velt, one of the three males, showed little self-control or foresight when the Work Machine was brought out: he wanted to cash in each chip as he earned it, and if not permitted to go shopping at the Chimp-O-Mat, he stopped working after amassing a very small pile. Bimba, a female, pumped the handle of the Work Machine with all the grim determination of a little old lady playing the slot machines at Reno or Las Vegas; she accumulated huge piles of chips, guarded them warily, and kept working even when she couldn't spend her chips until the next day. Bula, a stronger and more aggressive female, stole Bimba's chips, cashed them in for orange slices at the Chimp-O-Mat, and presented the whimpering victim with the sucked-out peels. Moos, a very intelligent male, was the most determined worker—he once pumped the eighteen-pound handle of the Work Machine 185 times in ten minutes—piling up chips for future use and fighting to defend them. For a time he worked so hard that laboratory staff members feared for his health.

All six chimpanzees caught the true spirit of civilization. In so doing, they managed to topple yet another shaky definition of man, as "the symbol-using animal." The chimps not only wheeled and dealed with man's favorite symbol but almost got ulcers while they were doing it. If we must insist on man's uniqueness, unlike Linnaeus who classified man and chimp as two species of *Homo,* we might label man "the credit-card–using animal." That definition seems unshakeable, at least for a while.

Back in their own market place where fruit is free for the taking, chimpanzees lead a casual, delightfully disorganized existence. Baboons march along in grimly military order, but chimps rove through the trees like bands of exuberant gypsies, trading gossip as they go. Any individual band of half a dozen adult chimps, plus dependents, splits and reforms itself constantly as little groups wander off on separate excursions; females always outnumber males, sometimes by a three-to-one ratio, and they are almost always draped with clinging babies. On encountering another band, they mingle peacefully or even merge for a time.

They give an impression of utter anarchy, but they are actually families who meet and socialize during the course of erratic rounds through vaguely defined territories. They also seem promiscuous, but there is a permanent marriage bond between male and female . . . and female . . . and female. Polygamy seems to be the rule, with little friction or jealousy among the co-wives, possibly because the master of the household usually looks the other way when one wife or another has her little fling with a passing bachelor.

To put it in roughly human terms, lady chimps practice occasional lighthearted adultery, like housewives frolicking with the delivery boy or the TV repairman—but they would never dream of running off with either, for they really love their husbands and they disapprove of divorce.

The word "love" may seem out of place, but it isn't. Anyone who has ever seen chimpanzees hugging, patting each other tenderly on back or shoulder, holding hands, or kissing mouth to mouth with their large sensitive lips, cannot doubt or deny that they know the spirit and the ways of love. It also seems impossible, after witnessing such scenes, to think of them as "mere animals."

Young chimpanzees experiment a great deal with various

217

sitting and recumbent postures; adults usually copulate in the old-fashioned mammal style with the male mounting from the rear. Whichever way they do it, the baby comes some eight months later—a delicate, helpless little two- or three-pound mannequin with pale-skinned, almost hairless limbs and torso. He starts teething at twelve to fifteen weeks, nurses for up to three years, attains puberty between his seventh and eighth year, and reaches social maturity at age twelve or thirteen. In captivity he lives only twenty to twenty-five years, usually succumbing to pneumonia and constantly bedeviled by the common cold, caught from humans. In the wild he may live forty to fifty years, providing he survives occasional encounters with leopards or snakes and the far more frequent threat posed by army ants.

Traveling in vast infernal legions, the safari ants sometimes march through the forest trees. Any chimp unfortunate enough to lumber across a column of ants while swinging to a new hold on a branch, is the victim of a sudden mass attack. He flees, screaming, to roll on the forest floor. If bitten badly enough, he dies of the massive inflammation that results.

Guenons and colobus monkeys, the chimps' fellow dwellers in the trees, usually avoid their larger neighbors. There is a popular native legend to the effect that Sokomutu once sued Kima (monkeys in general) for disturbing his nest-bound slumbers with their loud periodic cries. The monkeys lost the case and had to move out of the neighborhood. Less picturesquely stated, chimpanzees are irritated by any loud noise except when they are making it. Not unlike ourselves, they regard superior noise-making ability as a mark or prerogative of high social status, so they sometimes chase or at least outcurse the boisterous monkeys. The monkeys, in turn, wisely avoid taking undue liberties with next-door neighbors who outweigh them seven or eight to one: when chimpanzees swing into sight, the monkeys stop feeding and move on.

Although chimps feed on fruit for the most part, padding out their diet with nuts, leaves, buds, shoots, insects, birds' eggs, and occasional lizards, natives from the Burundi shores of Lake Tanganyika have told me that chimps will hunt and eat red meat. Such behavior seemed, until recently, to be on a par with legendary chimp-monkey lawsuits or fanciful tales of lust-maddened chimps and gorillas stealing women from native villages (a convenient way to explain sudden disappearances). Then Jane Goodall actually observed—at Tanzania's Gombe Stream Reserve, where forest meets savannah near the shores of Lake Tanganyika—chimpanzees picking off, killing, and devouring straying juvenile baboons, plus baby bushbuck, wild piglets, and red colobus monkeys. Despite this evidence, it must be emphasized that meat is a rarely-eaten gourmet dish, apparently favored by individual bands when they can get it without too much trouble but probably unknown to others. It seems to have a status comparable to that of snails or bird's-nest soup in America, and Wheaties or sukiyaki in France. Captive chimps, however, eat meat or almost any other kind of food, including spaghetti and even cheese, just as zoo- and circus-based elephants have learned to yearn for popsicles and chocolate bars. Zoo gorillas have also acquired a taste for meat, but free-living gorillas are another story.

Natives have sometimes claimed that gorillas will eat meat, especially human meat. But George Schaller, the outstanding zoologist who virtually lived with highland gorillas for nearly two years, getting to know them better than any native has ever done, never saw them eat meat, eggs, mice, lizards, or even insects. It may be possible that an isolated gorilla, here and there, has chewed for a moment on a piece of hunter. Gorillas do, after all, bite with their huge canines when they are forced to. I suspect, however, that he soon spat it out. Meat-eating seems like wildly unlikely behavior for a creature so specialized in diet that he will pass up the protein-rich insects which are enjoyed by almost every other primate from tree shrews to humans (including civilized gourmets who eat ants or grasshoppers dipped in chocolate, Mexican-style, as well as termite-toasting Pygmies).

Africa's really dedicated meat-eaters, Simba and Chui, have never been a major menace to chimpanzees. The savannah-dwelling lion and the forest-dwelling chimp who dislikes and shuns intense sunlight, almost never encounter each other except in a few fringe areas. Once, on an overcast day in the Congo's Upper Uele district where the Ituri borders the northern plains, I saw a lioness stalk a band of seven or eight chimpanzees who were foraging on the ground in a little thicket. I watched, terribly curious, as the lioness padded closer paw by paw with her belly close to the ground. But I'll never know what might have happened, for I simply couldn't stand it; the chimpanzee band, especially the baby-toting mothers, looked and acted like a gang of picniking humans. I gave a sudden Tarzan yell, shattering the suspense. The Sokomutu picnic literally exploded; chimps leaped for the trees as though shot from cannons, and the lioness fled, almost as terrified, in the opposite direction.

I never saw another lion-chimp encounter, but Azande tribesmen told me of lions actually killing chimps, sniffing dubiously, and then abandoning the dead bodies.

Leopards, who hunt through deep forest as well as wooded savannah, have far more opportunity but share the lion's disdain for human-tasting chimpanzee flesh. They prefer monkey meat, which tastes like goat but much sweeter, especially favoring colobus and baboon. When very hungry, a leopard may attempt to bag a chimp in the lower branches or along the mossy forest floor. But at night, when leopards are most active, the cautious chimps sleep up to a hundred feet off the ground—and they sleep very lightly.

Having only rudimentary callus pads on their rears or none at all, depending on the individual, chimps rarely sleep sitting up on branches like baboons or the amply padded gibbons. Like the Asiatic orangs who almost never come equipped with seat-pads, they select a forked limb and work for some four or five minutes, bending and interweaving branches, twigs, and vines to make a steady platform and adding sprays of leaves for comfortable bedding. They have no fixed sleeping sites like baboons but bed down at dusk wherever the day's travels have taken them. Baby chimps sleep with their mothers, young juveniles sometimes curl up in the mother's nest, and older children build their smaller nests close by.

Chimpanzees sometimes build tree nests in the daytime, when they want to rest and the forest floor is very damp from recent rain. They may then weave a little canopy over the nest to shade it from excessive sunlight, but they will not build elaborate "penthouses," as in the charming civilized myth helped along by the explorer Paul Du Chaillu, who gave an illustration in his book *Equatorial Africa* of an amazing but entirely imaginary structure that resembles a chimpanzee-style Pentagon.

Adult gorillas, especially the "silverbacks," or fully mature, majestically grizzled males, usually build rudimentary nests on the ground, hastily bending and breaking some weeds, twigs, and vines to form a raised rim around their bodies. As George Schaller has described, they sometimes make their nests on steep slopes and slide slowly downward as they sleep, often moving ten feet or more during the night. The whole process seems ludicrous but gorillas, like humans, seem to feel rather naked unless they have some kind of bed or bedding. Ngagi remembers, even as we do, his arboreal ancestors, and juvenile gorillas often build nests up to ten feet from the ground, bending branches inward on a forked limb but not interweaving or padding them with leaves like orangutans or chimpanzees. Females sometimes do the same, and, much more rarely, adult males will haul themselves into an easily climbed tree to build an off-the-ground nest.

Awakening at dawn in their own lofty nests, chimpanzees yawn, stretch, and scratch, then get on with the business of the day—a festive two-hour breakfast followed by three or four hours of traveling brunch, a midday rest, a long afternoon ramble punctuated by frequent snacks, and an enormous pre-bedtime supper. Considering the sheer amount of time they spend in eating or looking for food, it doesn't seem too surprising that their gifted ape brains never evolved to the level of creating true culture. The really astonishing thing is how very close they came.

Pygmy friends have told me that chimpanzees worship Toré, the Supreme Being who long ago made the Grand Forest. They say that the chimps pray once a day as they watch the sunset from the treetops, and that they sometimes dance during thunderstorms, stamping the ground and waving branches to propitiate the God who made forest, chimps, and rain.

The Pygmies have their own method of "stopping the rain." Like the civilized nineteenth-century French, they light a special ceremonial fire; by all the time-honored principles of sympathetic magic, it is supposed to dry up the downpour. The chimps are trying to do the same with their branches, say the Pygmies, but they are afraid to light the fire.

NYAMA

All Sorts of Animals

Leopards, lions, buffaloes, elephants, rhinos, hippos, crocodiles, baboons, chimps and gorillas. . . .

I have sketched, briefly and incompletely, the complexly interwoven lives of only ten animals: the hunters' Big Five, the "ugly" mammal and the "evil" reptile of the inland waters; and a primate trio whose intelligence might be recognized as fully human if they composed singing commercials, counted their calories, brushed after every meal, wore topless or bottomless bathing suits, carried lucky rabbits' feet, consulted horoscopes and peered into crystal balls, dabbled in politics, graft and bribery, falsified their tax returns, built the Bomb, worried about the Bomb, conducted their love-affairs via computer dating machines, purchased diamond rings, mink coats, weddings and divorces on the installment plan, squabbled about alimony and child support, sobbed out their troubles on a psychiatrist's couch, tried to escape from it all by "taking a trip" with LSD, attempted suicide and—for some mysterious reason!—prayed to be reincarnated. Ten animals . . . and there are more than five hundred African mammals, plus a vast assemblage of birds, reptiles, amphibians, fishes, insects, and other invertebrates, each as fascinating in its own hidden ways as a lion or an elephant. They are all animals, but there is no real word for animal in Swahili or in most Bantu tongues. The word employed in its place is *nyama*. It means "meat."

It would be easy, far too easy, merely to condemn the Africans for living in the midst of the world's richest, most magnificent fauna and seeing the animals as so many running, walking, flying, or crawling gobs of meat. But *nyama* is a human, not an African problem. Look at the implications of our own word "animal." Aside from the purely zoological definition—"any living thing capable of spontaneous movement and rapid motor response to stimulation"—I have found the following synonyms or connotations after a very brief search through dictionary and thesaurus: brutish, bestial, debased, gross, coarse, filthy, irrational, cruel, savage, merciless, bloodthirsty, and contrary to the nature and dignity of man. That smugly arrogant verbiage is even more appalling if you consider the origin of the word "animal." It was derived from the Latin *anima* and its predecessor, the Sanskrit *ana* or *animi*, meaning "soul."

For at least two millennia, allegedly rational men have been arguing as to whether "souls" have "souls." Not being a theologian, I wouldn't care to get involved in that monumental controversy. I would rather say, with Aristotle, "We ought to investigate all sorts of animals, because all of them will reveal something of nature and something of beauty."

I wish I had space enough to write an entire chapter on each of the little-known creatures who contribute "something of nature" to achieve the final biological balance. Instead, I can only give some thumbnail sketches of the strangest and most intriguing. Furred, feathered, or scaled, they are Africa's great eccentrics, all sorts of animals who live in all sorts of unexpected ways.

Digging away some nine to eighteen feet beneath the surface of the earth, Africa's most primitive and mysterious mammals riddle forest floor and savannah with their labyrinthine burrows, emerging at night to raid termite hills. Up to six feet long and averaging 140 pounds, the narrow-headed, daring-tongued, disk-snouted, long-eared, fat-tailed orycteropes look like the children of a complicated wife-swapping deal between anteater, pig, donkey, and kangaroo. The Boers called them aardvarks, or "earth-pigs"; the British styled them "ant-bears"; natives of the eastern Congo speak of them as *namulima;* and the Arabs name them *abu-delaf,* "father of nails," in honor of their massive claws, steel-hard and strong enough to smash open concretelike termite hills.

Baffled zoologists at first lumped the aardvark with two totally unrelated groups, the Old World pangolins and the New World armadillos, tree-sloths, and anteaters, in a hodgepodge zoological order called *Edentata* or "toothless ones." The name itself was absurd—aardvarks have twenty teeth, tree-sloths have eighteen, and armadillos have up to a hundred—and the animals involved had little anatomical resemblance beyond their long insect-licking tongues. They have since been separated into three distinct orders, but the aardvark's place among the mammals remains poorly understood. For a while scientists entertained the speculation that the Great African Enigma might be a sole surviving descendant of extremely primitive hoofed animals called condylarths who lived some sixty million years ago, in, of all places, Wyoming and New Mexico. Current opinion favors a connection with the chalicotheres—an almost equally ancient gang of fossils, distantly related to horses and rhinos, who traded in their hoofs for massive digging claws.

Namulima has somehow gotten a Western reputation for sloth and stupidity, perhaps because of his strange appearance and blinky-eyed daytime ways. He is, on the contrary, a lively and even playful character who roves about by moonlight, donkey ears twitching alertly while he moves, kangaroo-style, on the tripod of his hind legs and massive tail. His business is, of course, breaking open termite hills and licking up the startled insects with his long extensile tongue; he manages, however, to have a number of adventures between one termite hill and the next.

When mildly annoyed, Namulima sits up on his tail, ready to flail away with lethal claws at any caracal, serval, or other small predator who comes near him. When real danger threatens, usually in the form of lions, leopards, or meat- and hide-hunting humans, he can dig himself underground within minutes, shoveling with his forefeet and throwing huge clods of earth from between his hind legs; but he tries, whenever possible, to make it back to the labyrinthine halls of his burrow.

Legend after native legend tells of how the aardvark made

a treaty with the warthog or got married to a lizard or even swore a pact of friendship with the black mamba, simply because warthogs, lizards, rodents, snakes, hyenas, and a horde of other creatures take refuge, live, or prowl down in Namulima's old or current burrows. They are Africa's underground hotels, open to all comers, but the tenants sometimes check out rather suddenly.

Every family of warthogs has its own aardvark hole where the wary pigs sleep, hide out, bear babies and raise them. *Senge,* as he is called in Swahili, is a good-natured but rather timid sort of fellow, much less apt to stand and fight than the Indian wild boar. When disturbed, whole families or solitary old males literally hightail it to the burrow, fleeing to safety with their tufted tails stiffly erect. They enter hindfirst so that they can use their huge tusks to stave off enemy pursuit, and leopards rarely push the issue: full-grown male warthogs may weigh as much as 200 pounds and the leopard prefers, as with all sizable prey, to attack them from the rear. Lions may claw at the burrow like a pack of excited dogs, trying to dig out the holed-up pigs. If they succeed they have a fine pork dinner, but before the dinner fights back, often inflicting serious wounds before the lions seize and snap the neck.

At waterholes the warthog also approaches hindfirst, kicking at the edge with his back feet before turning to drink. He is stamping some salty crust into his drinking water—he doesn't like to take his salt straight—but Azande tribesmen say, observing that strange little ritual, that Senge has another reason. According to their legend, the first-created warthog saw a savage-looking creature lurking in a pool of still water. Appalled, timid Senge ran away to hide in his burrow. But he never forgot, warning all of his descendants to stir the water well before they faced it (so that they wouldn't have to see their own reflections).

Big-headed, broad-snouted, maned on the neck and back with bristling brownish hair, Senge has a pair of huge warty protuberances just below his eyes and another pair flanking his massive ivory tusks. Unlike those of true pigs, his tusks are upper canines, not lower ones; the paired warts protect his small, rather dim-sighted eyes as he ploughs up wild roots and tubers for a living. Timid as he is, he rarely ventures into village fields, but his smaller relative, the common bushpig, is much bolder; *Nguruwe,* like the roving hippopotamus, not only eats but tramples down and rolls upon the crops. He is one of Africa's most persistent and destructive pests, yet it is

Senge, the innocent possessor of the "ugly" warts, who has the ugly reputation.

Mfisi, who also makes his bedroom in the aardvark burrows, has a reputation so bad that he makes the much abused warthog sound like "man's best friend." Even Carl Akeley, that pioneering conservationist, condemned the hyena as "a filthy villain—vicious as a cutthroat," while Teddy Roosevelt wrote of his "foul and evil ferocity." More recently, Robert Ruark summed him up as a "stinking thief," "a living cemetery," and "a dirty joke on the entire animal kingdom."

I could go on for pages, quoting such hyena descriptions, but I shall restrict myself to one—all the more chilling for its brisk suburban tone—written by Paul L. Hoefler in *Africa Speaks,* the story of a documentary film company's 1928 motor truck travels across Equatorial Africa.

. . . I had lost all count of the number of hyenas killed, but now that we had made up our minds to continue the war against them, decided to keep a score. One idea led to another until in a short time we had invented a new game which we called "hyena golf." The rules were that the hyena must be at least two hundred yards away—the shooter being entitled to four trys. If he killed the hyena first shot, it was a hole in one; if it took two cartridges, an eagle; three bullets made a birdie, and four was par. . . .

Loathed and persecuted for his odd, ungainly looks and his carrion-eating habits, Mfisi is a scavenger by sheer necessity. Like the crocodile, he has a severe physical handicap and carries on in spite of it. The nature of their handicaps is, however, diametrically opposed: the half- to one-ton reptile has pathetically weak jaws and an immensely powerful rear, while the hundred-pound mammal—a relative of the civets and other primitive catlike animals—has the strongest jaws of any living carnivore and weak, almost crippled hindquarters. He can crush the shinbone of an ox with no more trouble than a dog chomping on a chicken wing, but his short hind legs hold him down to a fast shuffle rather than a run, and his blunt, non-retractile claws cannot be used like a cat's to seize and hold his prey.

Surrounded by fleet-footed game he cannot catch, the handicapped hyena has to compete for food with the world's smartest, best-organized, and fastest great cats, respectively leopards, lions, and cheetahs, plus a gang of lesser predators that includes the speedy wild dogs, servals, and caracals. He is outclassed on every side and, theoretically, should die of sheer starvation. But Mfisi, patient and determined, survives by prowling in packs and pulling down diseased, wounded, senile, or very young animals; shrewdly watching vultures and following lions in a dedicated quest for carrion; and feasting on the human corpses that are put out, traditionally unburied, from so many bush villages.

Each of these jobs represents a vital service rendered to the biological balance. His hunting, such as it is, provides a crude form of population and disease control, while his carrion-eating and especially his bone-crunching help to return the chemical elements of dead animal matter to the earth that gave and needs them.

I think, in the last analysis, that hatred and persecution of carrion-eaters must be linked to man's fear of death and longing for immortality. Human looks at hyena, the hardworking mortician of the savannahs, and sees the Grim Reaper waiting to carry him off to "the knell, the shroud, the mattock and the grave; the deep, damp vault, the darkness, and the worm," as the English poet Edward Young summarized mankind's most persistent phobia. Then, trying to negate his subservience to simple natural law, human blasts hyena—death's innocent scapegoat—with a high-velocity bullet.

My Masai brothers, who do not share civilized man's obsessive fear of death, take a different view of hyenas: accepting the inevitable, they call Mfisi the "Messenger of God."

Hyenas have also been condemned for unprovoked attacks on humans, a calculated risk they sometimes take when hungry enough; the fact that they eat, quite impartially, the bodies of dead hyenas has led to the accusation of cannibalism; and their custom of hunting in packs that operate in large part under cover of darkness has led man to suggest that hyenas are skulking cowards. I can hardly imagine, however, that a pack of human hunters would lay aside their rifles and attempt to drive hungry lions from their kill. Hyenas have been known to try it, and even to succeed.

Mfisi's famous laughter is a strange but very seldom-heard sound; most of the time, hyenas confine themselves to doglike yips, whines, and growls. One can, in fact, live in the African bush for months or even years without hearing hyenas really cut loose with their cackling, whooping, wildly shrieking laughter. No one really knows why they sometimes laugh, but the old cliché "laughing hyena" is an oddly apt one: easily tamed and trained, Mfisi is probably Africa's most playful, whimsically good-natured animal.

I had a pet hyena named Mfisi when I was stationed in Rutana, southeast Burundi. He used to sleep at the foot of my bed and he woke me up every morning by jumping onto my stomach and playing with the buttons of my pajama coat. When I got out of bed, I usually found that he had hidden my shoes. Then he watched with obvious enjoyment while I turned the house upside down searching for them. When he wasn't teasing me, he was trying to outwit tougher game—his good friend Ngugu, a baby baboon who rode around on Mfisi's black-spotted back as though the hyena were his mother instead of a "born enemy."

Eric was another pet hyena, equally playful and mischievous, who belonged to my friend Carr Hartley, the well-known and very humane game capturer of Rumuruti, Kenya. Eric wandered around Carr's unique animal farm, romping with the dogs and stealing anything he could get his teeth on —but always making sure that someone saw him in the act, for the whole object of the game was to lure a human into a wild sort of sport that might be called "hyena hide-and-go-seek."

Willy, another one of Carr Hartley's hyena pets, was a somewhat more controversial character. His name had to be changed periodically to Wilhelmina, then back to Willy again, for he/she apparently alternated like an oyster between male and female, fathering pups and giving birth to litters. It sounds, I know, like the wildest kind of hoax or fairy tale, but the hyena's eccentric anatomy and problematic sex life have been argued, endlessly and unresolvedly, since the days of Pliny the Elder.

Most zoologists deny the possibility of sex-changing in a mammal but admit, as they have to, that the rudimentary male organs are "very pronounced" in the female hyena. According to Dr. Hans Kruuk, who has been studying hyenas in the Serengeti area, it is only by dissection that a scientist can determine the sex of a spotted hyena before the animal is fully mature (up to two years). Natives, who usually mix acute observation and superb insights with the most erratic flights of fancy, variously claim that hyenas are homosexual, or alternately male and female, or capable of functioning as male or female whenever they choose. They also hold, and it is a very widespread belief throughout Equatorial Africa, that both hyena sexes suckle the young.

That last theory is the most likely, for all male mammals including man are fitted out with perfectly adequate suckling equipment. More remarkably, they have been known to use it. Charles Darwin long ago pointed out in *The Descent of Man:*

> The mammary glands and nipples, as they exist in male mammals, can hardly be called rudimentary. They are merely not fully developed and not functionally active. They are sympathetically affected under the influence of certain diseases, like the same organs in the female. They often secrete a few drops of milk at birth and at puberty. . . . In man and some other male mammals these organs have been known occasionally to become so well developed during maturity as to yield a fair supply of milk. . . .

Darwin went on to suggest, as others have, that male mammals of an earlier period "aided the females in nursing their offspring" and he recounted the ordeals of desperate men, left with motherless infants, who had tried to quiet their squalling babes by putting them to their flat chests, then found to their amazement that the intended pacifiers started to produce milk. Several human infants have been saved from death by this seemingly miraculous "father's milk."

Considering that men have wet-nursed infants, it hardly seems fantastic to admit the possibility that male hyenas should occasionally or even frequently give milk to their young. Such an unusual practice might have given rise to the native tales of homosexual or bisexual hyenas, but it doesn't solve the enigma of sex-switching Willy/Wilhelmina.

His/her case may have a totally different and even more startling explanation.

Birds have been known to reverse their sex even after reaching adulthood. Cocks have laid eggs and, it must be said, hens have laid hens and fathered chicks while doing it. Such enterprising hens, who grow spurs and start to crow before giving the ultimate proof, have been dissected and found to possess a diseased ovary almost completely transformed into a testis. Partial or complete sex reversals have also been recorded among mammals, even humans, and certain mammals show peculiar periodic transformations from male to near-neuter and back to male again: the testicles of an ermine out of season are only one-thirteenth of their mating size, and the testicles of rodents, bats, and insectivores move back and forth from body cavity to scrotum, shrinking and expanding as they change their seasonal position.

It may be possible that some female hyenas, even more hermaphroditic in the structure of their sexual organs than most members of their species, can function periodically as males. I won't believe it myself until there is unequivocal scientific proof, but neither will I deny it.

Twiga, the world's tallest animal, has two clearly defined sexes but usually chooses to ignore that fact, behaving with all the "gay" abandon of the ancient Greeks or the modern Greenwich Villagers.

I received only recently a sentimental valentine that showed two enchanting, soft-eyed, long-eyelashed giraffes "necking" together as giraffes sometimes do. The sender, an amiable but very refined lady, would have been shocked senseless had she known that there is no such tender-looking courtship between bull and cow giraffes: rubbing, winding or swinging necks, and jousting with sideways blows of head and neck, constitutes the amorous foreplay practiced by two bulls before one of them mounts the other. Sometimes groups of three to six bulls "neck" together, then mount each other indiscriminately.

It isn't lack of female company that prompts such strange performances. The herd cows are usually present in the background, watching with the somewhat bored air of housewives keeping each other company while "the boys" play a somewhat different game than poker. The cows, however, never indulge in homosexual behavior, confining themselves to platonic friendships and "sitting" with each other's babies.

When a bull giraffe makes advances to a cow—a much more socially productive form of behavior, resulting some fifteen months later in a six-foot-tall, 160-pound baby—he merely lays his head on her flank and licks or bites her tail. She urinates and he tastes the urine, apparently to determine if she is really in heat. The lead bull of the herd, which is usually composed of up to twenty individuals, permits subordinate bulls to go this far but tries to prevent actual matings. He defends his harem, which he has customarily neglected, with a tougher version of the "necking" tactic, dealing out heavy blows with his short, knob-like, skin-covered horns.

Bulls sometimes knock each other cold during these leadership battles, but they rarely use their bone-shattering hoofs against members of their own kind, reserving them for self-defense against predators. Since giraffes may reach maximum heights of eighteen feet or more, weighing up to one and a half tons, adults are never preyed upon by leopards. Chui knows his limits. Prides of lions may, however, take on a full-grown cow or bull, usually at a waterhole when tall Twiga "does a split" to reach the water.

His amazing neck, which makes bending down to drink such an engineering project, has only seven vertebrae—the standard number for virtually all mammals, including humans—but they are greatly enlarged and elongated. Since his heart has to pump blood up the tower of that neck to reach his brain some ten or twelve feet above, it is also large and massively constructed: a giraffe heart, equipped with three-inch-thick walls, is two feet long and weighs about twenty-five pounds.

With a blood pressure two to three times greater than the normal human standard, Twiga has to have specially adapted blood vessels. Otherwise, the rush of blood would burst the vessels of his brain whenever he lowered his head to drink or take a lick of salt. So he comes fully equipped with a complex group of arteries at the base of his brain—the so-called wonder net—which expands to reduce the pressure; and his one-inch-wide jugular vein, which carries blood *back* from the brain, is further fitted out with special valves that prevent the veinous blood from rushing backward when he bends.

The long-necked life has its complications, but it also has advantages. Twiga can reach food that nobody else can, using his dark-blue, two-foot-long, prehensile tongue to strip leaves off the loftier branches of acacia and mimosa trees. Living as he does on open savannah, his elevated viewpoint helps him to spot distant enemies—including his two great enemies, lions and men—and to gallop off in his poetic half-rocking, half-floating style at speeds of up to thirty-two miles per hour.

In the past, East African tribesmen feasted on Twiga's fine-tasting, succulent, and richly fat meat; dried what was left into giraffe jerky; grilled the long shank bones for their nourishing marrow; and tanned the thick hide into excellent, very durable leather. Today, when there are more and more mouths to feed, the meat is usually wasted. Rifle-armed poachers will shoot a giraffe, chop off the black-tufted tail, and leave the giant carcass to the lions, vultures, and hyenas. The tail is sold, for a dollar or so, to a dealer in animal curios who converts it into a souvenir fly-swatter.

I am not suggesting that giraffes be farmed for meat. There are far more suitable candidates for game-farming, including buffaloes and the easily domesticated eland. I am merely deploring, as usual, the money-minded manners and mores that have swept across Africa, destroying animals and traditional cultures alike. Understandably obsessed with naïve longings for our trashy "civilized" tradegoods, the Africans are selling their birthright for a mess of tin and plastic pottage: the poacher who kills a giraffe and sells its tail has earned enough money to buy a secondhand fedora hat, a couple of plastic bracelets for his wife, and a few more bullets to shoot a few more giraffes.

Chameleons, who climb among the vines and branches of the damper forest regions, are not mere *nyama* to be killed and eaten or killed and sold. Bantu and Sudanese tribesmen of the Ituri call them "sacred" but do not worship them—they fear and shun these utterly harmless and defenseless little lizards as omens and agents of black magic, possessed of the "evil eye."

Everything about *Kinyonga,* as they call him in Swahili, strikes the bush natives as weird and other-worldly. His color-changing, which so impresses Westerners, is only the smallest part of it: the Africans are far more troubled by his air of slow, profound deliberation as he moves from branch to branch, clamping and unclamping his four pincerlike feet, and the ominous, all-seeing way he rolls his ball-turreted eyes. He is looking for men, they say, so that he can steal or possess their human souls.

Actually, Kinyonga is looking for flies or moths—a far more practical and nourishing enterprise. He rolls each of his eyes independently, slowly turning the prominent globe with its thick protective lid until his pupil, situated beneath the tiny peep-hole in the center, focuses on an insect. Then, in utter contrast to the slow-motion style of all his other movements, his long tongue shoots out of his mouth with fantastic speed, catches the insect with its sticky club-shaped tip, and snaps back, dinner and all, into his mouth. Shooting range differs among the sixty-six species of chameleons—ranging from pygmies who are only three-and-a-half inches long from nose-tip to tail-tip to two-foot giants, variously equipped with horns, casques, and cockscomblike headgear—but the maximum is probably twelve inches.

Kinyonga's only real defense against animal enemies is his color-changing camouflage—mainly shades of green, blue, and yellow to match the foliage and brown or gray to blend with bark. If he is discovered and threatened, he anchors himself in place with clinging feet and prehensile tail, swallowing air to puff out his body, literally turning black with anger, snapping his little jaws, and making a sound somewhere between a hiss and the chirp or squeak of a very young bird.

The whole elaborate bluff, which sends humans running off in superstitious terror, fails to impress lizard-fancying mammals, birds, and snakes. Less sapient in their ways, they kill and eat the forest's animal magician with utter disrespect for the powers of his rolling "evil eye."

None of Africa's snakes, even the most venomous, shares the chameleon's reputation for unmitigated evil. *Nyoka,* as they are called in Swahili, enjoy a very different kind of supernatural status: they are regarded, cobras and mambas included, as reincarnated ancestors—wise and kindly creatures with a benevolent interest in the welfare of their human children.

Non-Africans, most of whom fear or loathe snakes as Africans fear chameleons, will probably find that attitude totally incomprehensible. According to civilized legend, every tree on the "Dark Continent" swarms with snakes and every snake is waiting to drop down and kill an unsuspecting human with his venomous fangs or crush him with his coils, especially the so-called man-eating python. The legend never bothers to explain, however, what the snakes do with human bodies, which are much too cumbersome for them to eat. Presumably, they just slither off, gloating with triumphant evil.

In reality, snakes are rarely seen and almost never attack humans, even in the tangled heart of the Ituri and other equatorial forests. They are too busy making a living, like everyone else, to waste their time and effort by behaving like a pack of characters from an old Tarzan film. When they are hungry they hunt for suitable prey, depending on their size and specific habits; when they are full they hole up to digest, very often in an aardvark burrow; when they see a human or any other large animal, they usually try to retreat; when they are cornered, most of them first try to bluff their way out of it; when they are attacked or stepped on, they at last bite.

Those alleged man-eaters, Africa's nonvenomous rock pythons, hunt instead for ground-fowl such as guinea hens and francolins, for rodents, wild piglets, dwarf antelopes, and, in general, any small mammal they can catch. As Africa's largest snakes, measuring up to twenty feet or more in length, they enjoy very high social status, especially in Burundi, where the *isato* have long been regarded as reincarnated queen mothers—a belief which may be connected with the female python's very maternal ways. She is one of the most devoted reptile mothers, collecting her newly laid eggs into a conical heap and coiling herself around it for the entire two-month incubation period. Endowed with a slower metabolic rate than the crocodile, she never even leaves to hunt up a meal.

When pythons catch their prey, they never kill by "crushing it to a pulp" as is commonly supposed: they smother it instead. Perhaps the best way I can describe their method is to tell of a strange, probably unique animal encounter I saw and photographed in Kenya's Nairobi National Park: the meeting of a python and an aardwolf.

The "earth-wolf," as the Boers called him, is no relative of the aardvark, but he practices some oddly parallel ways. His family ties lie with the civets, mongooses, and hyenas (he looks like a striped hyena reduced to the size of a large fox), but he is a timid, almost defenseless creature who digs his own burrow with heavy blunt claws and putters around by night, excavating termite hills and crunching the insects between his weak, almost rudimentary teeth. He is almost never seen outside the limits of South Africa, or seen in the daytime or, for that matter, seen at all.

Apparently the thirty-pound buff-and-black aardwolf had been searching for termite mounds in the long tussocky grass when the eight-foot python, patterned in gray and brown, seized the left foreleg in his teeth and threw his coils around the body. When I found them, the python had the slender, almost prehensile end of his tail wrapped around the aardwolf's neck and held its pointed muzzle between his jaws. Twitching and kicking feebly, the aardwolf slowly smothered to death with his nose inside the snake's throat. When he at last died of asphyxiation, the python took a quarter-turn on the head, dilating his jaws, to swallow the body with its legs toward his belly rather than his back.

His dinner seemed impossibly large, but it was within his powers: the bones of a python's upper and lower jaws can move outward and forward and the two halves of the lower jaw are connected at the chin by an elastic ligament alone. Each half-jaw acts separately as the snake engulfs his prey. He hooks the teeth on one side into the flesh; then, using the hold as a fulcrum, he moves the other half of his jaw forward, hooks his teeth into place and repeats the action again and again while salivating copiously to lubricate the swallowing procedure.

It took about two hours before the aardwolf's hindlegs and bushy tail disappeared completely into the snake's gullet. Then the python moved off slowly through the grass, his sinuous beauty marred by a large bulge that had been one of Africa's rarest, most elusive mammals.

My photos of the rock python and his unexpected dinner were published in the August 3, 1960, *East Africa Standard*. Six days earlier, the same newspaper had startled its readers with the headline: MONKEYS LATEST REFUGEES TO LEAVE CONGO. The accompanying story recounted the hectic arrival in Nairobi of Kikihibou, an owl-monkey; Spirou, a handsome crested mangabey; Sophie, who was no monkey at all but a baby chimpanzee; and their close primate relative, a fellow named Jean-Pierre Hallet.

The head monkey, if I may claim that title, also brought along two parrots and a Siamese cat, plus a car, truck, and trailer loaded with sculptured figurines and statues, masks, carved boxes and cups, drums, tamtams and other musical instruments, necklaces, bracelets, belts, amulets, anklets, earrings, armlets, tribal insignia, headdresses, combs, shields, spears, knives, axes, hoes, bows, arrows, swords, bill hooks, adzes, stools, paddles, baskets, trays, spoons, pipes, talismans, and fetishes—the world's largest and finest private collection of African artifacts.

To save that historic collection, I had to leave behind all the other animal friends I had tamed, trained, or studied at my Mugwata game park in the Congo and my backyard zoo in Kisenyi. It was painful, very painful, but I turned them loose to take their freedom, driving them into the bush when they repeatedly returned. Now they were all gone: Simba, Pierrot, Bella, Venus, Mbogo, and the rest, from the monkeys, lemurs, and baboons to the birds, antelopes, and zebras.

Their fate was problematic, their predicament symbolic. Nothing could have summed the temper of the Congo's new freedom better than a crew of tame animals wandering through a world gone wild with man's political intrigues, fratricidal warfare, murder, torture, raping, looting, and destruction. Humans were dying, senselessly and tragically, and animals were dying with them: during the first month of the Congo's independence, at least ten thousand elephants were slaughtered in the former sanctuaries, while naïve local politicians in Ruanda-Urundi, Kenya, Uganda, and Tanganyika, all scheduled for rapid independence, were making speeches of the F. K. Onama type: "If you are short of money, just shoot all the elephants and sell the tusks."

International conservation groups such as the World Wildlife Fund, the Washington-based African Wildlife Leadership Foundation (which contributes a half-million dollars yearly to conservation-education centers on African soil), and the East African Wild Life Society are trying heroically to stop the slaughter or at least to slow the rate of attrition. But the principles of conservation are poorly understood in parts of the world which have been civilized for centuries if not millennia. By the time the new nations of Tropical Africa achieve political stability and their peoples learn to respect the importance of the magnificent living creatures they call *nyama,* the animals themselves may have passed into oblivion —even familiar, seemingly common species such as lions and rhinos. We need some kind of *insurance* against that grim possibility.

I described in *Congo Kitabu* how I planned, in Nairobi, an ambitious project to re-establish the most meaningful elements of the African fauna in the United States of America: to build a scaled-down version of the Albert or Nairobi National Park in Southern California, where the animals could roam and breed freely as they had done on their ancestral terrain. There would be no cages, no bars, no kraals: unsurmountable barriers such as cliffs, pits, moats, lakes, and other natural fencing would separate the animals into compatible groups and prevent their escape. Visitors would explore the grounds in their cars, *discovering* free-living animals instead of watching captive specimens.

I planned also to establish a museum of tribal life where my ethnological collection could be displayed, and further, to bring living representatives of Africa's tribal cultures—native dancers, musicians, and craftsmen—to my proposed Congoland U.S.A., establishing them in authentic replicas of African villages. I had spent most of my adult life working with and for the Africans, and I wanted the Western world to see them as I had seen them; not as "primitives" or "savages" but as richly varied human beings with dignity and culture of their own.

Armed with those plans—officially approved by Kenya's Colonel Mervyn Cowie, Director of the Royal National Parks, and a host of other top officials—I boarded out my "monkey refugees," stored my collection in a Nairobi warehouse, and on August 22, 1960, boarded a plane at Nairobi

Airport, accompanied by Carr Hartley's going-away present: a big-eyed, long-tailed, six-ounce bushbaby. ". . . As the Super DC-7 took off from Nairobi," I concluded *Congo Kitabu*, "I had only one tiny animal and a vast, exciting dream hanging midway between *en-gop o eng-ai*—what my Masai brothers call the earth and the sky."

I came down with a bump in Southern California. What happened there to my proposed Noah's Ark has served as my direct inspiration for writing *Animal Kitabu*. Misunderstandings followed on the heels of misconceptions in a mad whirl of "African boa constrictors" and, of all things, "naked chimpanzees."

EPILOGUE:

Will Noah's Ark Finally Land in California?

"FRA I PROFUGHI DAL CONGO C'È UNA MODERNA ARCA DI NOÈ!" announced Rome's *La Voce Dell'Africa*. *"LE PÈRE NOÉ SERA DÉPASSÉ!"* exclaimed the Belgian magazine *Le Soir Illustré*. *"VOM KONGO NACH KALI-FORNIEN!"* thundered Munich's *Abendzeitung* under a flaming red headline.

Half the Continent talked excitedly of the new "Noah's Ark" while I engaged in four months of Congoland planning conferences with top European zoo authorities. Then I received my immigrant visa to enter the United States, and set sail for New York, arriving on December 10, 1960. I came on the giant liner *United States* instead of a home-made ark and I didn't bring a single animal with me: my monkey refugees remained in Nairobi and my bushbaby had been kidnapped by some Belgian relatives (mine, not his) who refused to give him back.

The "ark" was waiting to be loaded back in Africa, where its proposed passenger list—some 3,000 animals, ranging from birds, snakes, and small mammals to lions, elephants, and rhinos—was still roaming through the bush. Before the animals could be captured, shipped to a coastal port, quarantined and launched on their way to America, the Belgian Father Noah had to solve a set of problems that the Biblical Father Noah never dreamed of: I had to locate suitable and available land, obtain permits on federal, state, and county levels, and somehow find funds to finance the mammoth operation. Things must have been a lot simpler back on Mount Ararat.

My first stateside encouragement came from the late Dr. James Chapin, whose dedicated search had led at last to the discovery of the rare Congo peacock. Dr. Chapin was moved to the point of tears when we met in his office at New York's American Museum of Natural History and I described the carnage independence had brought to the Congo's national parks and game reserves. "They don't know what they're losing." he kept repeating. "It can *never* be replaced."

Deeply impressed with my conservation project, Dr. Chapin invited me to attend the annual meeting of the New York Zoological Society. President Fairfield Osborn and the assembled members discussed the project with warm enthusiasm; then, on January 10, 1961, I spoke on Congoland and conservation at the New York Explorers Club. The response was staggering. David M. Potter, President of Potter Aeronautical, immediately offered 2,000 acres of California land thirty miles south of Monterey, between Gamboa Point and Lopez Point, for my use in establishing a nonprofit sanctuary for the preservation of Africa's menaced wildlife.

It was almost unbelievable. Within thirty days of my arrival in the United States—thanks to David Potter's magnificent gesture—Congoland seemed to have found a home.

In a fever of activity, I conferred with mammalologists, ornithologists, herpetologists, ecologists, *et al.,* at the Museum of Natural History. Flying to Washington, D.C., I discussed quarantines and permits with the Department of Agriculture, health and sanitation problems with the Department of Interior, and six-month tourist visas for African tribesmen with the Department of State. Everything went without a hitch. Returning to New York, I plunged into another round of conferences with David Potter, Dr. Chapin, and Museum of Natural History authorities.

On February 8th, little suspecting the consequences of such

a simple action, I wrote to Thomas Hudson, Chairman of the Monterey County Board of Supervisors, requesting further information on the Congoland site. Then I left for California, heading first for a U.S. Customs warehouse at the San Pedro docks where my thirteen-ton collection of African artifacts was arriving from Mombasa on the steamship *Sarangan*. Days later, even as San Pedro and Los Angeles newspapers were front-paging my reunion with the collection and my plans for what they called "Operation Noah's Ark," a very different kind of Congoland story appeared in the *Monterey Peninsula Herald*.

The Monterey County Board of Supervisors hadn't bothered to answer my simple letter of inquiry; instead, without fully informing themselves as to the nature of the Congoland project, they had decided to oppose it. A special meeting of the Board had been held on February 21st at Salinas. As reported in the *Monterey Peninsula Herald*:

> Supervisor Frank Echeberria of San Ardo, in whose district the sanctuary would lie, summed up board feeling when he said: "It seems to me that they should set up the sanctuary in Africa. This doesn't look to me like the place for it."
>
> Echeberria complained that the sanctuary would develop into another Disneyland, and said the people in the area did not want it.

Both statements demonstrated the Board's lack of elementary information. Building a new sanctuary in Africa would have been a rather pointless enterprise when established game sanctuaries, even national parks, were fast becoming poachers' playgrounds. As for the Disneyland comparison, it was obvious but superficial. Congoland certainly had immense and valuable appeal as a tourist attraction, but it was intended and designed as a serious conservation project and approved as such by international authorities. Neither Colonel Cowie, Dr. Chapin, nor the General Consulate of Belgium would have lent support to a mere amusement park, even a good one.

Supervisor Echeberria had further suggested an ordinance banning African animals, and Board Chairman Thomas Hudson had "referred the matter" to the Monterey County Planning Commission. The Planning Commission wasted little time in planning, but declared that they could recommend an interim ordinance making a special-use permit necessary. "Presumably," the *Monterey Peninsula Herald* remarked, "if the ordinance were adopted, the permit would be denied."

Newspapers around the country received the story over the wire services, and the *Philadelphia Evening Bulletin* repeated Supervisor Echeberria's remark that "residents of the region might go wild themselves. It's not that they are against animals. They just don't like the idea of all those human tourists." The *New York Journal-American* and the *Philadelphia Inquirer* of the same date immortalized the Monterey Board's description of Congoland as an "African game preserve stocked with 3,000 animals from elephants to boa constrictors."

On March 6th, before I had time to mount organized opposition, the Monterey County Board of Supervisors rammed through Ordinance No. 1178, specifying in its Section 3 that:

> No person, firm or corporation shall hereafter, within the County of Monterey, use any land, or erect, construct or use any building, structure or enclosure for the purpose of maintaining a zoo or zoological garden or for the purpose of raising, maintaining, keeping or exhibiting of any wild animals unless and until a permit therefore shall have been first secured.

It would have been easier, I knew, to find boa constrictors in Africa than to obtain a permit from the wild supervisors of Monterey.

A month later, another Board of Supervisors met to discuss Congoland in another California county. Acting on the invitation of prominent Bakersfield farmer Lloyd Frick, whom I had met in the Congo, I presented a full outline of my project to the Kern County Supervisors at their regular public meeting. The response was wonderfully encouraging: they promised to adopt no prohibitive ordinances, assuring me that "the Board of Supervisors are very much interested and feel that the project will be an asset to the County of Kern. We extend to you our support and will help in any way within our jurisdiction."

There was no reason to doubt their sincerity or the area's potential as a site for Congoland. Predominantly agricultural, Kern County was famous for its cattle, potatoes, cotton, and grapes, and also produced most of the world's boron and a quarter of California's oil. Bakersfield, the county seat, had a modern civic center, a brand-new airport, a state college, a booming economy . . . and an unenviable reputation for hot summers and nothing special to do or see. All along the West Coast, Bakersfield was a virtual synonym for boredom, an oasis of mediocrity located midway between the tourist meccas of Los Angeles and San Francisco. Its people needed Congoland for further cultural and economic growth, and they apparently knew it.

So it was, early in June, 1961, that I moved to East Bakersfield and started looking for land. The first Congoland site was offered by a sprightly seventy-four-year-old ex-Britisher, Mrs. Ethel C. Joughin, who invited me to establish the African sanctuary on her 8,000-acre ranch in the Cyrus Canyon area. It was a splendid gesture on her part, but the Cyrus Canyon winters were extremely cold and the property was situated too far from Highway 99, creating access problems.

Considering climate, scenic values, and location, the Onyx Ranch, east of Lake Isabella, was a much more promising site. It was owned by the Oscar Rudnick Trust, comprising the Kern Valley Packing Company, the Paiute Packing Company, and the Rudnick Feed-Lot, all of them founded by pioneering meat-packer Oscar Rudnick and bequeathed to his eleven children. Marcus and Samuel Rudnick, the Successor Trustees, were both practical-minded but forward-looking businessmen who saw the great potential of Congoland for the entire area. They not only offered the use of the land but suggested that we go into partnership to establish Congoland as a commercial rather than a nonprofit enterprise.

Since the project's goals and plans would remain unchanged, I accepted, putting up my African collection as a guarantee of good faith. Marcus suggested that we move the collection to Bakersfield for public display in interim project headquarters. We decided after a short search to locate the new Congoland Museum and Headquarters in a huge building, a former supermarket-style hardware store on the corner of F Street and 29th Street in the Westchester section of Bakersfield within sight of Highway 99.

The rent was $750 per month, and I was not naïve enough to imagine that an African museum, especially an African museum in Bakersfield, would have the wide appeal of the Congoland project itself. So I planned to set up a small zoo in the museum's chain-link-fenced backyard, confident that the animals would attract enough visitors to keep the interim headquarters on a self-supporting basis.

My baby chimp Sophie had just arrived from Nairobi, making her Bakersfield debut at a gala luncheon given by Frederick Vajda, President of the Kern County Opera Company. She would be the charter member of the zoo, and I had already made preliminary arrangements to purchase baby lions, leopards, zebras, antelopes, and monkeys. Then I received an unexpected shock: zoning laws, I was told, prohibited the keeping of "wild animals" at the site of the new museum. I applied for a conditional-use permit and the hearing was held on September 20th at City Hall. Memories of Monterey County echoed through my mind as I heard the objections raised by a few local residents—the "wild animals" would escape and slaughter Bakersfield residents, etc., etc., etc. The permit was denied.

I was deeply troubled but, by now, thoroughly committed. The huge new headquarters had already been redecorated by a crew of carpenters and painters, and I had personally and singlehandedly unpacked, classified, and mounted five thousand artifacts in specially designed display cases. The Congoland Museum was scheduled to open on October 14, 1961, and Dr. René Devred, the future scientific and technical director of the Congoland project, was on his way from Washington, D.C. René, a top-ranking ecologist who also happens to be my brother-in-law, had just returned from a United Nations mission in Central America.

On the evening of October 13th, the Rudnicks and I gave a pre-opening party at the Congoland Museum, feting more than 120 guests with fine champagne. The next morning, official opening ceremonies were held: Bakersfield Mayor Gene Winer, armed with a Baluba circumcision knife from the collection, cut a woven-grass ribbon that stretched between two eight-foot-tall statues flanking the museum's plate-glass doors.

The admission charge was one dollar for adults or fifty cents for children, and the "maximum occupancy," as proclaimed by a wall placard, was 250 people. It was an overly optimistic regulation, for the largest crowd I ever had were the 120 pre-opening guests who came for free champagne. Now that the museum was officially open, I sat among my drums, masks, and circumcision knives, watching people stream in and out of Montgomery Ward's or the bowling alley across the street.

Adding to my troubles, I received some really bad news from Sam and Marcus Rudnick. The family's involvement in my African conservation project had created some dissention among the eleven brothers and sisters, and a majority were now opposed to my establishing the project on the Onyx Ranch. As Successor Trustees, Sam and Marcus had no choice. They told me I would have to find another site for Congoland and warned me to pare museum expenses to the bone, since Rudnick family funds were no longer available.

I contacted Floyd Ming, Chairman of the Kern County Board of Supervisors, and informed him of the new problem. We studied the situation together, and then drove to a 650-acre site on both sides of the Kern River between Hart Memorial Park and Lake Ming. In some respects, the land was even more suitable than the Onyx Ranch: it had the important advantage of being located only eight miles from Highway 99, with access to the highway by means of a four-lane road. Board Chairman Ming assured me that the right to lease the land—a part of the Kern River State Park, owned by the State of California and leased to the county—would present no problem once we had secured the approval of the State Park and Recreation Commission.

I started the necessary procedures, and then returned to my ailing museum. Business was desperately, pitifully slow. Sophie, playing in the backyard, was just about the only sign of life. She was apparently considered a pet rather than a wild animal, for the Zoning Board hadn't ordered her off the premises when they denied my permit. They had specifically forbidden keeping baby animals at the Congoland Museum, I reflected, but they hadn't said anything about *adults*.

Bearing that in mind, I bought Simba, as I called him, from a Kern County resident who specialized in livening up supermarket "grand openings" with a crew of trained animals. He had acquired Simba, born in the Fresno Zoo, but seldom used his services; a 400-pound, black-maned lion might make things just a little too lively at the Safeway or the Thriftimart—especially one that hadn't been tamed or trained.

Thus it was that Bakersfield awoke one morning to find itself presented with a *fait accompli*: somehow or other, a steel-barred arena had found its way into the fenced backyard of the Congoland Museum. It contained a huge, very wary non-baby lion and a rather large one-handed lion-tamer.

I had Simba gentled down within days, and I hung a big sign on the Museum's front door:

TODAY
OUR
GIANT AFRICAN
(BLACK MANE)
LION
ABOUT 400 LBS.
ALIVE
TAMED BY J.-P. HALLET

Simba was, after all, of African descent even though he was by birth a native Californian. He was not a member of the rare Indian sub-species, sprung of Gir Forest ancestors, and GIANT FRESNO LION would have been ridiculous.

Business boomed and I had every reason to believe that the Congoland Museum would, for the first time since its opening, break even on the month's operations. Then, just before Christmas of 1961, I received a yuletide greeting from municipal officials: they ordered me to remove my non-baby lion from the city limits of Bakersfield.

I could have done it very quickly and efficiently, for Simba was by now an obedient and trusting friend. But I staged instead a sort of lion-style Dreyfus Case, hoping that the resulting furor might at least stir renewed interest in the Congoland cause. "LION WANTS TO STAY IN BAKERSFIELD—LIKES IT HERE," the *Bakersfield Californian* announced on the front page of its December 23rd issue. Two large pictures showed Simba and me wrestling together as I tried, apparently, to push him into a small traveling cage. The farce went on for several days; then, reluctantly, I complied with the city's order, sending Simba into exile on a ranch in nearby Arvin.

Days later, when I received an official visit from a Bakersfield Police Department plainclothes detective, I thought at first that it was some sort of aftermath to the lion case. I learned, to my stupefaction, that I had just been accused of "cruel and inhuman" treatment toward Sophie. According to the complainant, a local lady, there was a "naked chimpanzee" in the backyard of the Congoland Museum; deprived of "warm and decent clothing," the chimp was sneezing pitifully.

I explained, and very patiently, that any animal is much healthier and happier without clothing; that Sophie was well-supplied with blankets which she used judiciously whenever she felt chilly; and that she had merely caught a slight head cold from a human visitor, as chimpanzees often do. I also suggested, and I believe with some justice, that the Bakersfield Police Department was better qualified to give out traffic tickets and chase purse-snatchers than to investigate the moral and physical welfare of champanzees.

The complaint was dropped. Barely two weeks later, by a stroke of irony, Sophie died of too much human attention rather than too little. Returning from a quick lecture trip to Fresno, I found the small museum staff gathered around Sophie's big backyard cage. She was huddled in the corner and the ground was strewn with bottles. Apparently the school children, who loved to watch the little chimp drink from a bottle, had surreptitiously given her at least a gallon of Coca-Cola. Unable to tolerate the sudden overdose of alkaloids, she died two days later, although the Bakersfield Veterinary Hospital worked heroically to save her.

The museum staggered on—a mournful place without Simba and Sophie. Then, on March 6, 1962, Congoland finally seemed to be on its way. On that date the Kern County Board of Supervisors authorized the County Counsel to confer with California state officials and obtain a concession-lease agreement with the state. The conference was held on April 26th at Ventura, where the Commissioners of the State Division of Parks and Beaches officially approved, unanimously and with great enthusiasm, the detailed plans of Congoland U.S.A.

The long "interim" was at last over. Now it was merely a question of arranging a few details before the lease agreement could be signed and I could expedite a large pre-incorporation subscription to float my African ark.

The *Los Angeles Herald-Examiner* ran a jubilant story headlined "MODERN DAY NOAH: BY TWOS AND THREES ACROSS SEAS"; the *Bakersfield Californian* printed the largest picture in its publication history, an artist's rendering of Congoland; the Jet Propulsion Laboratory of the California Institute of Technology devoted a page of its June *Bulletin* to "this exciting new cultural and scientific development"; and the Greater Bakersfield Chamber of Commerce officially endorsed the project.

Almost everyone in sight had approved of Congoland. There was no reason to suspect that difficulties would arise when the lease agreement was submitted to Kern County authorities. Those authorities were, after all, the same enthusiastic Board of Supervisors who had assured me, some thirteen months before, that they would help in any way within their jurisdiction and who had, indeed, cooperated all along the way.

When the Supervisors met, on July 17th, the unexpected happened. The Kern County Property Owners Association had filed a letter with the Board, stating that it would oppose the use of public tax money for the project. It was a pointless issue to raise, for the draft of the Congoland lease agreement specifically provided faithful performance bonds at every phase of construction, ensuring that no county funds would ever be spent on the project. But pointless as it was, the Board suddenly decided to submit the lease agreement to the

Kern County Parks and Recreation Committee for a recommendation, while appointing their own review committee to prepare a report and promising a decision—a final decision —on August 7th.

While the various reports, recommendations, and decisions were pending, the eleventh-hour controversy began to take shape.

Under the headline "CONGOLAND PLAN OPPOSED BY KERN SPORTSMEN," the *Bakersfield Californian* of July 26th reported that the Kern County Fish and Game Association had called on the Board of Supervisors to withhold approval, demanding that the proposed Congoland acreage be reserved for "public parks and recreation." Answered Mrs. Earlene Wright, a public-spirited citizen, in one of many pungent Letters to the Editor: "That land would do us a lot more good if a Congoland were put there, than waiting 20 years to put a few tables and benches, and some bar-b-ques."

On July 30th, the Kern County Property Owners Association publicly reaffirmed its opposition to Congoland and divulged the results of a comic-opera "investigation" into my character and personal history. Based for the most part on misinformation obtained in Monterey, the farrago of charges gave the impression that I was a reckless adventurer hell-bent on infecting California's cattle with "exotic diseases" and blithely unconcerned over "what might happen if some of the beasts got into nearby state parks."

The public protested against such tactics, rising to my defense in many, many indignant Letters to the Editor. But on August 2nd the Kern County Parks and Recreation Commission delivered a "negative recommendation" to the Board of Supervisors. Somewhat illogically, the commission praised the concept of Congoland but recommended that the acreage be reserved for future development as a "county recreation area"—presumably a dismal little gathering of picnic benches and refuse cans such as Mrs. Wright had complained of in her letter.

The final decision rested, however, with that same official body which had invited me to Bakersfield some fifteen months before—the Kern County Board of Supervisors. As reported in the *Bakersfield Californian*:

> Two supervisors, supporting a commission that admitted it had little or no time to study Jean-Pierre Hallet's proposed $7 million Congoland U.S.A., ignored the appeals of an overflow

audience and rejected a plan to lease 650 acres of the Kern River State Park for the project yesterday in the Civic Center.

A bare handful of people opposed to Hallet's plans were counted when Chairman of the Board of Supervisors Vance Webb called for a straw vote from the audience. With those few exceptions the packed Board room favored Congoland.

But Supervisors Charles Salzer of Bakersfield and W. Roy Woollomes of Delano rejected it. Approval needed a four-fifths vote of the Board. The votes of Supervisors John Holt of Arvin, Floyd Ming of Bakersfield and Vance Webb of Taft were not enough, although representing a majority of the Board. . . .

The two supervisors also ignored a petition signed by more than 3,600 Kern County residents within the last few days. It was submitted by Mrs. Frederick Vajda and said that in addition to providing entertainment and cultural advantages at a local level Congoland would give the county a tourist attraction "of great magnitude." . . .

Bakersfield citizens were, according to an August poll, in favor of Congoland by a margin of ten to one. They wanted a chance to vote on the issue in November, but the Congoland project wasn't put on the ballot. Instead, early in October, a whole series of special interest groups sounded off with anti-Congoland propaganda. The Kern County Milk Producers Association, the Kern County Farm Bureau, and the Kern County Veterinary Medical Association filed protests concerning "dangers to livestock" such as rinderpest, blue tongue, East Coast fever and Rift Valley fever, although the very stringent restrictions and quarantines enforced by the United States Department of Agriculture make it feasible and safe for American zoos to import exotic animals without menacing local livestock.

A private citizen, filing her own objection, apparently felt that Kern County had more to fear from the African tribesmen who would visit and work at Congoland on six-month tourist visas. As she stated in her letter of protest:

We are not prejudiced towards any race, but these natives will be of the most primitive sort, uninhibited, and foreign to our way of life. When they become bored and restless in their Congoland enclosure, and I presume they are to be restricted there, they will feel compelled to leave and venture into our community. I will not burden you with the numerous dangers that could result for us in that case; we can well imagine such an outcome. . . .

Frankly, I doubt that the lady would have had anything to fear, even from the most desperate African.

Had the people been given a voice, Congoland would have been voted in by a landslide. By actual poll, 90 per cent of them had wanted to see the African animal sanctuary established in Kern County, including a large enthusiastic group who had called themselves The Friends of Congoland. But the people had been defeated by a misinformed minority that lacked all understanding and sympathy for so-called wild animals. They had lost out to the "sportsmen" who wanted public lands reserved for hunting; to the association of property owners who lacked the vision to see what Disneyland had done for Anaheim, less than 150 miles away; to the cattlemen who feared "exotic diseases" from animals who had to be healthier than their own stock to pass federal quarantines and other requirements; and to the crackpots who denounced "naked chimpanzees" or worried about "uninhibited Africans" bursting into their bedrooms.

Kern County itself had been defeated, losing what a local paper prophesied that Congoland would bring to it—the "greatest boom since Lovely Rogers inadvertently discovered the Big Blue gold mine 100 years ago." But Congoland had *not* been defeated, merely delayed, for somehow and somewhere I knew I would find an open-minded, open-hearted Ararat to welcome Africa's animal refugees.

I closed the Congoland Museum in October, 1962, and started the enormous job of packing the thirteen tons I had unpacked some fifteen months before. Two months later, the world's largest and finest private collection of African artifacts was carted off on a hay wagon to its temporary haven, a vacant carpenter's shop offered by a faithful "friend of Congoland." Then, late in January, 1963, I received a brief communiqué which read:

Dear Jean-Pierre,
Please accept this letter as a formal demand for payment of $31,668.77 due us under our mortgage of items in your Congoland project. The interest has not yet been calculated. If payment is not made within 10 days, then we will take the necessary legal action.

Sincerely yours,
Rudnick Trust
Samuel Rudnick, Co-trustee

I was, by now, virtually penniless. There was little or no chance at all to save the mortgaged collection for a future Congoland. But it was more important, in the last analysis, to see the collection preserved intact and used as a tool for understanding Africa's rapidly disappearing tribal cultures. Only a top museum or university could handle that responsibility; there were, however, only ten days to work with . . . and the mills of large institutions grind even more slowly than the proverbial mills of God.

Looking for a solution, I asked advice from my good friend Maurice Machris, one of America's leading conservationists, who was then President of the Friends of the Los Angeles Zoo. Maurice was working on a project similar in some respects to my own, Animaland, which later came very close to realization on the Irvine Ranch in Orange County, only to bog down as Congoland had done in a muddle of local problems.

"That collection has to go to the University of California," Maurice said decisively. "Go to the top—call Murphy. If there's one man in California who can cut through all the red tape, it's Murphy."

Murphy was Dr. Franklin D. Murphy, the world-renowned scholar and educator who was and remains Chancellor of the University of California at Los Angeles. I had met him briefly before going to Bakersfield, and had come away deeply impressed by his rare blend of warmth, wit, and learning. What happened now was even more impressive. Hacking away at the undergrowth of institutional red tape, Dr. Murphy swiftly found private funds to acquire the epic collection for the University of California. University representative Clifford Dyrdahl journeyed to Bakersfield where he presented a check for $34,823.40 to the Rudnick Trust, and I was "reimbursed for crating, storage, shipping, insurance and other costs incurred."

While serving as temporary curator of the collection and consulting Africanist at the university's Westwood campus, I started work on *Congo Kitabu*. In writing it I tried to convey, within the framework of my personal experiences, some of the flavor and meaning of the old Africa, now passing away. I have written *Animal Kitabu* because I feel, especially in light of my Bakersfield experiences, that some understanding of Africa's so-called wild animals and their ways is vitally needed to stimulate and aid conservationist programs, Congoland included.

Since the birth of Christ—who said that not a sparrow

fell without God's knowledge—106 mammalian species have become extinct, 40 of them during the past half-century of industrial and scientific progress. Today, further menaced by exploding world population, some 250 rare mammals and 350 birds are menaced by extinction, from the little Madagascar aye-aye, a primate relative of man, to the world's largest mammal, the hundred-foot blue whale.

The World Wildlife Fund, established in 1961, has advanced four major reasons why the survival of other species than our own is vital to our human future, even in an age of computers and orbiting satellites. As stated by Dr. Fritz Vollmar, the international organization's Swiss Secretary-General:

1) With the tremendous strides toward urbanization of vast tracts of countryside, the city-dweller needs more and more the relaxation and enjoyment which nature and wildlife can give him.

2) Some species, already extinct because of man's interference with nature, could have provided a valuable source of food, particularly in some developing nations. They might also have been able to provide valuable information to the scientist.

3) Rare animals and birds can be of great economic value to under-developed countries, particularly as tourist attractions.

4) Man has an ethical and moral responsibility to preserve anything which lives on earth.

The last two or three generations of mankind have, by conscious intent or ignorant neglect, reduced the world's wildlife heritage to a tattered remnant of its former natural glory. It is up to our generation to decide what happens next. If we permit the wanton slaughter and pollution to continue, if we fail to control the ever-rising human population of the earth—in industrialized and "underdeveloped" nations alike —we shall not only sacrifice the lives of so-called wild animals but rob and degrade the future of mankind.

A White Hunter still operating in Kenya has advertised his services with a new slogan: "Go now to Africa. Your trophies and your pictures may be all of Africa's great game that your sons will ever see."

To hell with trophies. I would rather take away an arkload of animals, so that our sons can see them *alive*.

INDEX

254